CARS, TRAINS, SHIPS & PLANES

ABOUT THE AUTHOR

Clive Gifford is the winner of the Royal Society Young People's Book Prize and the School Library Association Information Book Award. He has written more than 150 books including **Wow! Science**, **Car Crazy**, and **Super Trucks**.

CARS, TRAINS, SHIPS & PLANES

A visual encyclopedia of every vehicle

WRITTEN BY **CLIVE GIFFORD**

DK India

Project Editor Sneha Sunder Benjamin
Project Art Editor Vaibhav Rastogi
Editor Medha Gupta
Art Editor Rakesh Khundongbam
Assistant Editor Isha Sharma
Assistant Art Editors Anusri Saha, Riti Sodhi
Jacket Designer Dhirendra Singh
Jacket Managing Editor Saloni Singh
DTP Designer Jaypal Chauhan
Senior DTP Designers Harish Aggarwal, Neeraj Bhatia
Picture Researcher Aditya Katyal
Managing Editor Rohan Sinha
Managing Art Editor Sudakshina Basu
Pre-production Manager Balwant Singh
Production Manager Pankaj Sharma

DK UK

Senior Editor Francesca Baines
Senior Art Editor Rachael Grady
Jacket Designer Mark Cavanagh
Jacket Assistant Claire Gell
Managing Editor Linda Esposito
Managing Art Editor Philip Letsu
Pre-production Controllers Nikoleta Parasaki, Gillian Reid
Production Controller Srijana Gurung
Design Development Manager Sophia MTT
Publisher Andrew Macintyre
Art Director Karen Self
Associate Publishing Director Liz Wheeler
Publishing Director Jonathan Metcalf

First published in Great Britain in 2015 by
Dorling Kindersley Limited
80 Strand, London WC2R ORL

Copyright © 2015 Dorling Kindersley Limited
A Penguin Random House Company
4 6 8 10 9 7 5
013–192634–September/2015

A CIP catalogue record for this book
is available from the British Library.
ISBN: 978-1-4093-4850-4

Printed in China

A WORLD OF IDEAS:
SEE ALL THERE IS TO KNOW

www.dk.com

CONTENTS

Foreword	6
Transport timelines	8
Land	**16**
Animal power	18
Camel caravan	20
Bicycle	22
Pedal power	24
Speed wheels	26
Sprint finish	28
Bike business	30
Fun on wheels	32
Extreme cycling	34
Mountain bike madness	36
Motorbike	38
Revving up	40
Bikes in battle	42
Scooting about	44
Three-wheelers	46
Road burners	48
Burning rubber	50
Jumps and flicks	52
Off-roaders	54
Fastest on two wheels	56
Easy riders	58
Car	60
Pioneering cars	62
Thrills and spills	64
Early racing cars	66
Machines with style	68
Fins and finery	70
Faster and faster	72
Fast and furious	74
The ultimate test	76
Fun in cars	78
Crazy cars	80
A spin across the waves	82
Family transport	84
Outdoor warriors	86

Convertibles and sports cars	88	On the farm	116	Dawn of diesel	134
Mini motors	90	Monster leap	118	Mainstream diesel	136
The Mopetta microcar	92	Construction and mining	120	Rail workhorses	138
Supercars	94	Tanks and tracks	122	Going electric	140
Luxury rides	96	Steam train	124	High-speed electric trains	142
Record breakers	98	Early steam	126	Bullet train	144
Dragster burn out	100	Mainstream steam	128	Urban railways	146
Truck	102	Flying Scotsman	130	Trams and trolleybuses	148
Tonnes of trucks	104	Diesel train	132	Hold on tight!	150
Special task trucks	106				
Shuttle crawler	108				
Bus stop	110				
Tractor	112				
Total tractor	114				

Water 152

Taking to the water	154	Sailing ship	160	City on the sea	178
World of watercraft	156	Sail power	162	World War ships	180
Over the top	158	Trade and exploration	164	Aircraft carriers	182
		War at sea	166	Modern warships	184
		Riding the wind	168	Submarine	186
		Steamship	170	Dive, dive, dive	188
		Steam meets steel	172	Need for speed	190
		Working ships	174	Fun and games	192
		Passenger carriers	176	A flying success	194

Air 196

Aeroplane	198	Eyes in the sky	226	Spacecraft	236
Taking to the skies	200	Helicopter	228	Launch vehicles	238
First planes	202	Whirlybirds	230	Space probes	240
The girl of nerve	204	Working choppers	232	Out of this world	242
Fighter planes	206	Air support	234	Lift-off!	244
Strike force	208				
Racers and record-breakers	210				
Jet fighters	212				
Super speed	214				
Seaplanes	216				
Light aircraft	218				
Plane spotting	220				
Coming in low	222				
Straight up and supersonic	224				

Glossary 246

Index 250

Acknowledgments 255

KTM 350 SX-F

Peel P50

New Holland T6.140

Foreword

Welcome to the world of fast cars and even faster planes, of mighty ships, awesome motorbikes, and heavy hauling trucks and trains. All these and many more machines that move around people, goods, and materials can be found in this bumper book of transport.

I have had a fascination with transport for as long as I can remember. My father flew gliders and worked for an early British airline that offered many people their first taste of air travel. I remember him taking me to an airshow when I was eleven to see an array of amazing aircraft –

from massive jet bombers to nimble aerobatic biplanes. I found them astonishing just as I did the giant trucks and two Ferrari supercars in the airshow's car park. I was hooked and have remained excited by all forms of transport ever since.

This book is packed with vehicles, craft, and vessels that have enabled people to travel further, faster, and with greater ease – from the slickest street bike to the most powerful diesel train. Many have played their part in changing people's lives, and how and where they work and live. Before the development of modern cars, trains, ships, and planes, few people travelled outside

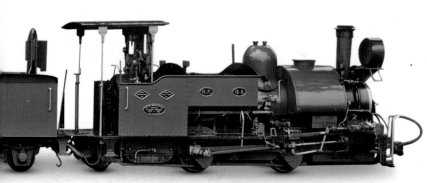

DHR Class B

De Dion-Bouton Type O

Bücker Bü133C Jungmeister

Montgolfier Hot-air Balloon

of their own neighbourhood and even fewer travelled long distances overseas. Today, coast-to-coast journeys that once took weeks take hours, while you can cross the planet in less than a day on a giant jet airliner. Shipping now connects all parts of the globe, enabling you to buy food grown on the other side of the world and many other goods besides. Advances in transport have helped people explore and settle new lands, make exciting discoveries about our world, and even blast off and leave the planet altogether to explore the marvels of space.

Clive Gifford

Throughout this book you will find scale boxes that show the sizes of types of transport compared to either a child or a US school bus.

Child = 1.45 m (4 ft 9 in) tall

US school bus = 11 m (36 ft) long

Unicycle

Sea-Doo® Spark™

John Deere 650K XLT

On the road

The first automobile was a steam-powered cart that set off in 1769 at a top speed of 4 km/h (2.5 mph). Over the years, many clever inventions have helped shape modern motor vehicles, and today, more than one billion whizz along the world's roads.

1769 French inventor Nicolas-Joseph Cugnot builds the first working automobile.

1868 The first road traffic lights are installed in London, UK. Not long afterwards, they explode!

1927

The Napier-Campbell *Blue Bird* sets a land-speed record of 314 km/h (195 mph).

Blue Bird

1876
German engineer Nikolaus Otto builds the first internal combustion engine.

1885
The Benz Motorwagen, the first wheeled vehicle powered by an internal combustion engine, takes to the road.

1850

1900

1894

In Germany, Hildebrand and Wolfmüller build the Motorrad, the first production motorcycle.

1871
The Penny Farthing, the first bicycle with big front wheels to boost speed, is designed.

1880
Several inventors develop so-called "safety bicycles" driven by a pedal and chain mechanism.

1908
The Ford Model T goes on sale in the USA. It becomes the first car to be mass-produced on an assembly line.

1916 The first fully working armoured tank, the Mark 1, goes into battle in France in World War I.

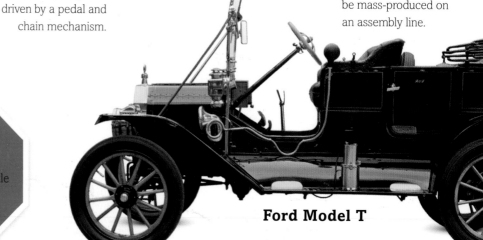

Ford Model T

1979 Bigfoot, the first monster truck, is developed in the USA by Bob Chandler for off-road adventures.

2013 British company FlashPark invents a talking parking ticket.

1938

The Volkswagen Type 1, or Beetle, rolls off the production line in Germany. Over the years, a further 21.5 million are built.

1997

Thrust SSC sets a world land-speed record of 1,228 km/h (763 mph), faster than the speed of sound.

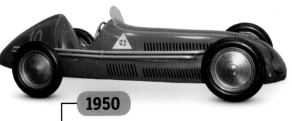

1950

The world's first Formula 1 World Championship is won by Italy's Giuseppe Farina in an Alfa Romeo 159.

1980

The world's longest recorded traffic jam of 170 km (105 miles) blocks roads in France.

1950

2000

1946

In Italy, Vespa produces its first scooter, sparking a fashion craze from the 1950s onwards.

1981

Stumpjumper, the first mass-produced mountain bicycle, goes on sale in the USA.

2005

A Bugatti Veyron sets the record for the world's fastest production car, clocking 407 km/h (253 mph).

1940

The Jeep is first introduced as a general purpose light truck.

Jeep

Bugatti Veyron

 **1949** Sierra Sam becomes the first fully formed crash test dummy, used to test the safety features of cars.

9

Along the tracks

Steam locomotives were known as "iron horses" when they started a transport revolution in the early 1800s, speeding up the movement of people and goods all over the world. Today, diesel and electric locomotives have taken over from steam.

1913
Grand Central Terminal opens in New York. The station has the most number of tracks – 67 in all.

1829
The first modern steam locomotive, the *Rocket*, built by Robert Stephenson, sets new speed records.

1830 The first inter-city steam passenger service, the Liverpool and Manchester Railway, begins.

1881
The first electric tram service begins in Berlin, Germany.

1770
Scottish inventor James Watt invents the compound steam engine, versions of which will power early locomotives.

1869
The first Transcontinental Railroad across the USA is completed – a total of 3,069 km (1,907 miles) of tracks.

1800

1850

1900

1804
The *Pen-y-Darren* locomotive is built by British inventor Richard Trevithick, for work in mines.

1863
The first underground city railway, the Metropolitan Line, opens in London, UK.

1906
The Simplon Tunnel, connecting Italy and Switzerland under the Alps, opens. It is the world's longest railway tunnel.

1914
Throughout World War I, railways prove invaluable for moving troops and supplies.

Pen-y-Darren locomotive

Golden Eagle **Trans-Siberian Express**

1916

The world's longest railway line, the Trans-Siberian Railway across Russia, is completed. It runs for 9,289 km (5,772 miles).

1937

German inventor Hermann Kemper develops magnetic levitation (maglev) as a force for moving trains.

1960

French Railways introduce the world's first 200 km/h (125 mph) service – the Le Capitole.

1964

The world's first bullet train, Shinkansen, connects Tokyo to other cities of Japan.

1984

In the UK, the world's first commercial maglev transport system opens, connecting Birmingham International Airport and nearby terminals.

1994
The high-speed Channel Tunnel Eurostar service begins from London to Paris.

2012

Tokyo metro carries 3.29 billion passengers in a year, making it the busiest metro system in the world.

1950

2000

1955

Initial trial of the English Electric *Deltic* locomotive take place – the most powerful diesel locomotive in the world.

1975

In the UK, the Inter-City HST becomes the fastest diesel-powered train in the world.

2007

An experimental French TGV sets the world record for the fastest electric train, with a speed of 574 km/h (357 mph).

2015

First passenger-carrying test run of Japan's new maglev train system. Trains reach speeds of 600 km/h (373 mph).

1938

The *Mallard* sets the world record for the fastest ever steam locomotive, at a speed of more than 200 km/h (125 mph).

1988 The world's longest underwater railway tunnel, the Seikan Tunnel, 53.9 km (33.5 miles) long, is built to connect two Japanese islands.

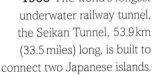

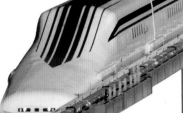

Across the water

Humans have been travelling by water for so long that it is impossible to know exactly when the first boats were built. While some have changed little over the centuries, today there are also hi-tech speedboats, mighty tankers, and giant cruise liners on the waters of the world.

Santa Maria

1768
Captain James Cook sets off from England to explore the South Pacific. His voyage takes three years and covers more than 48,000 km (30,000 miles).

1492
Explorer Christopher Columbus sails west from Spain in the *Santa Maria*. He crosses the Atlantic Ocean and lands in the Bahamas.

1661
The first recorded yacht race takes place, between the English King Charles II and his brother James, on the River Thames in London, UK.

1500

1600

1700

1510
The English ship *Mary Rose* is one of the first to be built with gunports – holes for cannons to fire through.

1620
The *Mayflower* leaves Plymouth, England, taking 102 pilgrims to settle in the New World (America).

Mayflower

1716
In the early 1700s, the waters of the Caribbean were at their most dangerous, as pirates plundered Spanish treasure ships.

1519
Portuguese navigator Ferdinand Magellan sets out with a fleet of five ships. Just one would make it back in 1522, having completed the first voyage around the world.

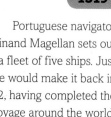

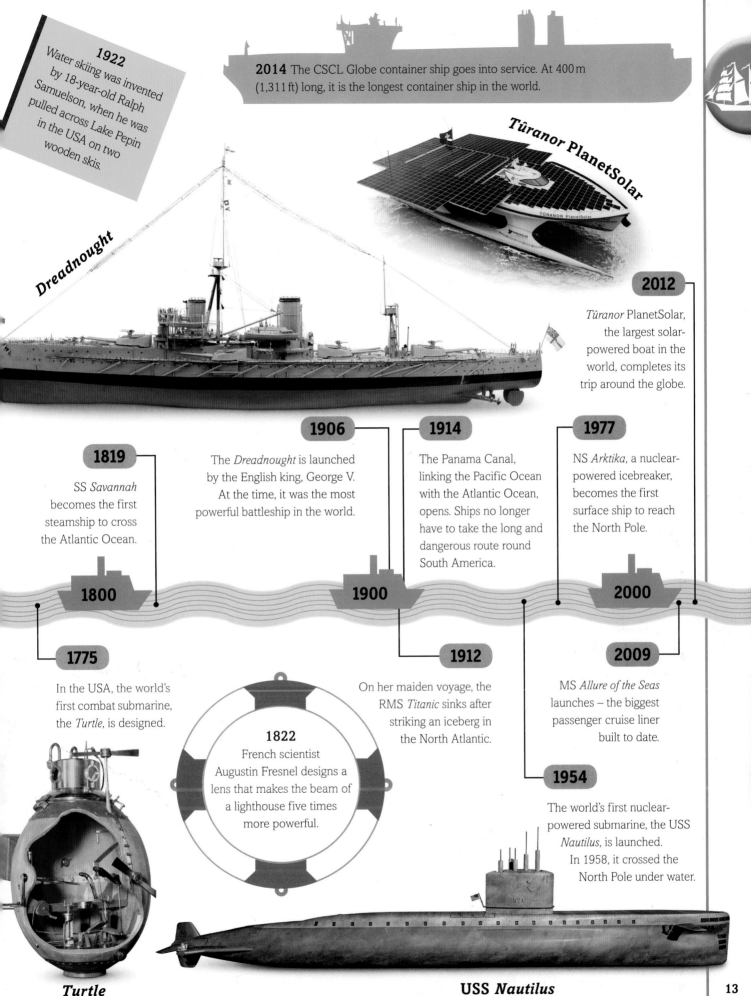

1922
Water skiing was invented by 18-year-old Ralph Samuelson, when he was pulled across Lake Pepin in the USA on two wooden skis.

2014 The CSCL Globe container ship goes into service. At 400 m (1,311 ft) long, it is the longest container ship in the world.

Tûranor PlanetSolar

Dreadnought

2012
Tûranor PlanetSolar, the largest solar-powered boat in the world, completes its trip around the globe.

1906
The *Dreadnought* is launched by the English king, George V. At the time, it was the most powerful battleship in the world.

1914
The Panama Canal, linking the Pacific Ocean with the Atlantic Ocean, opens. Ships no longer have to take the long and dangerous route round South America.

1977
NS *Arktika*, a nuclear-powered icebreaker, becomes the first surface ship to reach the North Pole.

1819
SS *Savannah* becomes the first steamship to cross the Atlantic Ocean.

1800

1900

2000

1775
In the USA, the world's first combat submarine, the *Turtle*, is designed.

1912
On her maiden voyage, the RMS *Titanic* sinks after striking an iceberg in the North Atlantic.

2009
MS *Allure of the Seas* launches – the biggest passenger cruise liner built to date.

1822
French scientist Augustin Fresnel designs a lens that makes the beam of a lighthouse five times more powerful.

1954
The world's first nuclear-powered submarine, the USS *Nautilus*, is launched. In 1958, it crossed the North Pole under water.

Turtle

USS *Nautilus*

Up in the air

Powered flight took off in 1903, when American brothers Wilbur and Orville Wright attached an engine to a glider and travelled through air for 12 seconds. This short flight blazed the trail for supersonic jets, giant airliners, and even spacecraft.

1913 Russian Pyotr Nesterov becomes the first pilot to fly a loop in the loop.

1785 Frenchman Jean-Pierre Blanchard and American John Jeffries fly across the English Channel in a balloon.

1783

In Paris, France, the Montgolfier brothers' hot-air balloon makes the world's first manned flight, lasting 25 minutes.

1900 The first rigid airship, the Zeppelin LZ1, makes its maiden voyage in Germany.

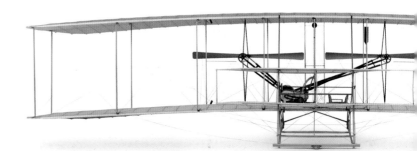

1903

The Wright brothers' first powered flying machine, the *Wright Flyer*, takes off in the USA.

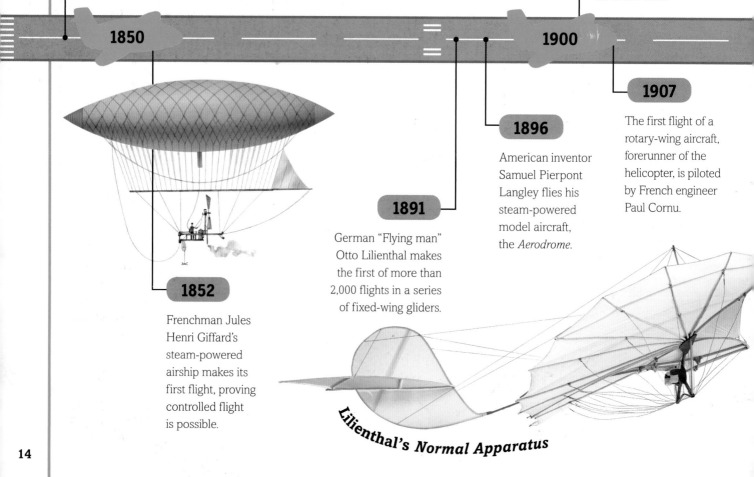

1850

1900

1907

The first flight of a rotary-wing aircraft, forerunner of the helicopter, is piloted by French engineer Paul Cornu.

1896

American inventor Samuel Pierpont Langley flies his steam-powered model aircraft, the *Aerodrome*.

1891

German "Flying man" Otto Lilienthal makes the first of more than 2,000 flights in a series of fixed-wing gliders.

1852

Frenchman Jules Henri Giffard's steam-powered airship makes its first flight, proving controlled flight is possible.

Lilienthal's Normal Apparatus

1930 A nurse by profession, Ellen Church becomes the first air stewardess.

Space Shuttle Columbia

1969

In the UK, the Hawker Siddeley Harrier becomes the first vertical-take-off-and-landing (VTOL) military jet in service.

1969

The US Apollo 11 spacecraft takes off for the Moon. Two of its astronauts become the first humans to walk on the lunar surface.

1981

Space Shuttle *Columbia* lifts off from Cape Canaveral, USA, for its first space mission. The Space Shuttle program continues until 2011.

1938

The American Boeing 307 Stratoliner, the first airliner with a pressurized cabin, helps make flying a pleasant experience for passengers.

1950

1952

In the UK, the first commercial jet airliner, the de Havilland Comet, enters service.

1961

Russian cosmonaut Yuri Gagarin becomes the first man in space. He orbits the Earth for 108 minutes onboard his Vostok 1 spacecraft.

1976

The UK/French supersonic airliner Concorde enters passenger service.

2000

2014

After a ten-year journey, the European Space Agency spacecraft *Rosetta* reaches a comet and lands a probe on its surface.

1927

American Charles Lindbergh makes the first nonstop flight across North Atlantic in his Ryan NYP *Spirit of St Louis*, a distance of more than 5,800 km (3,600 miles).

1949 A B-50 Superfortress makes the first nonstop flight around the world. It is refuelled in mid-air four times!

Animal power

Handler, called **musher**, *gives commands to dogs*

Husky sled Arctic region

Roman chariots pulled **by four horses** could race at speeds of 50 km/h (31 mph).

Wooden, spoked wheel

Chariot Rome 200 BCE

Leather harness

Canvas cover stretched over iron hoops to provide protection against weather

Reins are attached to the harness at the mouth

Straight backrest

Liverpool gig UK 1800s

Chuck wagon USA 1866

Conestoga wagon USA 18th and 19th century

The Glass Coach is used for the **weddings** of the British royal family.

Distinctive glass lanterns

The Glass Coach UK 1881

For thousands of years, people have harnessed the power of large animals to transport them and their goods. Oxen, dogs, horses, mules, and reindeer have all been used to pull sleds or haul wagons and, in some parts of the world, still do.

As early as 3000 BCE, animals were used to pull the first chariots into battle in the Middle East and Asia. Later, the Romans turned **chariot** racing into a sport, using lightweight designs, in which the driver rode from a small platform over the wheel axle. Wagons got bigger when pioneers set

"Rumble" seat for servant or groom

Arched hood can be raised or lowered

Spider phaeton
UK c.1890

Rubber tyres

Coachman's seat

Square landau
UK c.1890

Lead dogs find the trail and set the pace

Enclosed cab for passengers

Railway horse bus
UK c.1900

TENTERDEN STATION.

KENT & EAST SUSSEX R^{LY}

Iron hoop forms frame for a canvas cover

Chuck box – a set of drawers for storing goods

Flag with red cross indicates wagon was a medical vehicle

Wooden wheels with iron rims

Ambulance wagon
World War I 1914–18

off across North America in the 18th and 19th centuries. The four-wheeled, covered **Conestoga wagon** could carry five tonnes of food, tools, and belongings, and was usually pulled by oxen. Not long after, fully working kitchens on wheels, called **chuck wagons**, could be seen following cowboys as they herded cattle across the country. In the towns, small, lightweight carriages such as the **Liverpool gig** or the **Spider phaeton** carried up to two people on short journeys, while bigger carriages, such as the **Square landau** could transport four people in greater comfort.

CAMEL CARAVAN
Out of the way, there's a convoy coming through! It's made up of camels carrying salt – Ethiopia's white gold, mined from the Danakil Depression. Highly prized, both to flavour food and preserve it, salt is levered out of the giant salt flats at Danakil in slabs. These are then cut into blocks and lashed onto the backs of the camels, the ultimate desert pack animal.

Caravans (convoys) of pack animals – from camels, horses, and mules, to yaks, llamas, and even elephants – have been used throughout history to transport food, materials, and goods for trade. Camels are famed for their ability to withstand heat and a lack of water, making them perfect for cargo-carrying duties across hot deserts. This route across Ethiopia, from Danakil to the trading centre of Mekele, involves a 100 km (60 miles) trek across one of the hottest places on Earth, with temperatures soaring past 50°C (122°F). Salt caravans have crossed the Sahara for more than 2,000 years. In the past, thousands of animals made up the camel trains, but today 20 to 30 are more usual.

Bicycle

Bicycles are a fun and efficient way of getting around. A cyclist can travel around four to five times faster than a walker, using the same amount of energy. Although designs vary, most bicycles share common key parts. A chain, powered by a chainwheel and driven by pedals and cranks, transmits power to the rear wheel, which turns and drives the bicycle forward.

Saddle ❯ The bicycle's seat can be solid or padded for comfort. It is fitted to a seat post, which slides into the frame's seat tube.

Seat post

Rear brake cable

Seat tube

Rear brake

Wheel and tyre ❯ These support the weight of the bicycle and the rider. Different tyres have different patterns on their outer surface known as tread. This bicycle has smooth tread tyres for road racing. An off-road bicycle will have chunkier tread to provide better grip.

Gear cable

Rear derailleur ❯ The derailleur gear moves the chain to different gear cogs.

Spokes ❯ Thin and strong, spokes connect the wheel's rim to its centre, or hub. They allow wheels to be built that are strong but light in weight, and they let air through when the wheel faces the wind.

Chainwheel

Bottom bracket

Chain

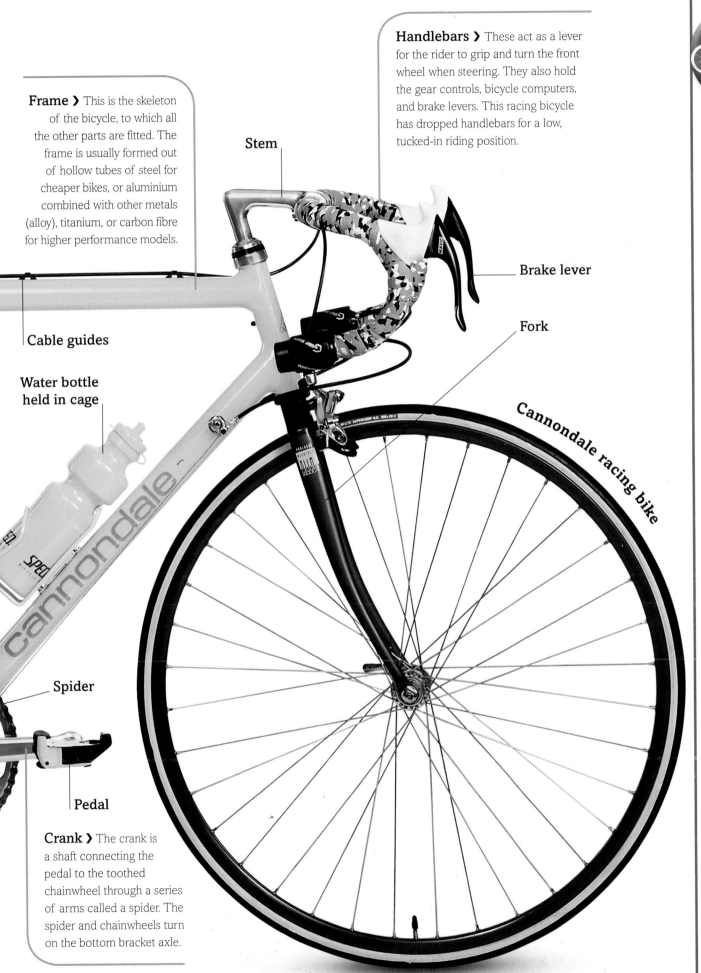

Frame > This is the skeleton of the bicycle, to which all the other parts are fitted. The frame is usually formed out of hollow tubes of steel for cheaper bikes, or aluminium combined with other metals (alloy), titanium, or carbon fibre for higher performance models.

Handlebars > These act as a lever for the rider to grip and turn the front wheel when steering. They also hold the gear controls, bicycle computers, and brake levers. This racing bicycle has dropped handlebars for a low, tucked-in riding position.

Stem

Brake lever

Fork

Cable guides

Water bottle held in cage

Cannondale racing bike

Spider

Pedal

Crank > The crank is a shaft connecting the pedal to the toothed chainwheel through a series of arms called a spider. The spider and chainwheels turn on the bottom bracket axle.

Pedal power

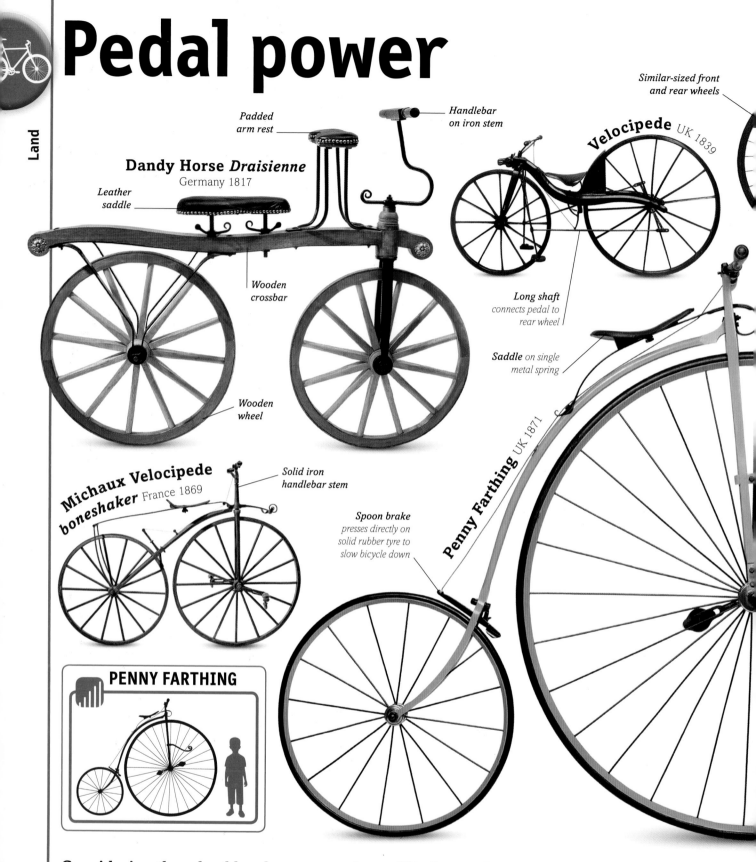

Similar-sized front
and rear wheels

Padded
arm rest

Handlebar
on iron stem

Velocipede UK 1839

Dandy Horse *Draisienne*
Germany 1817

Leather
saddle

Wooden
crossbar

Long shaft
connects pedal to
rear wheel

Saddle on single
metal spring

Wooden
wheel

**Michaux Velocipede
boneshaker** France 1869

Solid iron
handlebar stem

Spoon brake
presses directly on
solid rubber tyre to
slow bicycle down

Penny Farthing UK 1871

PENNY FARTHING

Considering the wheel has been around for more than 5,000 years, it is amazing to think that it was only 200 years ago that people finally got the idea of placing two wheels on a frame and creating pedal-powered personal transport.

The German Baron Karl Von Drais invented the **Dandy Horse** in 1817, which had a saddle and handlebars but was powered by a rider paddling his feet along the ground. It led to other human-powered machines, including the **Michaux Velocipede**, which had pedals fitted directly

Curved steel tubes *form a diamond shape*

Rover safety bicycle UK 1885

Penny Farthing front wheel *acts as a rear wheel*

Singer tricycle UK 1888

Straight front forks

Chain *links pedals and rear wheel*

In **1885**, the Rover bicycle won a **160 km** (99.4 miles) race in the UK in 7 hours, 5 minutes.

Large front wheel up to 1.5 m (5 ft) in diameter

Solid rubber tyre, replaced by pneumatic (air-filled) tyres from 1888

Swift safety bicycle UK 1887

Simple mudguard covered the small rear wheel

Curved front forks

Facile dwarf safety bicycle UK 1888

Singer safety UK 1888

In **1884**, Thomas Stevens crossed the **USA** on a **Penny Farthing**.

Saddle made of 40 m (131 ft) of woven cord weighs 100 g (3.5 oz)

Dursley Pedersen bicycle UK 1898–99

to the front wheel. The experience of its iron "tyres" on cobbled streets earned it the nickname *boneshaker*. **Penny Farthings** in the UK, France, and the USA had no chains or gears, but had bigger front wheels to boost speed. It perched the rider high above the ground, resulting in many falls. Alternatives were sought, including pairing two Penny Farthing front wheels together to form the rear wheels of the **Singer tricycle**, and using a chain-driven rear wheel, as in the **Rover safety bicycle**. This design ushered in the modern bicycle with wheels of similar size.

Speed wheels

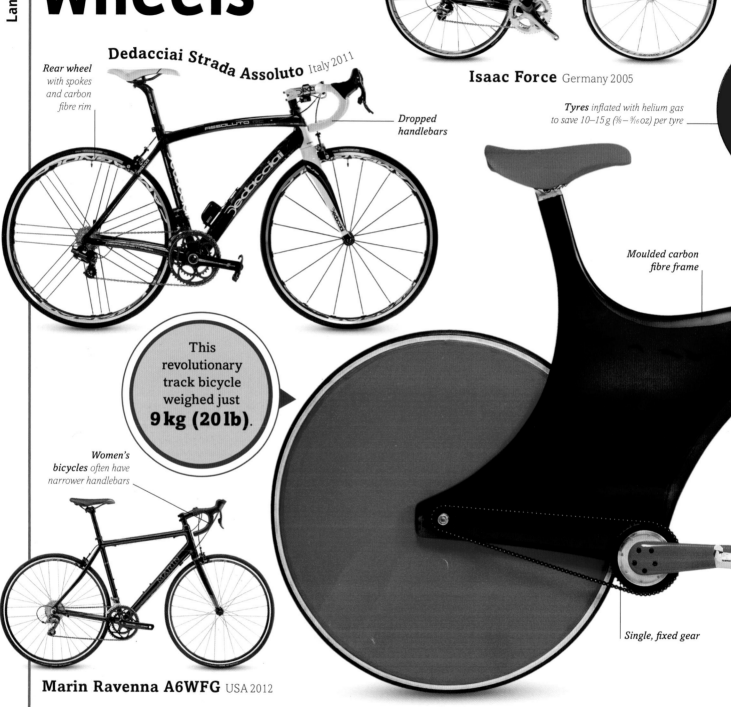

Seat post

Isaac Force Germany 2005

Tyres inflated with helium gas to save 10–15 g (⅜–⁹⁄₁₆ oz) per tyre

Dedacciai Strada Assoluto Italy 2011

Rear wheel with spokes and carbon fibre rim

Dropped handlebars

Moulded carbon fibre frame

This revolutionary track bicycle weighed just **9 kg (20 lb)**.

Women's bicycles often have narrower handlebars

Single, fixed gear

Marin Ravenna A6WFG USA 2012

If you have a need for speed, then a racing bicycle is for you. Designed for fast riding on smooth surfaces, racing bicycles are light in weight with a high seat and low, dropped, handlebars.

Not all racing bicycles are used for racing. Many are used by cyclists to commute rapidly to work or for a workout. Frames are designed for both men and women; the **Ravenna A6WFG** is a women's racing bicycle designed for endurance riding. Competition racing bicycles are designed with

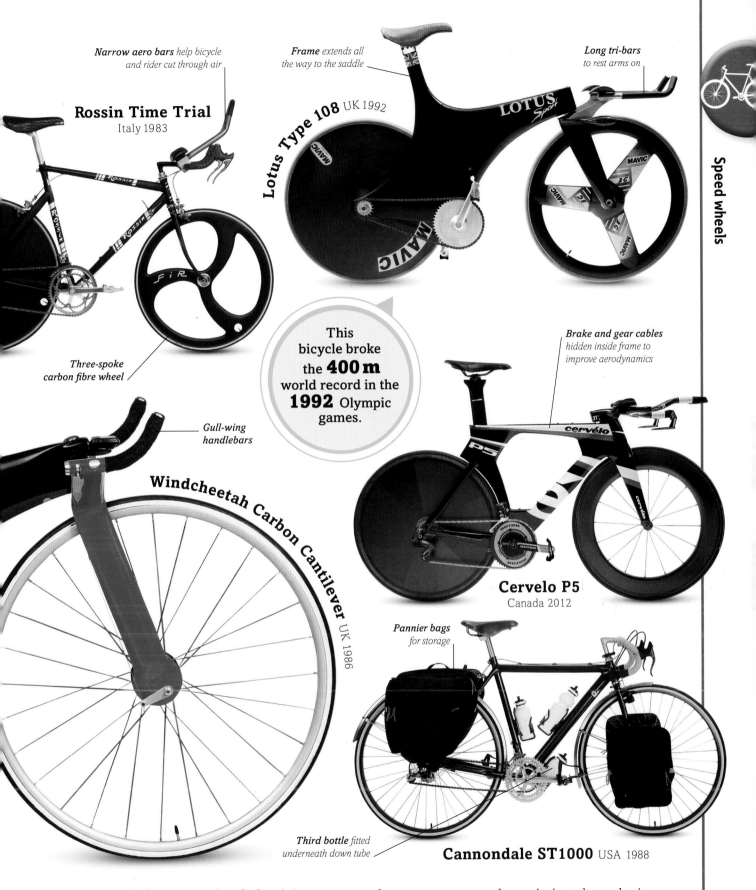

Narrow aero bars help bicycle and rider cut through air

Rossin Time Trial
Italy 1983

Frame extends all the way to the saddle

Lotus Type 108 UK 1992

Long tri-bars to rest arms on

Three-spoke carbon fibre wheel

This bicycle broke the **400 m** world record in the **1992** Olympic games.

Gull-wing handlebars

Windcheetah Carbon Cantilever UK 1986

Brake and gear cables hidden inside frame to improve aerodynamics

Cervelo P5
Canada 2012

Pannier bags for storage

Third bottle fitted underneath down tube

Cannondale ST1000 USA 1988

super-lightweight frames made of aluminium or titanium alloys, or carbon fibre. The **Assoluto's** carbon fibre frame weighs just 1.1 kg (2.4 lb), a little more than a baseball bat. Solid disc rear wheels are used on track racers, in time trials, and on triathlete's bicycles, such as the **Cervelo P5**, as

they are more aerodynamic (cut through air more easily) than wheels with spokes. Solid-bodied track racers, such as the **Windcheetah Carbon Cantilever**, appeared in the 1980s with a solid carbon fibre body and were tested in wind tunnels to ensure they were as aerodynamic as possible.

27

SPRINT FINISH
You can feel the pain just watching these sprinters pump the pedals at the end of another gruelling stage of the world's most famous bike race, the Tour de France. This stage – the tenth of the 2011 Tour – started 158 km (98 miles) back. In a photo finish, André Greipel of Germany (right) crossed the line a fraction ahead of Mark Cavendish of the UK (left). Both are given the time of 3 hours, 31 minutes, and 21 seconds.

The Tour de France takes place over three weeks every summer, and covers more than 3,500 km (2,175 miles), broken up into 21 stages. Each year, the route across France changes, sometimes entering other European countries, but it always challenges riders over all sorts of terrain, with stages on the flat, in the hills, and in the mountains. Around 20 teams take part, each with nine riders. The cyclists' times for each day are added together and the rider with the overall lowest time gets to wear the prized *maillot jaune* (yellow jersey). But there are also prizes for the fastest sprinter (green jersey), the fastest climber (red polka dot jersey), the fastest rider under 25 (white jersey), and for the fastest team.

Bike business

Wicker basket holds up to 25 kg (55 lb) of goods

Pashley Delibike UK 1948

Pannier contains emergency medical equipment

Response bicycle UK 2000

Butterfly screw can be loosened to fold frame in half

Folding stand supports the bicycle when parked

Flashing side lights on rack bag

BSA Airborne UK 1943

Toolbag hung from top tube of frame

Police mountain bicycle
Germany 2000s

...up bicycle is less than ... (22.4 in) in height and ... m (22 in) in length

There are more than **1,200 parts** in a Brompton Folding Bicycle.

Brompton Folding Bicycle UK 1981–83

Cycling may be lots of fun, but many people ride their bicycles to and from work, or use them to carry out their jobs. Bicycles offer a cheap, quick, and convenient way to get around, and to transport people and deliver goods.

In both crowded towns and cities, and isolated countryside areas, **police mountain bicycles** allow officers to get to a crime scene rapidly. **Response bicycles**, with their pannier bags filled with lifesaving medical equipment, can get through traffic or crowds to reach a patient where

Container for letters and small parcels

Hooded canopy provides shade

DHL Parcycle Netherlands 2014

Penang Trishaw Malaysia 1980s

Seat for up to two passengers

Canopy keeps ice cream shaded from Sun

Cart handle acts as bicycle's handlebars

Tricycle ice cream cart India 1980s

Height and angle of the saddle can be adjusted for maximum comfort

Brake and gear cabling hang loose, so the bike can be folded

Luggage rack can hold large bag

Small wire basket to carry shopping

Public bicycle China 2000s

Small, 40.6-cm- (16-in-) wheel

larger vehicles cannot go. The **BSA Airborne** was used by British troops during World War II – its frame folded in half when two butterfly screws were loosened. Folding bicycles, such as the **Brompton Folding Bicycle**, continue to be used by thousands of commuters. Delivery bicycles are equipped with baskets or carriers to carry cargo. The **DHL Parcycle** fits a giant container onto a bike to carry parcels. Bicycles can also be modified, and their frames attached to carts or carriages, such as the **ice cream cart** and the pedal-powered **Penang Trishaw** taxi.

31

Fun on wheels

Unicycle France 1800s

Padded seat supports back

Velocar France 1933

Windcheetah SL Mark VI Speedy UK 1981

Backrest includes lockable boot and rear lights

Kingcycle UK 1990s

Riders experience **"rubber legs"** every time they try a new style of bike and use new muscles.

Dropped handlebars with brakes for the rider at the back

Santana Triplet USA 2000s

If you think all bicycles feature just one rider sitting upright, supported by two wheels, think again! Many variations on the bicycle's basic design have been attempted for greater speed, more comfort, or just for fun.

A **Unicycle** has a single wheel, turned by pedals, and demands great balance from the rider to stay on. Three-wheelers are easier to ride, and some, such as the **Pashley Tri.1**, even offer a platform to carry large loads. Tandem bicycles, such as the **Dawes Galaxy Twin**, have two riders pedalling,

Joystick

Brakes on front wheel

Body shell and bicycle weigh 37.2kg (82lb)

Kingcycle Bean UK 1984

This slick bicycle has **joysticks** instead of **handlebars** for steering.

Twike Switzerland 1995

Hinged windscreen acts as a door

Electric motor, plus pedal power, gives top speed of 24km/h (15mph)

Handlebars gripped under rider's knees

Twin seats

Sinclair C5 UK 1985

Platform to carry loads

Pashley Tri.1 UK 2013

Hinged frame folds up for storage

Luggage rack

Dawes Galaxy Twin UK 2008

Timing chain links two set of pedals and chainwheels

but only the front rider steers. The **Santana Triplet** has saddles for three riders, with a long chain linking each rider's chainwheel to ensure smooth pedalling. In recumbent bicycles, riders sit or lie down with their legs out in front. The bicycle is low and can slip through air at high speed.

The **Windcheetah *Speedy*** was cycled the length of the UK in just 41 hours, 4 minutes, and 22 seconds. Some recumbents fit a body shell around the rider to let air flow past more smoothly. In 1990, the **Kingcycle Bean** set a world speed record of 76km/h (47 mph) over one hour.

33

Extreme cycling

Trek 8900 Pro USA 1990

Suspension allows front forks to telescope down into lower tubes when hitting bumps

Gear changer on the handlebar helps select between the bicycle's 15 gears

Single gear cog on rear wheel

Specialized Stumpjumper
USA 1981

Raleigh Kool Max UK 2000s

Frame made of carbon fibre tubes fitted to aluminium joints

6.4-cm- (2.5-in-) wide tyre for excellent grip in sand, dirt, and mud

Some mountain bicycles have up to **30 gears** to speed over different conditions.

Fat Chance Yo-Eddy USA 1991

Shock absorber cushions bumps

Trek 6000 USA 1991

Toe straps secure rider's feet on pedals

Hydraulic (fluid-operated) disc brakes

Stumpjumper FSR Pro USA 2004

While ordinary bicycles can be ridden off-road, their smooth tyres and slender frames are not suitable for rough stuff. When bikers in the USA began redesigning bicycles for better off-road performances in the 1970s, mountain biking was born!

The first mountain bicycle made on a large scale was the **Specialized Stumpjumper**. Only 500 were initially produced, but they started a revolution! Soon, many manufacturers came up with their own designs. The **Trek 6000** had a lightweight, all-aluminium frame, while the **Trek**

Rubber grips on handlebar

Derailleur gear system has 20 different gears for rider to select from

Front forks have suspension that can slide as much as 99 mm (3.8 in) to cushion bumps

Cushioned saddle with plastic covering

Marin Nail Trail
USA 2014

Large frame

Rigid forks

Chainguard stops clothing from snagging on chain

Reflector fitted to wheel spokes

Foot peg for stepping on when performing tricks

Saddle set low so that rider's weight is over rear wheel

MBM Instinct BMX stunt bicycle Italy 2000s

Haro Freestyler BMX racing bike USA 2012

8900 Pro's frame was made of carbon fibre to keep its weight down. Many mountain bikes are fitted with suspension systems. Hardtail bicycles (with rigid frames), such as the **Marin Nail Trail**, have front forks that lessen the impact of bumps and landings. In contrast, full-suspension bicycles, such as the **Stumpjumper FSR Pro**, have shock absorbers for both wheels. BMX bikes are strong, small-wheeled bicycles, some of which are raced over dirt tracks. Freestyle (stunt riding) BMX bikes, such as the **MBM Instinct**, are built for doing tricks and out-of-the-saddle moves.

MOUNTAIN BIKE MADNESS
MTB freerider Louis Reboul launches his mountain bike off a giant 16-m- (52-ft-) high ramp during the Red Bull Rampage 2014. He twists the bike and his riding position in mid-air to pull off a perfectly judged landing. One mistake and the result could be disastrous, with a huge drop onto the hard, unforgiving sandstone below.

Mountain bike (MTB) freeriding involves riders pulling moves and tricks as they take on a challenging run, full of dramatic natural features and, sometimes, man-made obstacles such as large ramps. Competitors ride bikes with full suspension on both wheels to allow for heavy impacts on landing, and their runs are judged for speed, control, and the execution and complexity of their tricks. These can involve full 360° spins, backflips, and no-hands riding. Held on the edge of Zion National Park in Utah, USA, the Red Bull Rampage is an annual invite-only tournament for some of the hottest freeriders in the world. Each gets to pick their own route along the almost vertical drops of ridges and cliffs.

Motorbike

Bikes were first fitted with engines in the 19th century and have never looked back! Today, millions enjoy the fast, convenient travel and the freedom of the open road or trail that motorbikes provide. This **Yamaha XJR 1300** is called a "naked" bike, as its engine is not hidden behind body panels. With a top speed of 210 km/h (130 mph), it is faster than many cars.

Chassis ❯ The frame to which other parts of the motorbike are attached, the chassis helps keep the wheels in line for good handling. It is usually made of steel or a combination of metals (alloy).

Rear seat ❯ Big motorbikes have a seat long enough for a passenger, who can grip the handle behind the seat.

Yamaha XJR 1300

Indicator light

Shock absorber ❯ A coil-spring and oil-filled cylinder cushion the bike and rider over bumps in the road.

Rear wheel ❯ This is driven by power from the engine through a shaft or belt, or on this motorbike, a metal chain similar to a bicycle chain.

Exhaust pipe ❯ The exhaust pipe channels waste gases from the engine out behind the bike.

Side mirrors ›
Mounted on the handlebars, these allow the rider to see what's going on behind the bike.

Throttle › Controlled by twisting the right handlebar, the throttle controls the flow of fuel and air mixture into the cylinders in the engine. More air means more power and a higher speed.

Windshield

Fuel tank ›
The tank holds the fuel and pumps it to the engine.

Headlight › Powered by the motorbike's alternator, this lights up the road ahead.

Front wheel › Fitted with an air-filled tyre, this wheel is steered by the handlebars.

Front forks

Brake disk

Engine › Fuelled by petrol, the engine generates power, which is transmitted to the rear wheel. This engine generates around 107 horsepower, as much as a hatchback car.

Revving up

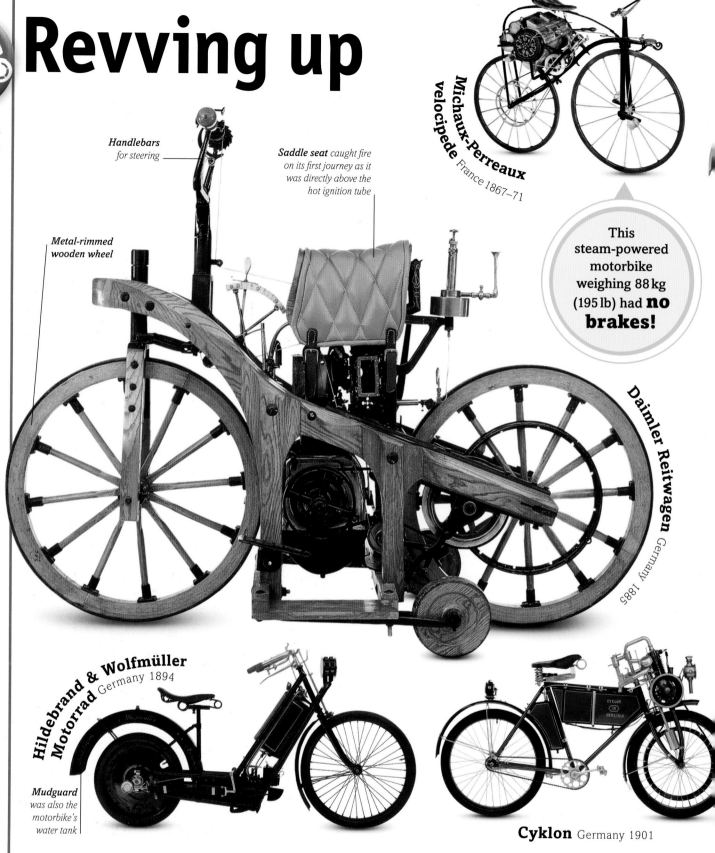

Michaux-Perreaux velocipede France 1867–71

This steam-powered motorbike weighing 88 kg (195 lb) had **no brakes!**

Handlebars *for steering*

Saddle seat *caught fire on its first journey as it was directly above the hot ignition tube*

Metal-rimmed wooden wheel

Daimler Reitwagen Germany 1885

Hildebrand & Wolfmüller Motorrad Germany 1894

Mudguard *was also the motorbike's water tank*

Cyklon Germany 1901

The first powered motorbikes used a small steam engine to drive the rear wheel, but motorbikes made a great leap forward once internal combustion engines were built small enough to attach to a bicycle-styled frame.

With its 0.5 horsepower engine, the **Daimler Reitwagen** is considered the first "real" motorbike, although it was crafted out of wood. It proved to be an uncomfortable ride due to its wooden wheels and lack of suspension. The faster **Motorrad** was the first widely built motorbike,

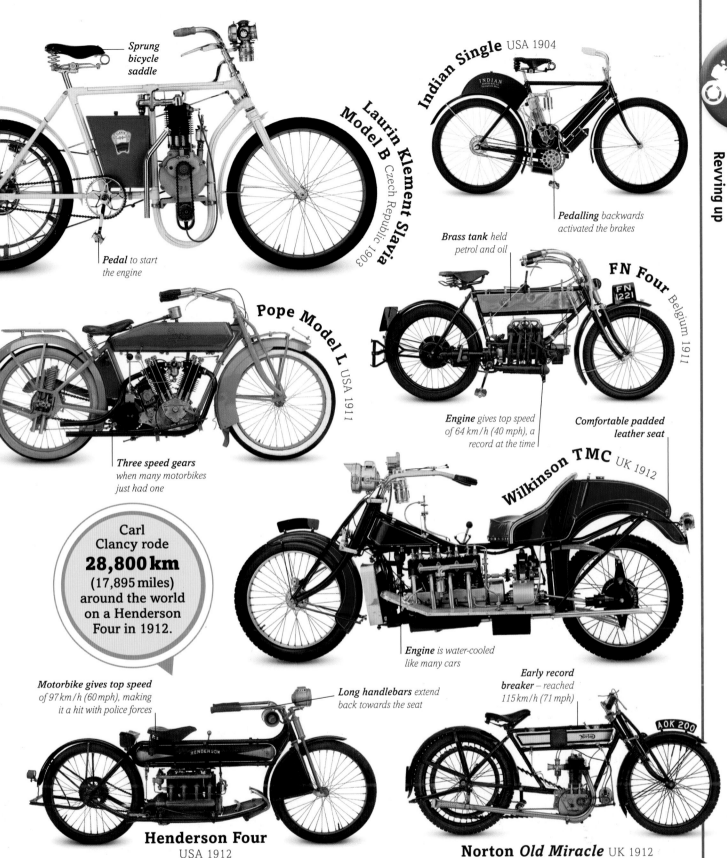

Sprung bicycle saddle

Laurin Klement Slavia Model B Czech Republic 1903

Pedal to start the engine

Indian Single USA 1904

Pedalling backwards activated the brakes

Brass tank held petrol and oil

FN Four Belgium 1911

Engine gives top speed of 64 km/h (40 mph), a record at the time

Pope Model L USA 1911

Three speed gears when many motorbikes just had one

Carl Clancy rode **28,800 km** (17,895 miles) around the world on a Henderson Four in 1912.

Comfortable padded leather seat

Wilkinson TMC UK 1912

Engine is water-cooled like many cars

Motorbike gives top speed of 97 km/h (60 mph), making it a hit with police forces

Long handlebars extend back towards the seat

Early record breaker – reached 115 km/h (71 mph)

Henderson Four USA 1912

Norton *Old Miracle* UK 1912

with around 2,000 built. Some early motorbikes had their engines mounted in strange places. The **Cyklon's** engine sat in front of the rider and drove the front wheel round, while the **Indian Single's** engine was so low that riding over a bump could knock it. Over time, engines were built with more than one cylinder. The **Pope Model L** had two cylinders and cost as much as a Ford Model T car, while the **FN Four** was one of the first motorbikes with four cylinders. The four-cylinder **Wilkinson TMC** was designed for long-distance touring with a padded leather seat, but it had no front brake.

Bikes in battle

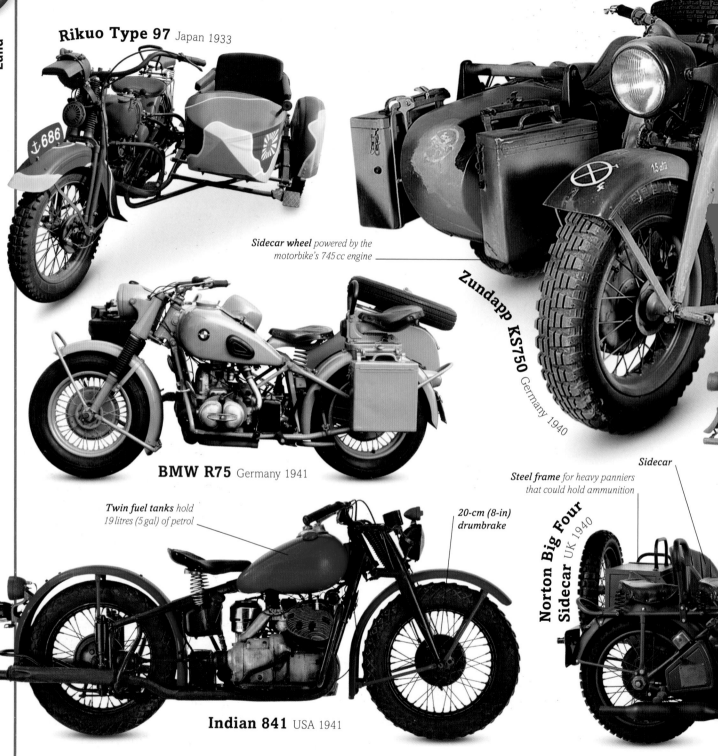

Rikuo Type 97 Japan 1933

Sidecar wheel powered by the motorbike's 745 cc engine

Zundapp KS750 Germany 1940

BMW R75 Germany 1941

Twin fuel tanks hold 19 litres (5 gal) of petrol

20-cm (8-in) drumbrake

Steel frame for heavy panniers that could hold ammunition

Sidecar

Norton Big Four Sidecar UK 1940

Indian 841 USA 1941

As motorbikes became faster, sturdier, and more reliable, they were adopted by armed forces in their thousands. World War II saw heavy motorbike use, as scouts, in convoys, and as couriers, delivering messages and transporting people.

Many World War II motorbikes were adapted civilian models. More than 70,000 **Harley-Davidson WLAs** were made for the American forces, while 126,000 **BSA M20s** were built by the UK and its allies – making it the most produced motorbike of the war. A pre-war Harley-Davidson

Motorbike could carry three soldiers and their weapons at speeds up to 95 km/h (59 mph)

Cannister, with the bike fitted inside, is just 33 cm (13 in) in diameter

Parachute

Welbike UK 1942

BSA M20 UK 1942

A
Welbike
could be put
together in just
11 seconds.

Rear-wheel
canvas panniers

Holster to hold rifle
or machine gun

US ARMY

Norton 16H Desert Duty UK 1942

Harley-Davidson WLA USA 1942

Metal sheet
"bash plate"
to protect engine

The 60 kg (130 lb)
motorbike could be easily dropped
by parachute or carried by a glider

HTO 23

Small engine used
1 litre (0.26 gal) of fuel
per 53 km (33 miles)

Royal Enfield WD/RE125 *Flying Flea* UK 1948

built in Japan, the **Rikuo Type 97** served Japanese forces during wartime. Its sidecar was engine-powered, improving travel over rough ground, a feature also found in the sidecar of the **Norton Big Four**, used as a scout by British soldiers. The 420-kg (930-lb) **Zundapp KS750** was one of the biggest World War II sidecars. In contrast, the 32-kg (71-lb) **Welbike** could be folded inside a cannister, dropped from a plane, and parachuted to the ground. Another lightweight, the *Flying Flea* was used to carry messages when radio contact was impossible.

Scooting about

Steering column folds down when not in use

Autoped USA 1915

155 cc engine directly over the front wheel

Enclosed 202 cc engine mounted under the seat

Cushman Auto-glide
USA 1938

Lockable boot

Large windshield

Rear wheel is 25 cm (10 in) in diameter

Exhaust pipe

Lambretta LD150 Italy 1957

MTP 325

Padded bench saddle seats two

Vespa Rally 250
Italy 1976

Saddle that can seat two people

More than **60 million** Super Cubs have been built – the most produced motor vehicle ever.

Air vents help cool engine, which can propel scooter to speeds up to 113 km/h (70 mph)

Honda Super Cub C100
Japan 1958

Scooters are small motorbikes with a step-through design and the driver's seat above an enclosed engine. The term "mopeds" once meant motorized bikes that had to be pedalled to start, but now applies to small scooters with 50 cc or lesser power engines.

The **Autoped** was one of the first scooters; its engine drove the front wheel using gears. The **VéloSoleX 45**, an early moped, had an engine that powered a ceramic roller that gripped the top of the front wheel to turn it. Lightweight and fuel efficient, scooters and mopeds, such as the

Safety cell crumples in crash to protect rider

BMW C1 200 Germany 2001

This scooter can go from **0 to 100 km/h** (62 mph) in under **7 seconds**.

Hooded instrument panel

Honda PCX 125 Japan 2010

Front wheel fitted with hydraulic brake

BMW C Evolution Germany 2014

Large lithium-ion battery powers electric motors and can be recharged in 4 hours

Scooter travels 100 km (62 miles) on a single charge

Small fuel tank holds 5 litres (1.3 gal) of fuel

Carrier with storage box

Steel luggage rack

VéloSoleX 45 France 1949

Motobécane Mobylette France 1986

Hinged seat with compartment underneath

Headlight fitted into the plastic fairing

Yamaha Jog RR Japan 2011

PGO PMX Naked Taiwan 2011

Honda Super Cub, proved to be a cheap form of transport in the post-war years. A craze for stylishly designed Italian scooters in the 1950s and 1960s led to the popular **Lambretta LD150** with its large windshield, passenger seat, and top speed of 80 km/h (50 mph). Scooters and mopeds are still in demand. The **Yamaha Jog** and the **PGO PMX**, powered by small 50 cc engines, are aimed at young riders. Future scooters may be enclosed with a roof, such as the **BMW C1 200** concept, or be powered by electric motors, like the **BMW C Evolution**.

Three-wheelers

Ariel Tricycle UK 1898

Fuel tank

Single-cylinder engine propelled bike to 39 km/h (24 mph)

Top box holds tools and spare clothing

Raleigh Raleighette Tandem Tricar UK 1904

Passenger seat in front of the driver

Steering wheel instead of handlebars

Coiled radiator tubes filled with water to cool engine

Rexette 5HP UK 1905

Rear light

Front fender

Harley-Davidson Servi-Car GE USA 1969

Police siren

Chopper-styled wide, padded seat

Honda Stream Japan 1982

Not all motorbikes have two wheels. Ever since bikes were first developed, engineers have experimented with three-wheeled machines, which are easier to learn to ride, have more space for engines or loads, and come with an extra tyre for better grip.

Early three-wheelers were pedal-powered tricycles fitted with an engine. The **Ariel Tricycle** used the space between the rear wheels for the engine. Some manufacturers preferred to power a single rear wheel, so they placed a pair of wheels in the front. Both the **Rexette 5HP** and **Raleighette**

Honda Goldwing EML Trike
Japan/Netherlands 1994

Vandenbrink Carver One Netherlands 2007

Short, plastic, windshield deflects air up and over rider's head

Three-wheeled car-like body tilts up to 45 degrees, with wheels staying on the road

Each Can-Am front wheel has its own **suspension** to ride out **bumps**.

Motorbike weighs 152 kg (335.1 lb), a quarter of the Carver One

Can-Am Spyder Trike
Canada 2011

Yamaha Tricity
Japan 2014

Twin six-spoked wheels with 35 cm (13.8 in) diameter

Tricar had rear-wheel drive, and used the space above the front wheels to fit a passenger chair. The popular **Harley-Davidson Servi-Car GE** served police forces and breakdown mechanics from the 1930s to the 1970s. In contrast, the **Can-Am Spyder** is built for fun and has as much power as a small hatchback car. Advances in technology have brought in new three-wheelers that can tilt their bodies as they turn. The **Vandenbrink** is like a three-wheeled car, with a fully enclosed cockpit and twin rear wheels, while the **Yamaha Tricity** resembles a motorbike, with twin wheels in front.

Road burners

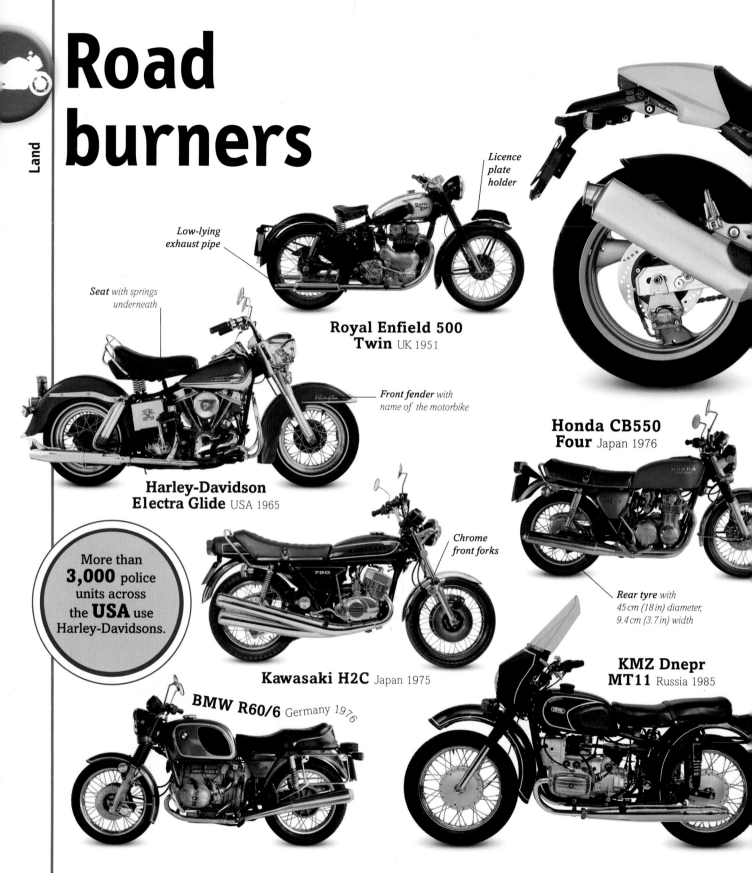

Low-lying exhaust pipe

Licence plate holder

Royal Enfield 500 Twin UK 1951

Seat *with springs underneath*

Front *fender with name of the motorbike*

Harley-Davidson Electra Glide USA 1965

Honda CB550 Four Japan 1976

More than **3,000** police units across the **USA** use Harley-Davidsons.

Chrome front forks

Rear tyre *with 45 cm (18 in) diameter, 9.4 cm (3.7 in) width*

Kawasaki H2C Japan 1975

BMW R60/6 Germany 1976

KMZ Dnepr MT11 Russia 1985

Various types of motorbikes have been designed for road use, from standards to cruisers. Most standards offer a relatively upright riding style and have smooth tyres. Cruisers are bigger, with a reclining back and relaxed riding position for long rides.

Standard motorbikes are ideal for riding around town and for short journeys. Popular mid-sized engine bikes in the 1970s included the **BMW R60/6** and the **Honda CB550**, with a top speed of 164 km/h (102 mph) from its 500 cc engine. For long-distance riding, cruisers are more

Ducati M900 Monster Italy 1994

Powerful headlight

Harley-Davidson FLSTF Fat Boy USA 1999

A **Fat Boy** starred in the **Terminator 2** movie.

Long exhaust pipe from engine cylinder

Large, twin, 32-cm- (12.6-in-) diameter brake discs for high braking power

BMW R1200 RT Germany 2005

Yamaha FZS1000 Fazer Japan 2002

21-litre (5.5-gal) fuel tank

Engine gives top speed of 217 km/h (135 mph)

Instrument panel on top of fuel tank

Long bench seat is 74 cm (29 in) above ground

Triumph Bonneville UK 2011

Triumph Thunderbird UK 2010

popular. The **Electra Glide** was the first big Harley-Davidson motorbike to have an electric engine starter. The **Thunderbird**, manufactured in UK, was Triumph's first belt-driven motorbike since the 1920s. Muscle bikes have powerful engines and are shaped to look as up-to-the-minute as possible. The **Ducati M900** stands out with its large, sculpted fuel tank and unusual triangular frame. Other road motorbikes have picked up design elements from classic machines, such as the **Harley-Davidson Fat Boy** and the **Triumph Bonneville**.

Burning rubber

Oil tank fitted in front of fuel tank

129 km/h (80 mph)
Scott Super Squirrel UK 1927

Heavily sprung saddle

153 km/h (95 mph)
Norton International 30 UK 1936

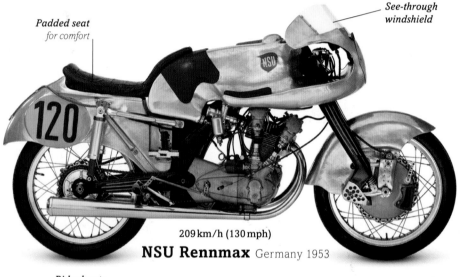

Padded seat for comfort

See-through windshield

209 km/h (130 mph)
NSU Rennmax Germany 1953

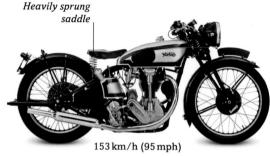

The RC166's engine could turn at **20,000 rpm**, which is 333 turns every second!

Windshield

Rider has to lean over large aluminium fuel tank

Three of the motorbike's six exhaust pipes

Honda RC166 Japan 1966

286 km/h (178 mph)
Moto Guzzi V8 Italy 1957

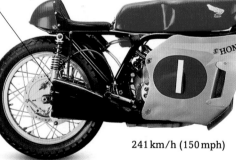

241 km/h (150 mph)

Racing motorbikes are built and tuned for ultimate performance, and maximum speed, acceleration, and braking power on the track. Sports bikes also boast high performance, but are used on roads. Some mimic the style and features of racers.

Early racing motorbikes, such as the **Scott Super Squirrel** and the **Norton International 30**, competed in different kinds of races, from track races to time trials. In 1934, the Nortons finished first, second, third, and fourth in the famous Isle of Man TT (time trial). Track racers compete

Kawasaki Dragster UK/Japan 1977

Low fairing with built-in windshield

Two Kawasaki 850 cc motorbike engines work together

354 km/h (220 mph)

Sculpted seat for low riding position

Suzuki RG500 Japan 1986

Bimota Mantra Italy 1996

237 km/h (147 mph)

201 km/h (125 mph)

The Dragster could reach **240 km/h** (149 mph) in just **7.7 seconds**.

Wide, slick, treadless tyre for racing on smooth tracks

320 km/h (200 mph)

Honda CBR1000RR Fireblade Japan 2009

Yamaha YZF R1 Japan 1998

Aprilia RSV4 Italy 2011

275 km/h (171 mph)

Single racing exhaust made of titanium metal

290 km/h (180 mph)

according to their type and engine size. The **Honda RC166** weighed 112 kg (247 lb) and had a 250 cc engine, yet it could race at speeds up to 241 km/h (150 mph). Modern racers, such as the **Aprilia RSV4**, are packed with electronic wizardry. An RSV4 rider can adjust the motorbike's suspension, gearbox, and engine performance while riding. Manufacturers sometimes produce road-going versions of their successful racers. The **Suzuki RG500** was based on the racing RG500s, which had won four 500 cc Grand Prix World Championships in seven years.

JUMPS AND FLICKS

Woooah! Pedro Moreno pulls a spectacular mid-air move during the 2013 freestyle competition in Zurich, Switzerland – the largest freesport event in Europe. Moreno is a professional freestyle motocross (FMX) rider. This is a sport in which motocross riders perform routines, throwing stunning shapes and pulling wicked tricks in the air as their bikes leap off giant ramps.

Freestylers use modified motocross racing motorbikes with a number of adjustments. These include shaving the foam saddle down to narrow it, replacing components with lighter variations, and re-routing cables to avoid getting boots tangled up in them as they perform their tricks and moves. These can be spectacular, such as full backflips by both bike and rider, "the cliffhanger", where the rider hooks his or her toes under the handlebars, and "the tsunami", where the rider performs a handstand over the handlebars while keeping the bike horizontal! Riders can also twist in the air, grab the saddle, and even let go of the bike completely, but they must nail a safe landing to get top marks from the judges.

Off-roaders

Harley-Davidson Hillclimber USA 1930

Raised mudguard to keep mud and water from flinging up

BSA Gold Star Scrambler UK 1959

Metal chains wrapped around rear tyre to grip loose ground

Hollow aluminium **wheels** meant this motorbike could **float** in water!

Rokon Trail-breaker USA 1963

Large, steel cargo rack

Chain driving front wheel

Husqvarna Enduro Sweden 1973

284

Race number

CZ 250 Motocross Czech Republic 1974

35

Knobbly, deep-tread tyre for gripping soft ground

Road-legal bike weighs 109 kg (240.3 lb)

10.6 litres (2.8 gal) plastic fuel tank

Suzuki Enduro PE250X Japan 1981

Off-road motorbikes let you get away from the traffic, unless you are competing in a motocross race with 30 or 40 riders over a bumpy dirt course. Off-roaders are tough and strong, and equipped with plenty of suspension to soak up impacts.

The **Rokon Trail-breaker** is the only widely produced motorbike to offer an all-wheel drive. Other off-roaders rely on rear-wheel drive and chunky tyres with deep tread to grip sand or mud. The **KTM 65SX** is ideal for 8 to 13 year olds, but young riders may progress to a top motocross bike

Speedway bikes take under **3 seconds** to accelerate from **0 to 100 km/h** (62 mph).

Small tank holds enough methanol fuel for four laps of racing

Forks steeply angled to give more response when steering

Weslake Speedway UK 1981

Honda Africa Twin Japan 1990

Twin headlights

Motorbike can travel 600 km (372.8 miles) on one tank of fuel

Yamaha XT Tenere Japan 2010

KTM 65SX Austria 2011

Long-travel front forks

Aluminium exhaust silencer tucked up under seat rear

Motorbike gives top speed of 80 km/h (50 mph)

KTM 350 SX-F Austria 2012

such as the **KTM 350 SX-F**. KTMs won the Motocross MX2 World Championships from 2008 to 2014. Enduro bikes, such as the lightweight **Suzuki Enduro PE250X**, race off-road but are usually used for competing over longer courses than motocross. Adventure motorbikes are big off-roaders with large fuel tanks, such as the **Yamaha XT Tenere**, which is based on the bike that won the Dakar Rally seven times. Speedway bikes, such as the **Weslake Speedway**, have no brakes and just one gear. They are raced in laps on a tight, oval dirt track in competitions.

Fastest on two wheels

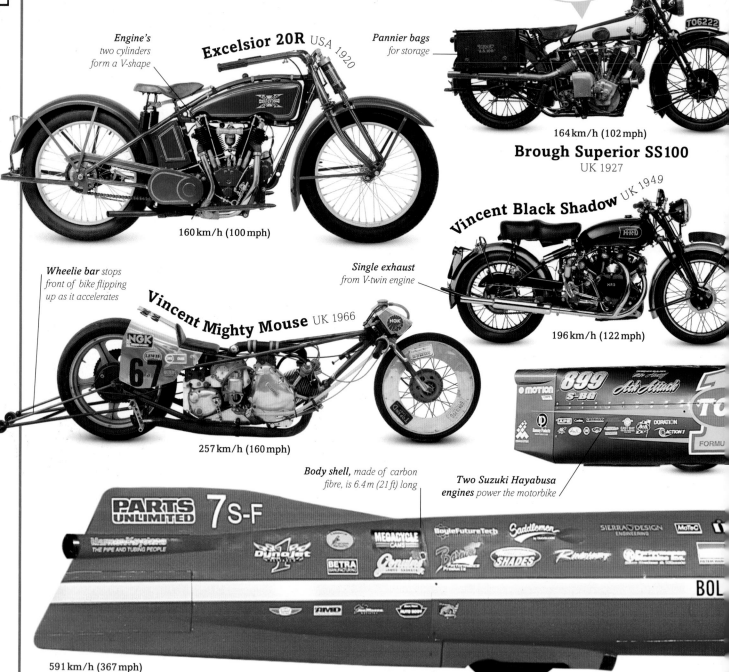

A 1929 **SS100** once sold for **£315,000** ($480,000) at auction.

Engine's two cylinders form a V-shape

Excelsior 20R USA 1920

160 km/h (100 mph)

Pannier bags for storage

164 km/h (102 mph)

Brough Superior SS100
UK 1927

Vincent Black Shadow UK 1949

Single exhaust from V-twin engine

196 km/h (122 mph)

Wheelie bar stops front of bike flipping up as it accelerates

Vincent Mighty Mouse UK 1966

257 km/h (160 mph)

Body shell, made of carbon fibre, is 6.4 m (21 ft) long

Two Suzuki Hayabusa engines power the motorbike

591 km/h (367 mph)

Ever since motorbikes were built, they have been raced or tested to see just how fast they would go. Designers, engineers, and riders would push everything to the limit to squeeze every drop of speed from their magnificent machines.

The **Excelsior 20R** was one of the first motorbikes to reach 160 km/h (100 mph). It was overtaken by the **Brough Superior SS100** and later the **Vincent Mighty Mouse**, which became the fastest single-cylinder motorbike when it raced along drag strips in the 1960s. Most modern

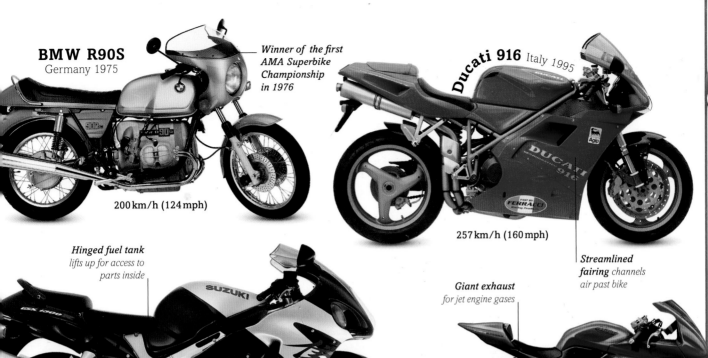

BMW R90S
Germany 1975

Winner of the first AMA Superbike Championship in 1976

200 km/h (124 mph)

Ducati 916 Italy 1995

257 km/h (160 mph)

Streamlined fairing channels air past bike

Hinged fuel tank lifts up for access to parts inside

299 km/h (186 mph)

Suzuki GSX 1300R Hayabusa
Japan 1999

Powerful disc brakes

Giant exhaust for jet engine gases

402 km/h (250 mph)

MTT Turbine Superbike
USA 2001

Giant 1,441 cc engine has power of two cars

Top 1 Ack Attack USA 2004

606 km/h (376 mph)

301 km/h (187 mph)

Kawasaki ZZR1400 Japan 2011

BUB Seven Streamliner USA 2006

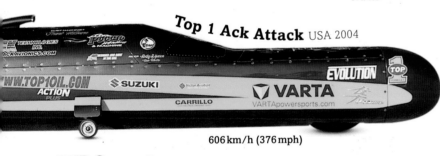

SPEED Top three record breakers

Top 1 Ack Attack
606 km/h (376 mph)

BUB Seven Streamliner
591 km/h (367 mph)

MTT Turbine Superbike
402 km/h (250 mph)

motorbikes have engines with multiple cylinders. The **Ducati 916** won four World Superbike Championships with its twin-cylinder engine, while the four-cylinder **Suzuki GSX 1300R Hayabusa** was the fastest production motorbike of last century, and the **Kawasaki ZZR1400** is the fastest so far. Even faster are modern streamliners, motorbikes with low-slung aerodynamic bodies inside which riders lie flat. The **BUB Seven Streamliner** was the first to break 563 km/h (350 mph) in 2006, while the **Top 1 Ack Attack** is currently the world's fastest motorbike.

Easy riders

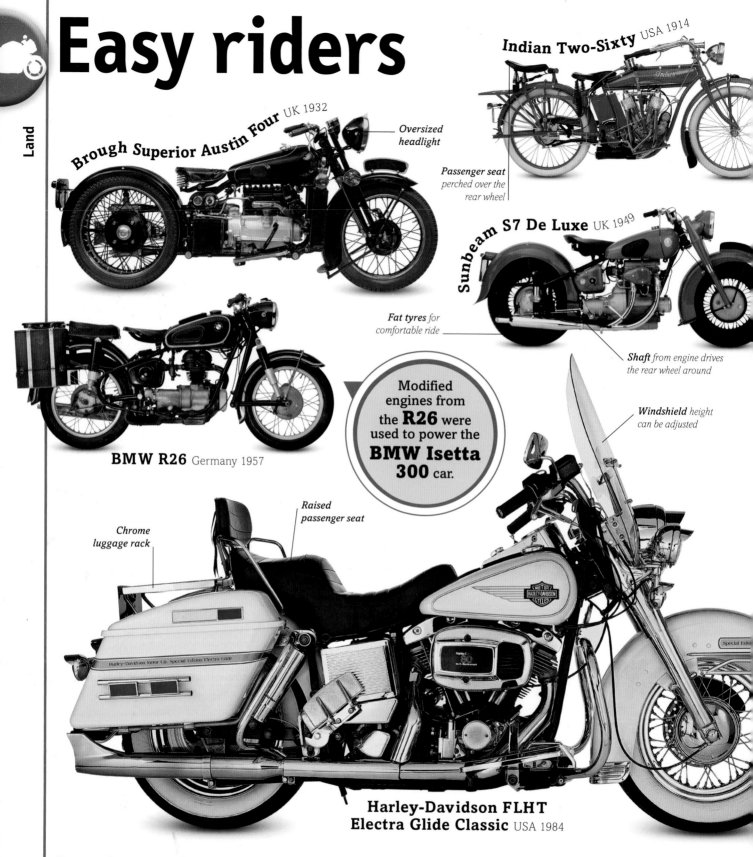

Indian Two-Sixty USA 1914

Brough Superior Austin Four UK 1932

Oversized
headlight

Passenger seat
perched over the
rear wheel

Sunbeam S7 De Luxe UK 1949

Fat tyres for
comfortable ride

Shaft from engine drives
the rear wheel around

BMW R26 Germany 1957

Modified
engines from
the **R26** were
used to power the
**BMW Isetta
300** car.

Windshield height
can be adjusted

Raised
passenger seat

Chrome
luggage rack

**Harley-Davidson FLHT
Electra Glide Classic** USA 1984

Large, heavy, and powerful, touring and
sports-touring motorbikes are designed for
comfortable long-distance riding. Some of
these big beasts are the last word in luxury,
with high-quality audio systems and
comforts not found on other motorbikes.

Early big motorbikes often copied features usually
found in cars. The **Indian Two-Sixty** was the
first bike to come with electric lighting as a
standard feature. The **Brough Superior Austin
Four** used an engine and a gearbox from a car to
drive two closely set rear wheels for a smoother

Cruise control *allows motorbike to travel at set speed*

Honda Goldwing GL1500 Japan 1999

Suzuki M1800R Intruder Japan 2007

Harley-Davidson CVO Softail Convertible USA 2010

Carbon fibre body panels

1,078 cc engine *gives top speed of 315 km/h (196 mph)*

MV Agusta F4CC Italy 2008

Cast aluminium front wheel

Adaptive headlight *changes brightness according to conditions*

Costing **£196,755** ($300,000), this bike comes with a **£13,117** ($20,000) watch.

Twin disc brakes, *normally found on racing motorbikes*

Air bag *inflates in 0.1 seconds during crash*

BMW K1600GT Germany 2011

Frame *made of light but strong titanium metal*

Ecosse Titanium USA 2011

Honda Goldwing GL1800 Japan 2014

ride. In the 1970s and 1980s, big motorbikes got even larger and heavier. The **Electra Glide Classic** weighed more than 335 kg (738.5 lb) empty. Modern luxury motorbikes continue to offer innovative features. The **Honda Goldwing GL1500** comes with foot heaters and some feature an in-built jukebox. The **BMW K1600GT** has heated seats and handlebar grips for cold weather, and an onboard computer with a colour touch screen. The **Honda Goldwing GL1800** has an electric reverse gear and an air bag for the rider.

Car

The car revolutionized transport in the 20th century and more than half a billion cars are found on the world's roads today. While some are powered fully or partly by electric motors, most cars use an internal-combustion engine in which fuel and air are mixed and burned to produce power to drive the wheels. The **Toyota Yaris** (or the *Vitz*) is a popular, small family car, with more than 200,000 manufactured every year.

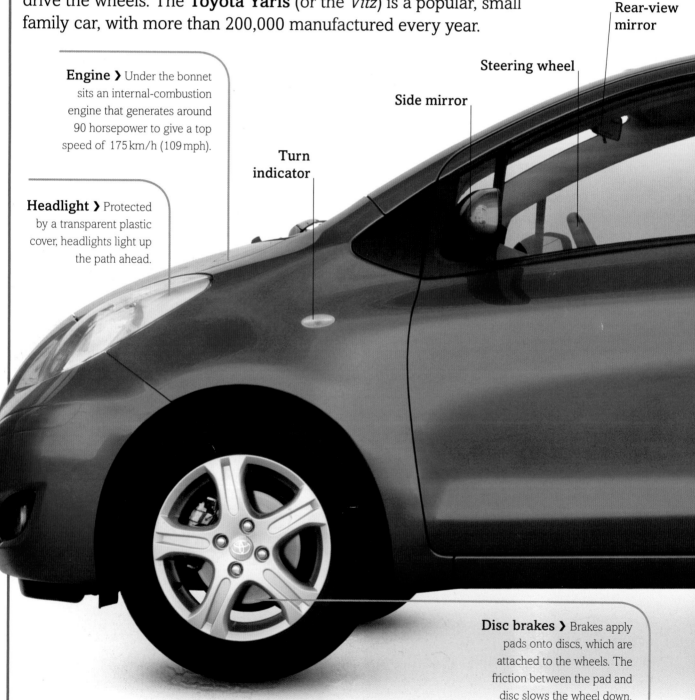

Engine ❯ Under the bonnet sits an internal-combustion engine that generates around 90 horsepower to give a top speed of 175 km/h (109 mph).

Headlight ❯ Protected by a transparent plastic cover, headlights light up the path ahead.

Turn indicator

Side mirror

Steering wheel

Rear-view mirror

Disc brakes ❯ Brakes apply pads onto discs, which are attached to the wheels. The friction between the pad and disc slows the wheel down.

Hatchback ❯ A full-height rear lifting-boot door gives this car 272 litres (71.8 gal) of storage space. Cars with a rear door like this are known as hatchbacks.

Interior ❯ Inside the car, the driver and passengers are protected by a number of airbags, which inflate when there is a severe impact, to cushion the occupants. The Yaris has front and side airbags.

Radio aerial

Toyota Yaris/ _Vitz_

Rear indicator and brake light

Passenger door ❯ These are fashioned out of steel panels, aluminium, or carbon fibre. This car is fitted with remote central locking. The driver presses a button on the key to open or close the locks on all four doors.

Pioneering cars

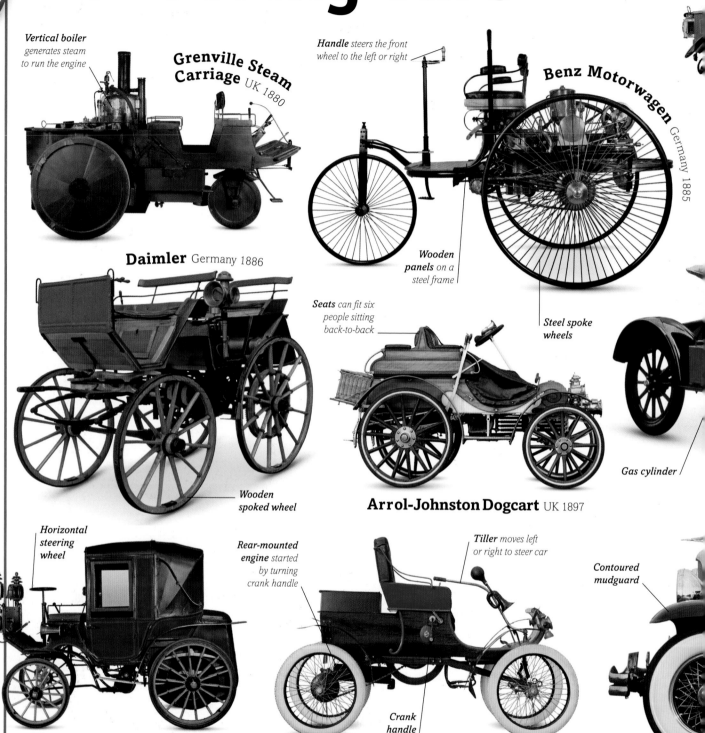

Vertical boiler *generates steam to run the engine*

Grenville Steam Carriage UK 1880

Handle *steers the front wheel to the left or right*

Benz Motorwagen *Germany 1885*

Daimler *Germany 1886*

Wooden panels *on a steel frame*

Seats *can fit six people sitting back-to-back*

Steel spoke wheels

Wooden spoked wheel

Arrol-Johnston Dogcart UK 1897

Gas cylinder

Horizontal steering wheel

Rear-mounted engine *started by turning crank handle*

Tiller *moves left or right to steer car*

Contoured mudguard

Crank handle

Daimler Cannstatt
Germany 1898

Oldsmobile Curved Dash USA 1901

Early attempts to take to the road were in steam-powered vehicles, such as the Grenville Steam Carriage. It took the development of reliable internal-combustion engines fuelled by petrol to produce the first popular cars.

The inventor Siegfried Marcus constructed an early four-wheel car with a petrol-driven internal combustion engine, but Karl Benz was the first to get a patent for his vehicle, the three-wheeled **Benz Motorwagen**. The **Daimler**, a motorized horse carriage, appeared shortly after. Soon more

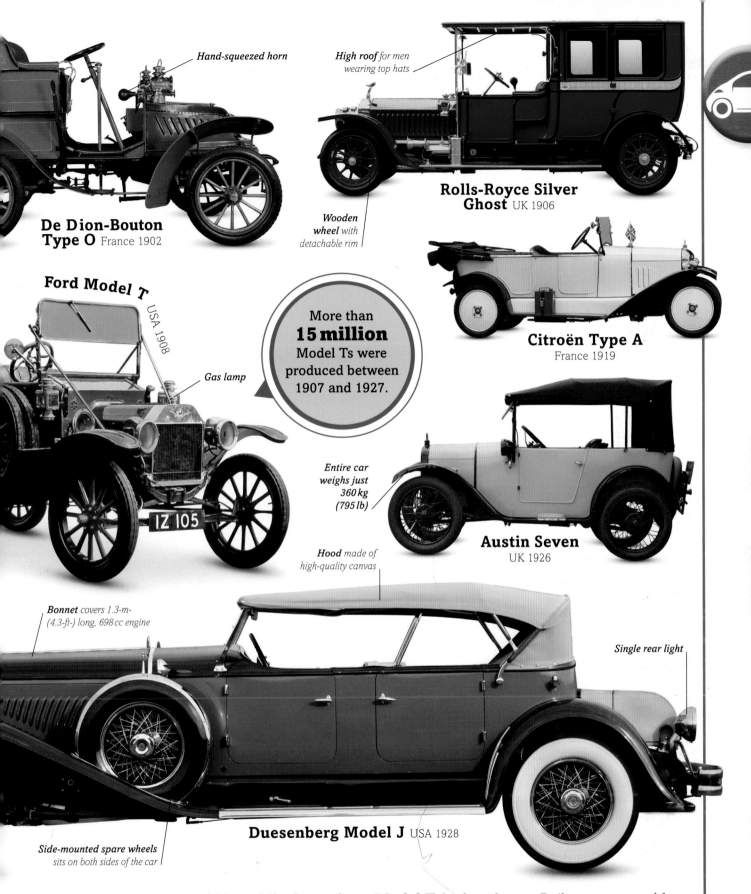

Hand-squeezed horn

De Dion-Bouton Type O France 1902

High roof for men wearing top hats

Rolls-Royce Silver Ghost UK 1906

Wooden wheel with detachable rim

Ford Model T USA 1908

Gas lamp

IZ 105

More than **15 million** Model Ts were produced between 1907 and 1927.

Citroën Type A France 1919

Entire car weighs just 360 kg (795 lb)

Austin Seven UK 1926

Hood made of high-quality canvas

Bonnet covers 1.3-m- (4.3-ft-) long, 698 cc engine

Single rear light

Duesenberg Model J USA 1928

Side-mounted spare wheels sits on both sides of the car

car makers emerged. The **Oldsmobile Curved Dash** was the world's first mass-produced car, with more than 19,000 sold. Some early cars had rather primitive features. The engine of the **Arrol-Johnston Dogcart** was started by pulling on a rope, and many cars, including the **Ford Model T**, had gas lamps. Built on an assembly line, the Model T made motoring affordable for the masses. The 1920s saw an explosion in car design, from the **Duesenberg Model J**, driven by American gangsters and movie stars, to the compact **Austin Seven**.

THRILLS AND SPILLS
At first, this dramatic tangle of men and machines looks like a horrible accident. In fact, it's all fun and games. A clue is the ball on the ground on the right of the picture and, if you look closely, you can see that the two passengers in the cars are wielding mallets. Welcome to the sport of "auto polo", and a crunch moment during a game in Florida, USA, in 1928.

Polo is usually played by riders on horseback. In the USA in the early 1900s, the sport was given a mad makeover when the horses were replaced with cars. It is said that the inventor was a Ford automobile dealer who came up with the idea as a publicity stunt, and it caught on. The game was played by two teams, each made up of two cars and four players, and their steeds were stripped-down Ford Model Ts. The driver was held in place with a seat belt, while his malletman leaned out and tried to hit a basketball into a goal. The cars tore around the field at furious speeds up to 64 km/h (40 mph), while the referee chased the action on foot. By the end of the game, most of the cars were destroyed.

Early racing cars

Some early racing cars had a **mechanic** onboard to make repairs.

Small, round windscreen known as monocle

Cylindrical fuel tank

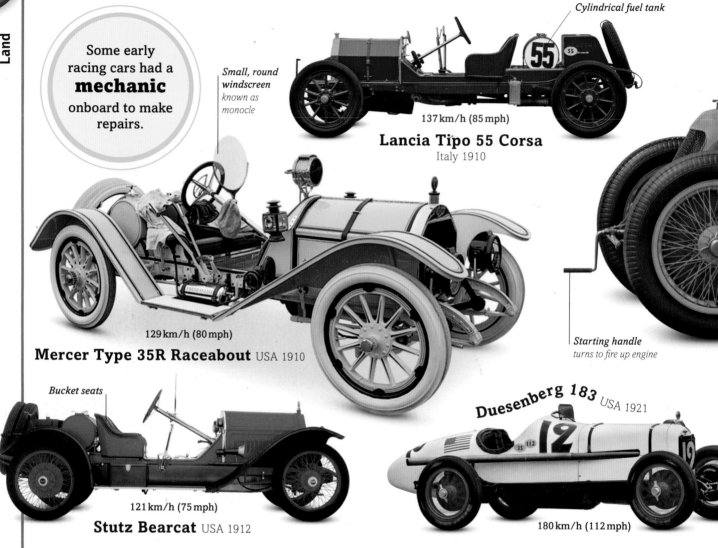

55

137 km/h (85 mph)

Lancia Tipo 55 Corsa
Italy 1910

129 km/h (80 mph)

Mercer Type 35R Raceabout USA 1910

Starting handle turns to fire up engine

Bucket seats

121 km/h (75 mph)

Stutz Bearcat USA 1912

Duesenberg 183 USA 1921

12

180 km/h (112 mph)

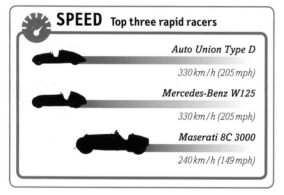

SPEED Top three rapid racers

Auto Union Type D

330 km/h (205 mph)

Mercedes-Benz W125

330 km/h (205 mph)

Maserati 8C 3000

240 km/h (149 mph)

Bugatti Type 35B France 1927

Eight-spoke cast aluminium wheels

204 km/h (127 mph)

As soon as cars were built in numbers, people became keen to race them. Early racing tested speed as well as reliability, as early cars broke down a lot. But, advances in technology quickly saw racing cars develop into speed demons.

Some early racing drivers turned into car builders. Italy's Vincenzo Lancia, who won the 1904 Coppa Florio race, manufactured the **Lancia Tipo 55 Corsa**. Across the Atlantic, the **Stutz Bearcat** won 25 of the 30 races it entered, while the **Mercer Type 35R Raceabout** won

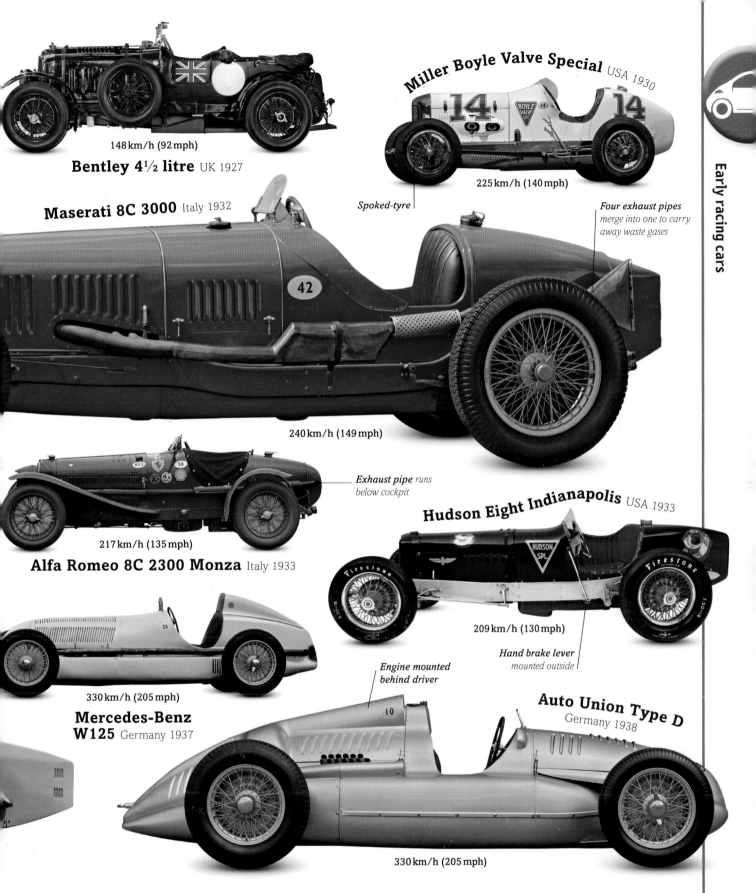

Bentley 4½ litre UK 1927

148 km/h (92 mph)

Miller Boyle Valve Special USA 1930

225 km/h (140 mph)

Spoked-tyre

Four exhaust pipes merge into one to carry away waste gases

Maserati 8C 3000 Italy 1932

240 km/h (149 mph)

Exhaust pipe runs below cockpit

217 km/h (135 mph)

Alfa Romeo 8C 2300 Monza Italy 1933

Hudson Eight Indianapolis USA 1933

209 km/h (130 mph)

Hand brake lever mounted outside

330 km/h (205 mph)

Mercedes-Benz W125 Germany 1937

Engine mounted behind driver

Auto Union Type D Germany 1938

330 km/h (205 mph)

five of its first six races in 1911. Racing cars remained box-shaped until after World War I, when sleeker, more rounded shapes started to emerge. In 1921, the **Duesenberg 183** became the first all-American car to win a Grand Prix race in Europe. Stunning speedsters, such as the **Alfa Romeo 8C 2300 Monza** and the **Bugatti Type 35B**, were produced throughout the 1920s and '30s. Type 35 cars won more than 1,000 races and battled it out with German cars such as the **Mercedes-Benz W125**, which dominated the 1937 European Grand Prix Championship.

Machines with style

Mercedes-Benz 500K Special Roadster Germany 1934

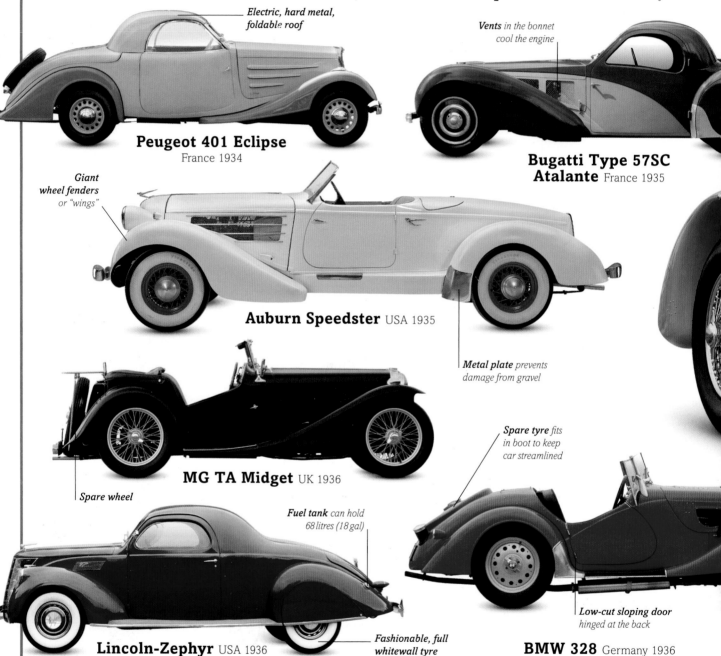

Electric, hard metal, foldable roof

Peugeot 401 Eclipse
France 1934

Vents in the bonnet cool the engine

Bugatti Type 57SC Atalante France 1935

Giant wheel fenders or "wings"

Auburn Speedster USA 1935

Metal plate prevents damage from gravel

MG TA Midget UK 1936

Spare wheel

Spare tyre fits in boot to keep car streamlined

Fuel tank can hold 68 litres (18 gal)

Lincoln-Zephyr USA 1936

Fashionable, full whitewall tyre

Low-cut sloping door hinged at the back

BMW 328 Germany 1936

In the 1930s, some cars got slick and sleek as research revealed the importance of airflow around a car, especially at higher speeds. Streamlining vehicles to improve performance resulted in some stylish and eye-catching designs.

The **Lincoln-Zephyr** created a sensation at the 1936 New York Auto Show with its teardrop shape, while on the road, the **Auburn Speedster** roared, with a 148 horsepower engine that generated a top speed of around 160 km/h (100 mph). While some European sports cars

Side-opening, folding bonnet

Cord 810 USA 1936

Alfa Romeo 8C 2900B Coupé Italy 1938

A mere **seventeen** of the elegant Bugatti Type 57SCs were ever built.

Long, sweeping wheel fender

Leather strap holds engine bonnet down

Delage D6-75 France 1938

FYE 415

Retractable windscreen

Enclosed rear wheel

A **Darl'Mat** won the 2-litre- (0.5-gal-) class **Le Mans** 24 Hour race in 1938.

Peugeot 402 Darl'Mat France 1938

stayed boxy, such as the **MG TA Midget**, others like the **Alfa Romeo 8C 2900B Coupé** were designed with sweeping, rounded body shapes. The exotic **Peugeot 402 Darl'Mat** showcased extreme streamlining with a lightweight aluminium body and an advanced gearbox.

The sleek **Mercedes-Benz 500K Special Roadster** was packed with advanced features for its time, including electric door locks, turn indicators, hydraulic brakes, and separate suspension systems for each wheel for a comfortable ride.

Fins and finery

Rear compartment seats four people on two rows of facing seats

Mercedes-Benz 300 Germany 1951

Buick Roadmaster
USA 1951

**Cadillac Series 62
Club Coupé** USA 1952

7,046cc engine with a top speed of 177km/h (110mph)

Armstrong Siddeley Sapphire UK 1953

Big fins were pioneered by Cadillac

Large tailfin contains the fuel cap of the 87-litres (23-gal) fuel tank

Front doors open at the back, the opposite way to the rear doors

Chrysler New Yorker
USA 1957

Large tailfin rises up from main body

Studebaker Silver Hawk USA 1957

The 1950s saw an incredible boom in the USA, and 30 million more cars had taken to its roads by the end of the decade. Cars went from being everyday transport to chrome-covered status symbols, packed with innovative new features.

Germany's first post-war luxury car, the **Mercedes-Benz 300**, seated six people and was called the *Adenauer* after the West German chancellor who fitted a writing desk inside one of his 300s. In contrast, the American **Buick Roadmaster** was a riot of two-tone colour and

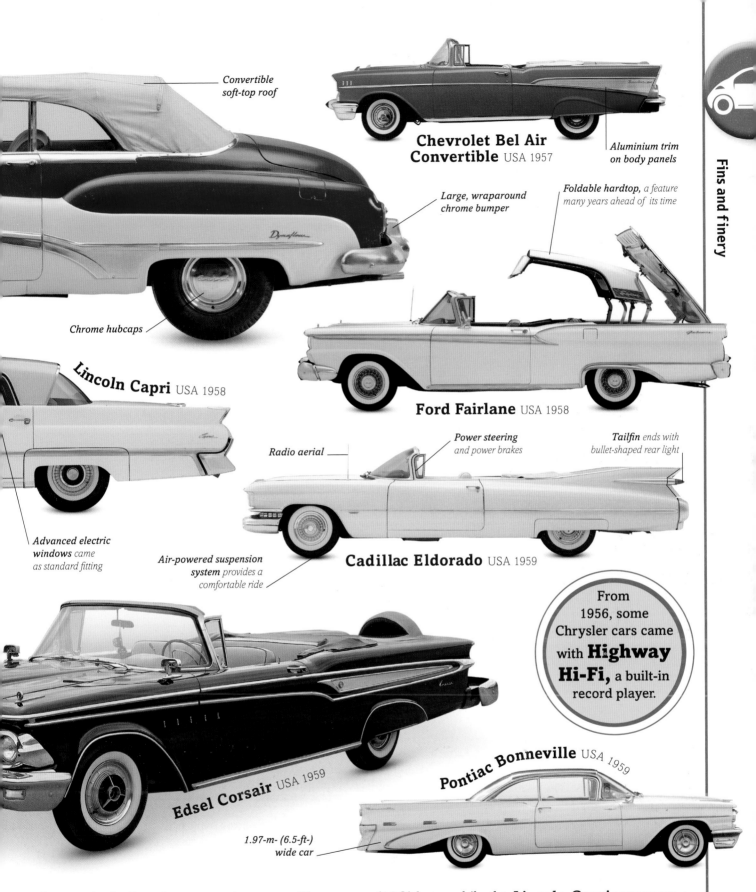

Convertible soft-top roof

Chevrolet Bel Air Convertible USA 1957

Aluminium trim on body panels

Large, wraparound chrome bumper

Foldable hardtop, a feature many years ahead of its time

Chrome hubcaps

Lincoln Capri USA 1958

Ford Fairlane USA 1958

Radio aerial

Power steering and power brakes

Tailfin ends with bullet-shaped rear light

Advanced electric windows came as standard fitting

Air-powered suspension system provides a comfortable ride

Cadillac Eldorado USA 1959

From 1956, some Chrysler cars came with **Highway Hi-Fi,** a built-in record player.

Edsel Corsair USA 1959

Pontiac Bonneville USA 1959

1.97-m- (6.5-ft-) wide car

chrome, including chrome engine vents. The USA had entered the jet-aircraft age and this was reflected in the design of many cars such as the **Pontiac Bonneville,** with its futuristic styling and large tailfins. Some cars also grew in length. The **Chrysler New Yorker** was over 5.5 m

(18 ft) long, while the **Lincoln Capri** was more than 5.8 m (20 ft) long. Automatic transmission was popular in big cars such as the **Chevrolet Bel Air Convertible,** which also had fuel injection and luxurious styling. It remains one of the most collectable cars from the fifties.

Faster and faster

Single, two-eared wheel nut for quick replacement

Mercedes-Benz W196 Germany 1954

Removable steering wheel

196

10

Large 200-litre (53-gal) fuel tank carries 50 per cent methanol

Large stabilizing fin

Maserati 250F Italy 1954

63

Jaguar D-Type UK 1956

83

Driver's headrest

Aston Martin DBR1 UK 1956

101

5

This Formula 1 racer won **8 Grand Prix** between 1954 and 1960.

Roll bar to protect driver if car turns over

Huffaker-Offenhauser Special USA 1964

MG **LIQUID SUSPENSION** Special

Racing car design developed greatly from the 1950s onwards. Engineers and designers were constantly looking for improvements to increase speed, enhance handling, and boost performance in order to be the first over the finish line.

Track racing began in the 1950s with mostly front-engined racing cars, such as the **Maserati 250F** and the **Mercedes-Benz W196**, which won the Formula 1 (F1) Championships in 1954 and 1955. By the end of the 1950s, rear-mounted engines became all the rage

Lotus 49 UK 1967

Ford GT40 MKII USA 1966

Lola-Cosworth T500 UK 1978

Nose fitted with low front wing

FIRST NATIONAL CITY
TRAVELERS CHECKS

Benetton-Ford B193 UK 1993

Carbon fibre body

UNITED COLORS
OF BENETTON.

Adjustable rear spoiler

Williams-Renault FW18 UK 1996

Williams-Renault FW18 won **12** of the **16 F1 races** in 1996.

Holden VR Commodore SS Australia 1993

Windshield clipped in for easy removal

Large, aerodynamic wing keeps the car stable at high speed

Chevrolet Monte Carlo USA 2000

3,000 cc engine gives top speed of 354 km/h (220 mph)

Front wing ensures car grips the track

F1 and Indy Cars. Sports car racing, too, witnessed change. Open cockpit cars such as the **Jaguar D-Type**, which won the Le Mans 24-hr endurance race in 1955, 1956, and 1957, were replaced by cars with a roof. The sleek **Ford GT40 MkII** finished first, second, and third at Le Mans in 1966. In some parts of the world, track racing featuring modified saloon and sedan cars gained popularity. A **Holden VR Commodore SS** won the 1995 Australian Touring Car Championships, while the **Chevrolet Monte Carlo** was driven by many NASCAR racers.

Fast and furious

Bentley Speed 8 UK 2001

Rear wing deflects air to keep car stable

Le Mans 330 km/h (205 mph)

Aston Martin DBR9 UK 2005

Le Mans 299 km/h (186 mph)

Powerful headlights for night-time racing

Audi R10 Germany 2006

Le Mans 339 km/h (211 mph)

Radio transmitter sends information about the car's performance to race team

Roll cage frame protects driver if car rolls over

BMW M3 GT2 Germany 2008

Le Mans 290 km/h (180 mph)

Ferrari F2008 Italy 2008

Powerful disc brakes can stop a car at 200 km/h (124 mph) in three seconds

Modern high-speed racers packed with electronics are designed and modelled on computers, and tested in wind tunnels to ensure their design offers maximum performance. No expense is spared on these sleek speed machines.

All successful racing cars must be fast, but different forms of racing place different demands on the vehicle. A power-packed rally car must be rugged and able to handle roads, tracks, and rough ground. The World Championship winning **Volkswagen WRC Polo R** can accelerate from

Heated, wide, rubber tyres improve performance

Hinged side window acts as door

Lola Aston Martin LMP1 UK 2009

Le Mans 336 km/h (209 mph)

Formula 1 322 km/h (200 mph)

McLaren-Mercedes MP4/23 UK 2008

Chevrolet SS USA/Australia 2013

Large roof flaps lift up to ground car during crash

NASCAR 316 km/h (196 mph)

F1 drivers **shift gears** more than **3,600** times in a Grand Prix race.

Indycar Series 370 km/h (230 mph)

Team Penske Dallara/Chevrolet USA 2014

Volkswagen WRC Polo R Germany 2014

Rally 201 km/h (125 mph)

Formula 1 322 km/h (200 mph)

Mercedes AMG Petronas W05 Germany 2014

Formula 1 341 km/h (212 mph)

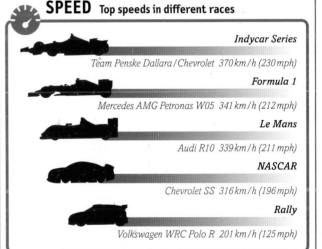

SPEED Top speeds in different races

Indycar Series
Team Penske Dallara/Chevrolet 370 km/h (230 mph)

Formula 1
Mercedes AMG Petronas W05 341 km/h (212 mph)

Le Mans
Audi R10 339 km/h (211 mph)

NASCAR
Chevrolet SS 316 km/h (196 mph)

Rally
Volkswagen WRC Polo R 201 km/h (125 mph)

0–100 km/h (0–62 mph) in 3.9 seconds. Cars built for endurance racing must be very reliable. In 2009, the **Lola Aston Martin LMP1** raced 5,084 km (3,159 miles) in 24 hours at Le Mans. Its driver, Tom Kristensen, also won the race a record nine times in the **Bentley Speed 8** and the **Audi R10**. Danica Patrick, in a **Chevrolet SS**, became the first woman to win pole position for NASCAR's Daytona 500. Lewis Hamilton won the World Championship with the **McLaren-Mercedes MP4/23** in 2008, and again in 2014, with the **Mercedes AMG Petronas W05**.

THE ULTIMATE TEST

Powering through giant sand dunes, some more than 20 m (66 ft) high, is just one of the many challenges facing this Monster Energy X-Raid Mini in the 2013 Dakar Rally. Considered the toughest test of car and driver on the planet, competitors race across more than 8,500 km (5,280 miles) of the toughest terrain imaginable, from rocky pavements to giant deserts and forest trails.

The Dakar was first held in 1979 across the unforgiving Sahara in Africa, but since 2009 it has run through South America. More than 400 cars, motorcycles, quad bikes, and trucks take part in each race, but less than 60 per cent of these reach the finish line. This Mini is built tough and equipped with four-wheel drive, a powerful engine giving it a 178 km/h (111 mph) top speed, and tanks able to hold up to 400 litres (106 gallons) of fuel. Driver Stéphane Peterhansel is a Dakar legend. He won the motorcycle class of the rally six times before switching to cars. Over two solid weeks of phenomenal off-road racing in his Mini, Peterhansel won the 2013 Dakar – his fifth victory in the car class.

Fun in cars

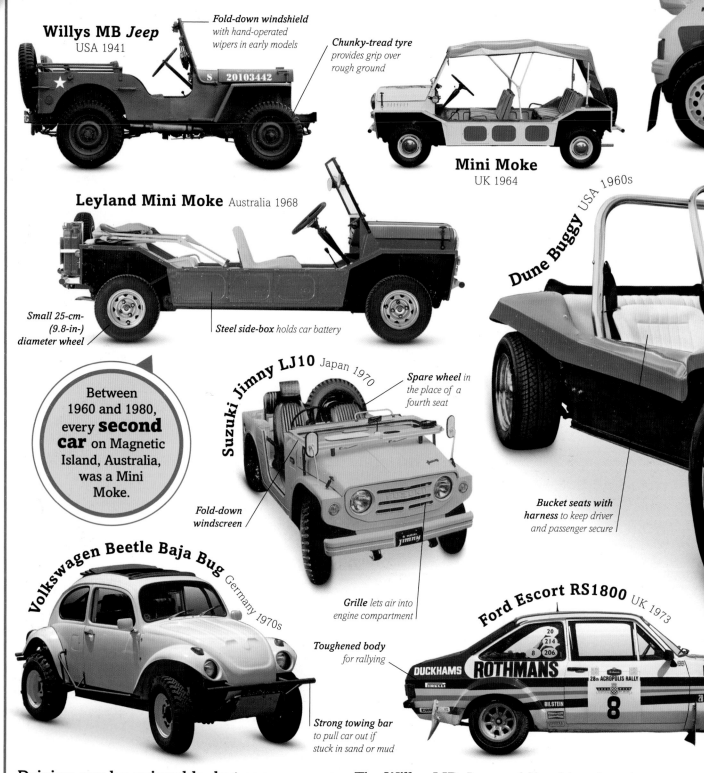

Rear spoiler

Willys MB *Jeep*
USA 1941

Fold-down windshield with hand-operated wipers in early models

Chunky-tread tyre provides grip over rough ground

Mini Moke
UK 1964

Leyland Mini Moke Australia 1968

Dune Buggy USA 1960s

Small 25-cm- (9.8-in-) diameter wheel

Steel side-box holds car battery

Between 1960 and 1980, every **second car** on Magnetic Island, Australia, was a Mini Moke.

Suzuki Jimny LJ10 Japan 1970

Spare wheel in the place of a fourth seat

Bucket seats with harness to keep driver and passenger secure

Fold-down windscreen

Grille lets air into engine compartment

Volkswagen Beetle Baja Bug Germany 1970s

Toughened body for rallying

Ford Escort RS1800 UK 1973

Strong towing bar to pull car out if stuck in sand or mud

Driving can be enjoyable, but some cars are more fun than others! A number of cars have been modified, or designed from scratch, to offer a fun drive on open roads, across stretches of sand, or along trails and rally courses.

The **Willys MB *Jeep*** could be driven just about anywhere, with more than 600,000 produced during World War II. Civilian Jeeps followed until 1986 when they were replaced by the **Jeep Wrangler**, which allowed drivers to switch between two- or four-wheel drive. Several fun

Fuel cap of 290-litre
(76.6-gal) fuel tank

V12 engine from
a Lamborghini
Countach supercar

**Lamborghini
LM002** Italy 1986

**Peugeot 205 T16
Evo 2** France 1985

Steel half-door

Spare wheel

Rear door for
passengers to enter

Jeep Wrangler
USA 1987

Heavy-duty suspension
to withstand bumps

MCC Smart Crossblade France 2002

Cut-out sides offer
open-air driving

Doors are optional
on this two-seater

The
Crossblade has
**no doors, no
windscreen,
and no roof.**

Secma F16 Sport France 2008

cars started life as military prototypes, such as the **Lamborghini LM002**, an off-roader with a four-wheel drive, air conditioning, and a roof-mounted stereo. The **Leyland Mini Moke**, in contrast, was a bare bones vehicle with no frame around the driver. **Dune Buggies** were tailor-made for beaches, while some modified cars, such as the **Baja Bug**, had raised bodies and strong suspensions to overcome the most difficult terrains. Buggy-styled cars are still made today, such as the **Secma F16 Sport**, which has plastic body panels and a convertible roof for rainy days.

79

Crazy cars

Lightweight plywood body

Leyat Hélica France 1919

Brooke Swan UK 1910

Whitewash came out of the back to simulate bird droppings

Aluminium disc-wheel

10.4-m- (34-ft-) long wings

Aerocar USA 1954

BMW Isetta 600 The Detonator Germany 1958

This **James Bond** car can race in reverse gear at speeds above 180 km/h (112 mph).

Gull-wing doors

DeLorean DMC-I2 UK 1981

Body made of brushed stainless-steel

Colourful, hot-rod paint scheme

Aston Martin Vanquish UK 2002

Machine guns

Wienermobile USA 2004

Oscar Mayer

KE02 EWW

Rockets fire from radiator grill

Think all cars are simple, straightforward boxes-on-wheels? Think again! Over the years, designers and engineers have let their imaginations run riot, and some outrageous and surprising designs have left the drawing board and turned into reality.

Some of these wacky machines, such as the **Brooke Swan**, which hissed hot water and steam out of its beak, were wicked one-offs built for eccentrics, or for movies such as the **Batmobile Tumbler**. The **Flatmobile**, however, was made to break records. At just 48.2 cm (19 in) tall, it is

Batmobile *Tumbler* USA 2005

Four rear tyres

LOWEST STREET CAR

48.2 cm (19 in) tall

Home-made jet engine from a Volvo F10 truck turbocharger

Flatmobile UK 2007

Terrafugia Transition USA 2009

Electromagnets lock wings into place

The Transition can **convert** from a car to a plane in under **60 seconds**.

Cockpit has an aircraft control stick and a car steering wheel

Toyota FV2 Japan 2013

Controlled by driver's body movements

Giant Buick-Rover V8 engine fitted to the rear

Cab shaped like a hot dog

Small cockpit pod

Onda Solare Emilia 3 Italy 2013

Solar panels produce more than 1,200 watts of electricity to drive motors

the lowest street-legal car in the world. Flying cars are among the craziest of all, but the **Aerocar** and **Terrafugia Transition** did work, using folding wings and a pusher-propeller at the rear to thrust the car forward. The **Leyat Hélica** couldn't fly but was pushed into action by an aircraft propeller and could reach speeds of up to 170 km/h (106 mph). Some strange-looking cars are experiments to test out ideas, such as the solar-powered **Onda Solare Emilia 3**, or the **Toyota FV2**, whose body can change colour to reflect the driver's mood!

A SPIN ACROSS THE WAVES

Is it a car? Is it a boat? The answer is it's both!

The WaterCar Panther is an American amphibious vehicle equally at home on water as it is on land. When on a lake, river, or bay, its engine powers jet thrusters that suck in water and then push it out behind the craft, propelling it forward at speeds up to 70 km/h (43 mph).

On the road, the car's 3.7-litre (1-gal) Honda Acura engine powers the Panther's rear wheels, giving it a top speed of around 128 km/h (80 mph). The 4.6-m- (15-ft-) long waterproof, Jeep-shaped body can carry four people and is sculpted out of fibreglass fitted to a steel frame. Parts of its body are filled with incredibly lightweight Styrofoam to help it float. When reaching the water, the driver only has to pull a knob to engage the jet thrusters and press a button. The Panther does the rest, using its hydraulic suspension system to retract its wheels up into its body. This all takes under 15 seconds! Once on the water, the Panther can glide with ease and can even tow a water skier or wakeboarder for a bit of watery fun!

Family transport

Radio aerial

Engine at the rear of car

Hillman Imp UK 1963

The Cortina was **the UK's bestselling** car from 1972 to 1981.

Ford Cortina MK I GT UK 1963

Chrome hubcaps

Oldsmobile Starfire USA 1964

5.5 m (17.9 ft) long

Fake air vents, only for show

Austin Maxi 1750 UK 1969

Rear seats fold flat to form cargo area

Morris Marina UK 1971

Fuel tank can hold 52 litres (13.7 gal) of petrol

A family car needs to be economical, and have space for four to five people, as well as for plenty of storage. Many manufacturers work hard to build affordable cars that have the perfect balance of space, performance, and price.

Family cars in the 1960s, such as the **Oldsmobile Starfire**, were often based on a three-box design, with an engine compartment, passenger cabin, and large boot. The **Hillman Imp** changed things by putting the engine in the rear, while early hatchbacks, such as the **Austin Maxi 1750**,

Volkswagen Golf GTI Germany 1975

Front wheels drive
110-horsepower engine

Fiat Strada/Ritmo Italy 1978

Top speed of just
93 km/h (58 mph)

Front-wheel
drive

Trabant East Germany 1989

Engine gave top speed
of 100 km/h (62 mph)

OF·921 A

Peugeot 406 France 1995

Body panels made
of recycled materials

Volvo V70 T5 Sweden 1997

Mercedes-Benz A-Class MKII Germany 2004

Top speed of
218 km/h (135 mph)

came with a sloping rear door to offer more versatile storage space. The affordable **Morris Marina** was built to compete with the highly popular **Ford Cortina**, which was bought by more than two million customers, mostly in the UK. Sleeker family cars appeared from 1970s,

with more hatchbacks such as the **Fiat Strada/ Ritmo** and the **Volkswagen Golf GTI**, which launched a new class of cars – the hot hatch. These offered a hatchback design with a faster, sportier output than most family cars. More than 29 million Golfs have been built to date.

Outdoor warriors

Spyker 60HP
Netherlands 1903

Wheels powered by
8-litre (488-cu in) engine

Jeep Wagoneer USA 1972

Low height
to enable easy
loading of cargo

Rear seats fold down to
create large cargo space

Subaru Leone Estate Japan 1972

*Car switches
between four- and
two-wheel drive*

Audi Sport Quattro Germany 1983

*Top speed of
248 km/h
(154 mph)*

*Low rear
spoiler*

Daihatsu Sportrak Japan 1987

*Small 2.2 m (7.2 ft)
wheelbase*

Turbocharger boosts
engine power to
185 horsepower

STEEP CLIMB

*Some 4x4s
can tackle
angles of
up to 45°*

Lancia Delta Integrale
Italy 1987

Most cars transmit power from their engine to either the front or rear wheels, but not four-wheel drives. Known as "4x4s", these cars direct power to all four wheels, offering better grip on slippery roads and tricky off-road conditions.

In 1903, the **Spyker 60HP** used the first four-wheel drive on a petrol-fuelled car. However, only military and special purpose off-road 4x4s, such as Land Rovers, were built in large numbers until the 1960s and 1970s. The **Subaru Leone Estate** was one of the first everyday 4x4s. It was designed

Land Rover Discovery series II UK 1998

Rubber impact bumper

Top speed of 158 km/h (98 mph)

Volvo XC90 Sweden 2002

Open cargo area

Electronic suspension
allows car to have better
grip for twisting roads

Range Rover Sport UK 2005

Lincoln MK LT USA 2005

Fold-down tailgate

Hummer H3 USA 2005

Mounted rear
tyre takes length
to 4.8 m (15.7 ft)

The H3 was the **smallest** among the Hummer models, and the **only** one to be built by **GM**.

Saturn Outlook USA 2006

Three rows
of seats
accommodate up
to eight people

mainly for driving on roads in all conditions, with some light, off-road action. In the 1980s, rallies became dominated by fast, rugged 4x4s, such as the **Lancia Delta Integrale** and the **Audi Sport Quattro**, which won many World Rally Championship titles between them. By then, the first sports utility vehicles (SUVs) had emerged. These rugged cars, such as the **Daihatsu Sportrack** and **Volvo XC90**, had high-set bodies for better ground clearance over bumpy roads. The powerful **Hummer H3** can drive through water up to 60 cm (24 in) deep.

Convertibles and sports cars

Soft-top roof had to be folded by hand

MGB Convertible UK 1962

Austin-Healey 3000 MKIII UK 1963

Wire-spoked wheels

Porsche 911 Germany 1965

Ford Mustang Fastback USA 1965

Small, narrow boot just wide enough to hold spare tyre

Rear-mounted engine

Ferrari Dino 246GT Italy 1969

Headlight with transparent plastic cover

559 VF

Fast to accelerate and quick to brake, sports cars are built to thrill. Mostly two-seaters, they offer higher performance and sharper handling than everyday cars. Convertibles have a folding roof for open-top driving on sunny days.

There's no mistaking the love for sports cars – old and new! The first generation of **Chevrolet Corvettes** were built in 1953 and the seventh generation came out in 2014. Over 820,000 high-performance **Porsche 911s** have been built, while **Ford Mustang Fastbacks** were

Datsun 260Z Japan 1973

Pontiac Trans Am USA 1975

Large V8 engine under steel bonnet

Turning indicator lights

Chevrolet Corvette USA 1980

The 260Z series was one of the world's **best-selling** sports car in the 1970s.

Long, sloping bonnet

Mazda MX-5 (MkI) Japan 1989

Alloy wheel fitted with disc brake

Fibreglass body on top of aluminium frame

More than **940,000 MX-5s** were sold by 2015.

Lotus Elise UK 1996

Morgan Aero 8 UK 2001

Audi TT Roadster Germany 1999

Louvres channel air over front brakes to keep them cool

amongst the two million Mustangs sold in the first two years of production. Many Mustangs in the late 1960s and 1970s were fitted with large V8 engines to offer the brute force provided by fellow muscle cars such as the **Pontiac Trans Am**. Sports cars fitted with smaller engines, even if not as powerful and fast, also proved fun to drive due to their light weight. The **Mazda MX-5** weighed 890 kg (1,962 lb), while the **Lotus Elise** tipped the scales at just 725 kg (1,598.4 lb). The popular soft-top **MGB Convertible** sold half a million models in the UK alone.

89

Mini motors

1 Volkswagen Beetle Germany 1945

Rear engine air-cooled via vents

4.1 m (13.5 ft) long

Front of car opens out as a single door

2 BMW Isetta 300 Germany 1955

2.3 m (7.5 ft) long

3 Messerschmitt KR200 Germany 1956

2.8 m (9.3 ft) long

Shallow doors open out at the front

4 Frisky Family Three UK 1958

3.1 m (10.2 ft) long

The Subaru 360 took **37 seconds** to do 0–97 km/h (0–60 mph).

5 Subaru 360 Japan 1958

6 Austin Mini Seven UK 1959

Space for four seats

2.95 m (9.7 ft) long

7 Peel P 50 UK 1963

1.3 m (4.3 ft) long

Car has a handle at the back for driver to pull it into parking spaces

Small is beautiful when you need a car to dodge and weave through narrow city streets, and to squeeze into the smallest parking spaces. Light in weight and easy on the pocket, their small engines make these mini motors cheap to run.

Partly inspired by the success of the **Volkswagen Beetle**, a wave of tiny cars hit the roads in the 1950s and 1960s. The compact **Messerschmitt KR200** could accommodate only a driver and one passenger, while the egg-shaped **BMW Isetta 300** had two front wheels placed close

8 Reliant Robin UK 1973

3.3 m (10.8 ft) long

SIZE Small to large

Small boot *area above engine*

10 Fiat 500 Italy 2007

3.5 m (11.5 ft) long

Single *front wheel*

9 Smart City-Coupé Germany / France 1998

2.5 m (8.2 ft) long

11 Tata Nano India 2009

Fibreglass roof

Petrol cap *underneath bonnet*

nano twist

3.1 m (10.2 ft) long

12 Renault Twizy ZE France 2012

2.9 m (9.7 ft) long

Storage space under bonnet as engine in the back

Small 32.5-cm- (1.1-ft-) long *wheels*

Scissor doors open upwards

2.3 m (7.5 ft) long

...o bonnet, and a motorcycle engine ...hind the seat. Many three-wheeled ...h as the **Reliant Robin** and the **Frisky** ...**Three**, could be driven on a motorcycle ...While the Frisky sold only in hundreds, ...es of the hugely popular **Austin Mini**

Seven reached more than four million by 1976. Today, mini cars such as the **Smart City-Coupé** and the **Tata Nano** are popular in crowded cities. However, all of them still dwarf the **Peel P50**, the world's smallest car, which weighs a mere 59 kg (130 lb).

THE MOPETTA MICROCAR

In 1958, the passionate German car designer Egon Brütsch decided he was going to build the world's smallest car for the International Bicycle and Motorcycle Exhibition in Frankfurt that year. His idea was to use a new material called fibreglass to make two shell-like panels, which would fit together to form an egg-shaped microcar.

Brütsch built the prototype of the Mopetta overnight, but he did not have time to sort out the mechanics before the exhibition, so the microcar was displayed up high, away from prying eyes. Success at the show meant Brütsch then had to make his design work. The result was a single-seat three-wheeler that was 1.75 m (5.8 ft) long and 0.9 m (3 ft) wide and had a 50 cc engine that took it to a top speed of 35 km/h (22 mph). With its fibreglass body, Brütsch thought the car would also work as a boat. Although publicity photographs showed the Mopetta crossing a shallow stream, it could never be made fully watertight. Sadly, the Mopetta never took off and only 14 were ever made.

Supercars

Lamborghini Countach, LP 400 Italy 1974

274 km/h (170 mph)

Engine mounted sideways just behind driver's seat

Lamborghini Miura Italy 1966

285 km/h (177 mph)

Lamborghini Diablo Italy 1990

325 km/h (202 mph)

Marcello Gandini designed the Miura before he turned **28**.

Rear wing keeps wheels on the ground at high speeds

Driver sits in the centre and slightly in front of two passenger seats

McLaren F1 LM UK 1995

370 km/h (230 mph)

Five-spoke magnesium wheels fitted with tyres specially made for the car

0–100 KM/H (0–62 MPH)

Caparo T1
2.5 seconds

Porsche 918 RSR Spyder
3.0 seconds

Koenigsegg CCX-R
3.1 seconds

Pagani Zonda Italy 1999

Body panels made of light but strong carbon fibre

354 km/h (220 mph)

Some cars are just too hot to handle. These high-performance sports cars, known as supercars, are phenomenally fast and often very expensive. Hand-crafted in small numbers, they offer the last word in speed and handling.

The first supercar emerged in the 1960s. High-performance cars such as the **Lamborghini Miura** had sleek lines, powerful engines, and were built low to the ground. Miura's successor, the **Countach, LP 400**, was just 1.1 m (3.6 ft) tall. Some supercars were made of high-tech

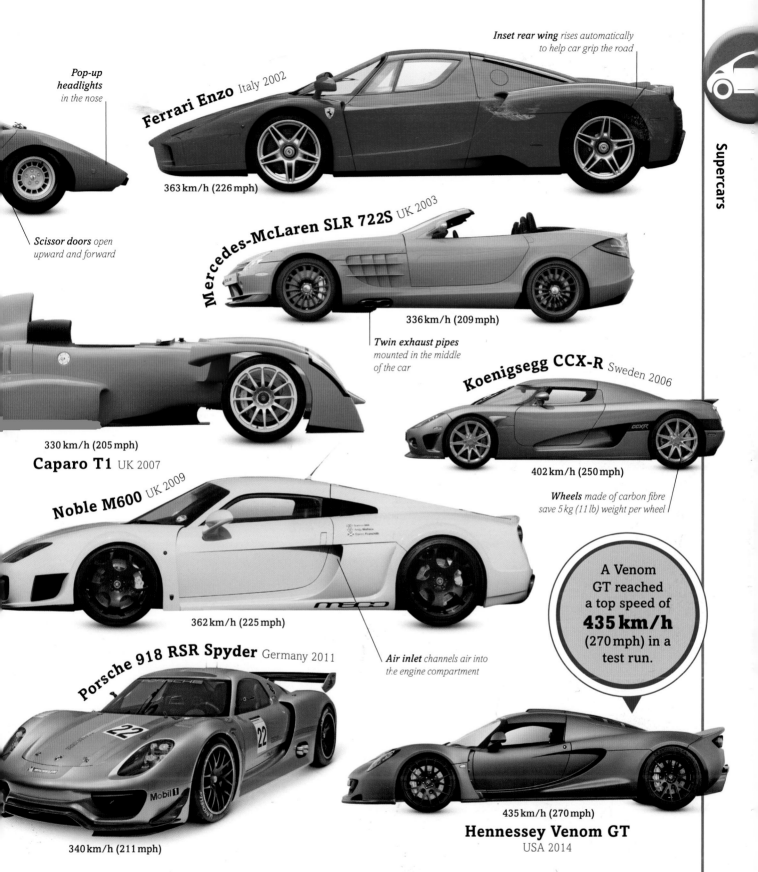

Pop-up headlights in the nose

Ferrari Enzo Italy 2002

Inset rear wing rises automatically to help car grip the road

363 km/h (226 mph)

Scissor doors open upward and forward

Mercedes-McLaren SLR 722S UK 2003

336 km/h (209 mph)

Twin exhaust pipes mounted in the middle of the car

Koenigsegg CCX-R Sweden 2006

402 km/h (250 mph)

330 km/h (205 mph)

Caparo T1 UK 2007

Wheels made of carbon fibre save 5 kg (11 lb) weight per wheel

Noble M600 UK 2009

362 km/h (225 mph)

A Venom GT reached a top speed of **435 km/h** (270 mph) in a test run.

Porsche 918 RSR Spyder Germany 2011

Air inlet channels air into the engine compartment

435 km/h (270 mph)

Hennessey Venom GT USA 2014

340 km/h (211 mph)

material to keep their weight down, with the 470 kg (1,036 lb) **Caparo T1** being the lightest. The heavier supercars compensate with incredibly powerful engines. The **Hennessey Venom GT** can deliver up to 1,244 horsepower, which is 10 times the power of a hatchback. The **Noble M600's** twin turbochargers give it a top speed of 362 km/h (225 mph), while the **McLaren F1 LM** can hit 370 km/h (230 mph). Some supercars feature the latest in racing car technology, such as the **Mercedes-McLaren SLR 722S**, which has fly-by-wire brakes.

Luxury rides

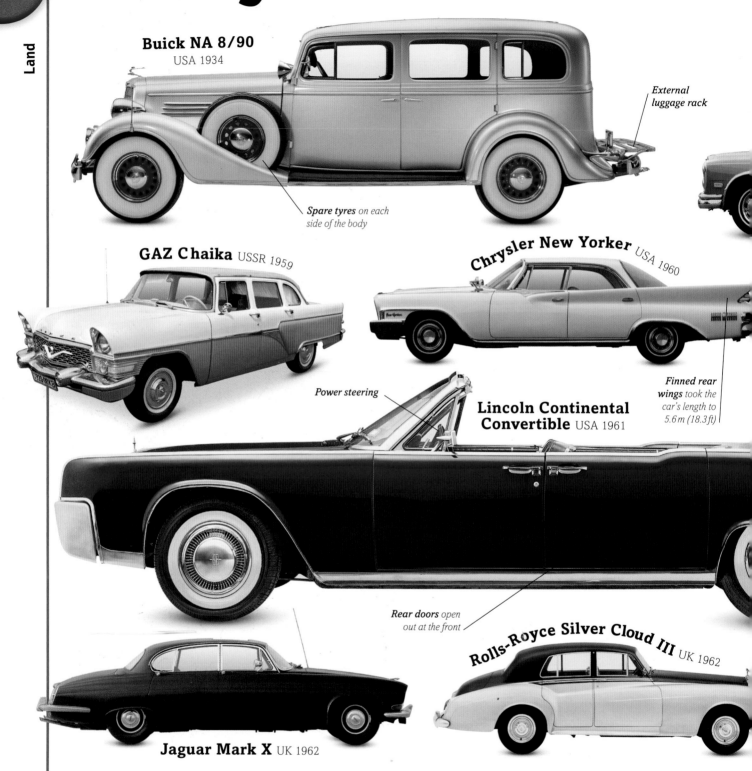

Buick NA 8/90
USA 1934

External luggage rack

Spare tyres on each side of the body

GAZ Chaika USSR 1959

Chrysler New Yorker USA 1960

Finned rear wings took the car's length to 5.6 m (18.3 ft)

Power steering

Lincoln Continental Convertible USA 1961

Rear doors open out at the front

Rolls-Royce Silver Cloud III UK 1962

Jaguar Mark X UK 1962

The last word in comfort, luxury cars are often packed with the most advanced driving and passenger features. These grand, super-expensive cars offer a quiet, cushioned ride for the rich, the powerful, and the famous.

Celebrities and dignitaries did not have to shut the doors of the **Mercedes-Benz 600**. This 2.6-tonne car did it for them! Owners ranged from the Pope and presidents of many countries to the rock 'n' roll legend Elvis Presley. In Communist Soviet Union, the 5.6-m- (18.3-ft-) long, seven-

Checker Marathon USA 1963

A rugged taxi, but stretched for style

Mercedes-Benz 600 Germany 1963

Fuel tank with 45 litre (11.9 gal) capacity fitted inside each rear wing

Daimler DS420 UK 1968

Car accelerates from 0–100 km/h (62 mph) in under 7 seconds

Bentley Continental R UK 1991

Rolls-Royce Phantom Drophead UK 2007

Fold-up roof stored in rear of car

The Phantom Drophead was available in **4,300** different **colours**.

Cadillac STS V8 USA 2009

Sensors alert the driver if the car drifts out of its lane

seater **GAZ Chaika** was the car of choice for politicians, while the stately **Daimler DS420** was used by the British, Swedish, and Danish royal families. The car was based on the **Jaguar Mark X**, which came with a wood-panelled interior, plenty of legroom, and fold-down picnic tables.

Some **Rolls Royce Silver Cloud IIIs** had cocktail bars and televisions, while the **Lincoln Continental Convertible** turned heads with its convertible, four-door design. The statue on the hood of the **Rolls-Royce Phantom Drophead** sinks into the bonnet when the car is locked up.

Record breakers

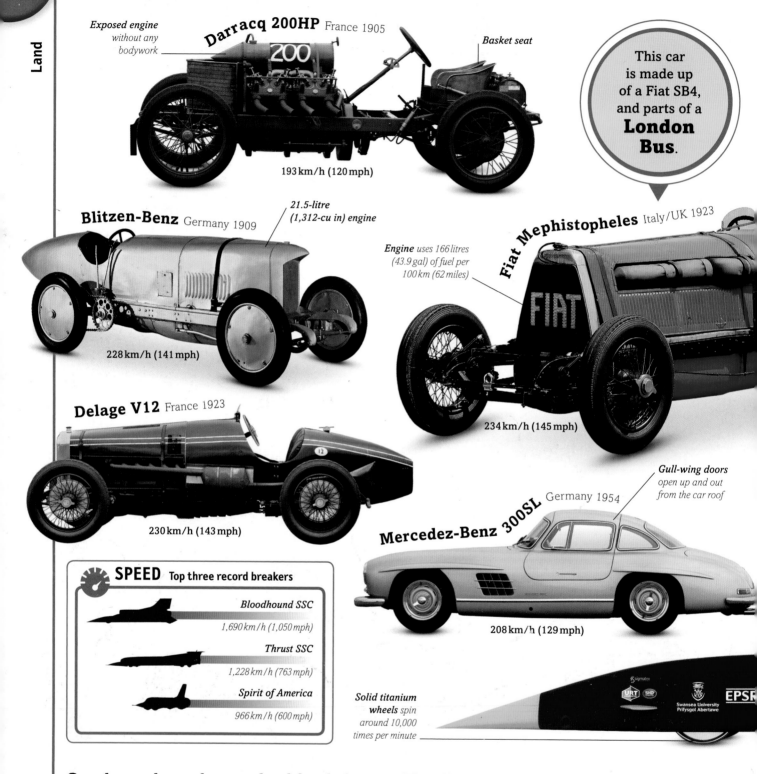

Darracq 200HP France 1905

Exposed engine without any bodywork

Basket seat

193 km/h (120 mph)

This car is made up of a Fiat SB4, and parts of a **London Bus**.

Blitzen-Benz Germany 1909

21.5-litre (1,312-cu in) engine

228 km/h (141 mph)

Fiat Mephistopheles Italy/UK 1923

Engine uses 166 litres (43.9 gal) of fuel per 100 km (62 miles)

FIAT

234 km/h (145 mph)

Delage V12 France 1923

230 km/h (143 mph)

Mercedez-Benz 300SL Germany 1954

Gull-wing doors open up and out from the car roof

208 km/h (129 mph)

⏱ **SPEED** Top three record breakers

Bloodhound SSC
1,690 km/h (1,050 mph)

Thrust SSC
1,228 km/h (763 mph)

Spirit of America
966 km/h (600 mph)

Solid titanium wheels spin around 10,000 times per minute

URT SHD | Swansea University Prifysgol Abertawe | EPSR

Cars have always been valued for their speed. Some people have built one-off fast cars in an attempt to break land-speed records, while car manufacturers have competed to produce the fastest production cars.

The **Blitzen-Benz** was the first car with an internal combustion engine to break the 200 km/h (124 mph) barrier. In 1924, the **Delage V12** held the land-speed record for six days before it was broken by the **Fiat Mephistopheles** with a bomber aircraft engine. The **Bluebird CN7**, also

Bluebird CN7 UK 1962

Sculpted front for air intake

648 km/h (403 mph)

Body fairing covers large 1.3-m- (4.3-ft-) diameter wheel

Spirit of America Sonic 1 USA 1965

SPIRIT OF AMERICA

GOODYEAR

966 km/h (600 mph)

11.5-m- (37.7-ft-) long body

Ferrari 365 GTB/4 Daytona Italy 1968

280 km/h (174 mph)

Exhaust pipes run along the side

Chain-driven rear wheel

Thrust SSC UK 1997

Rolls-Royce Spey jet engine

1,228 km/h (763 mph)

Bugatti Veyron Super Sport Germany/France 2012

431 km/h (268 mph)

Tyre can run flat for up to 50 km/h (31 mph)

Tailfin

Bloodhound SSC UK 2015

Castrol **EDGE**   **Rolls-Royce**   AMADA   JAIVEL   ThyssenKrupp

ROYAL AIR FORCE   RiS   Institution of MECHANICAL ENGINEERS

UWE BRISTOL   STP   ARMY BE THE BEST

JAGUAR

1,690 km/h (1,050 mph)

with an aircraft engine, was the last record-breaking car with wheels driven directly by the engine. Record breakers since then, such as the current holder **Thrust SSC**, are propelled by jet engines. The **Bloodhound SSC** team is hoping that their machine, using a Jaguar car engine, a jet engine, and a rocket engine, will set a new record at supersonic speeds. The **Mercedes-Benz 300SL** set a record for fastest production car in 1955, which was broken by the **Ferrari 365 GTB/4**. The **Bugatti Veyron Super Sport** is the current fastest production car.

DRAGSTER BURN OUT

Vrrrm, Vrrrm! Dave Gibbons revs up his Rough Diamond T dragster at the UK's Santa Pod Raceway in 2014. These mean machines race along straight pieces of tarmac track, known as drag strips, in high-speed races that last as little as five or six seconds. Blink and you'll miss the contests between these epic racers – the fastest-accelerating cars in the world.

Dragsters feature ridiculously powerful engines that burn an explosive fuel mixture. The most powerful, found in a class of dragster called Top Fuel, can generate a staggering 8,000 horsepower. That's more than the power created by all of the first 10 NASCARs or Formula One cars on a starting grid put together. This phenomenal force carries dragsters from 0 to 160 km/h (100 mph) in less than 0.8 seconds. After two or three seconds, they're rocketing along at more than 400 km/h (250 mph) while the fastest can cross the line at 500 km/h (310 mph). Dragsters need plenty of braking assistance, usually provided by large parachutes that open out behind the car to generate drag and slow it down.

Truck

Trucks come in many shapes and sizes. Articulated trucks come in two parts. At the front is a tractor, containing the engine and driver's cab. It is connected to the cargo-trailer by a pivoting joint, which allows the truck to go round tight corners. The **Kenworth C540** is a powerful long-distance truck that can haul a fully loaded trailer over long distances.

Sleeper cab ❯ This cab contains a bed, storage space, and, often, cooking facilities for long-distance truckers.

Kenworth C540

WALKER · BROS ·

Trailer side-curtain

Semi-trailer ❯ This is called a semi-trailer, because it does not have a front set of wheels. It is designed to hook up to the tractor. This model is a curtain-sider, with fabric side panels that can be pulled aside for loading or unloading.

Wheels ❯ Two sets of tractor rear wheels support the weight of the trailer.

Side lights

Fuel tank

Cab light

Exhaust stack ❯
Vertical exhaust pipes
release waste gases
from the engine.

Windscreen

Rear-view
mirror

Radiator grille ❯
The grille lets in air
to cool the large
diesel engine that
powers the truck.

NILRAH EQUIPMEN
407-855-870
ORLANDO, F

KENWORTH

BE·16·88

MARLINS

Steps to
driver's cab

Fender

Bumper

Tonnes of trucks

Chimney from steam engine ——

Wallis & Steevens Wagon 7279 UK 1912

Thornycroft Type J UK 1917

THE SOUTHERN COUNTIES AGRICULTURAL TRADING SOCIETY Lᵀᴰ CORN & SEED MERCHANTS WINCHESTER.

TELEGRAMS. FARMERS.
TELEPHONE. 382

Flatbed to carry sacks, boxes, or other loads

During World War I, some Type Js were fitted with **guns** to shoot at enemy aircraft.

Solid-rubber tyres

Two-doored cab seats only one

Piaggio Ape Model D Italy 1967

Frame for protective cover

Subaru Sambar Kei truck Japan 1969

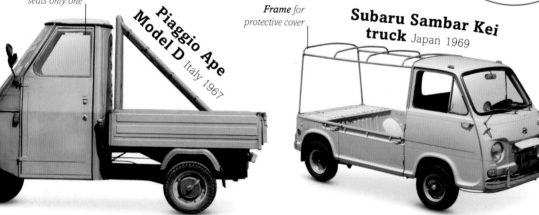

151

Tree logs carried in trailer from forest to lumber mill

Chevrolet C10 USA 1960s

Driver's cab contains sleeping bunk in roof

Renault TR 280 France 1971

There are almost as many types of trucks as there are jobs they perform – from whisking parcels around town, to hauling farm animals, cars, or goods on trailers. The first motorized trucks ran on steam power, but today most have diesel engines.

In Japan, tiny Kei trucks, such as the **Subaru Sambar,** carry small cargos around cities, while in Italy, the even smaller **Piaggio Ape Model D** runs on three wheels, with a motorbike engine powering its rear wheels. Pick up trucks, such as the **Chevrolet C10**, are often just a little larger

MCD DAF 85 Netherlands 1992

Mercedes-Benz 1838 tanker truck Germany 1996

DAF XF105 Netherlands 2008

Racing
DAF 85 trucks
reach speeds of up
to **160 km/h**
(100 mph) on
race tracks.

Rear supported
by three sets
of wheels

Large 13-litre
(793-cu in) engine
situated below driver's cab

Vertical
exhaust

Radiator grille

Volvo Bobtail semi-truck Sweden 2011

Living quarters
contain bed for driver

Western Star 4900EX USA 2001

than a saloon car, and have an open cargo bed behind the driver's cab. Many large trucks, such as the **Volvo Bobtail** and **Western Star 4900EX**, are designed to haul a range of trailers carrying very different loads. These trucks have a tractor unit with a driver's cab and an engine, and are articulated, which allows the truck to turn around tight corners. Trailers can be box-shaped, open, or specialized, such as the ramped car transporter hauled by the **MCD DAF 85**, or a tanker containing liquid pulled by the **Mercedes-Benz 1838**.

Special task trucks

Three-seater cab *can be entered from the roof*

Alvis Stalwart UK 1966

Underside of vehicle *is waterproof to travel through water*

Douglas P3 UK 1970

Aircraft Engineering

Water-and-foam cannon *can fire hundreds of litres of liquid per minute*

Walter Snowfighter USA 1972

56

Gloster Saro Javelin UK 1987

4

B·A·A
Stansted
Airport Fire Service

JAVELIN
E69 KDF

Large blades *push snow to the sides*

Telescopic ladder *can extend upwards to reach into multistorey buildings*

Large hopper *to collect refuse*

Six-wheel drive *with engine powering all wheels*

MIAMI-DADE
59
American La France Metrostik 75 USA 2000

Outrigger *provides stable base when ladder is extended*

Extended cab *carries firefighters and equipment*

M A HAZ MAT TEAM

MIAMI INTERNATIONAL AIRPORT
MIAMI-DADE
FIRE RESCUE

FD 228

I'm a fuel efficient hybrid automated garbage truck
Miami-D·de green

While some trucks are designed to be versatile and carry a wide range of loads, others are designed and purpose-built to do one job and do it extremely well. Meet some of the more extraordinary special task trucks.

Every airport has tugs, such as the **Douglas P3**, which can pull a giant aircraft into position, and crash tenders such as the **Gloster Saro Javelin**. These high-speed firefighting vehicles often have four-, six-, or eight-wheel drive and can rush to a stricken aircraft to cover it in water and foam.

Powerful crane can lift smaller tow trucks

Kenworth W900 tow truck
Australia 2007

Flashing warning lights

Mercedes-Benz Citaro ambulance Germany 2009

Ambulance

Driver's cab windows are protected from branches and debris by metal mesh

John Deere 843K USA 2010

KEEP BACK 300 FT / 90 M

JOHN DEERE

843K

Citaro is the **largest** civilian ambulance, with space for **20 patients**.

Giant tyres support weight of the 12,696-kg (27,990-lb) vehicle and its load

Holder C270 Germany 2010

Vertical exhaust pipe

Autocar E3 refuse truck USA 2011

Hyundai 700S-7E South Korea 2012

Rapidly spinning brushes remove dirt

Special purpose trucks are also found every day on city streets. Road sweepers, such as the small **Holder C270**, can turn their cabs to sweep around tight corners, while refuse trucks, such as the **Autocar E3**, collect and compact rubbish in their rear hoppers before taking it to dumps or recycling centres. The **Walter Snowfighter** can clear roads of snow, and the **Kenworth W900** lifts and recovers broken-down vehicles. Out in the countryside, tree fellers such as the **John Deere 843K** use powerful saws and grippers to fell and remove trees.

SHUTTLE CRAWLER
Meet the ultimate heavy hauler – NASA's gigantic Crawler Transporter. This picture shows it inching the Space Shuttle *Discovery* from the Vehicle Assembly Building to Launchpad 39B at the Kennedy Space Center in Florida, USA, in 2005. Fully loaded, the Shuttle spacecraft weighs more than 2 million kg (4.4 million lb) so it takes a serious machine to carry such an extreme load.

NASA's two Crawler Transporters, nicknamed Hans and Franz, were built in the 1960s to carry Saturn V launch vehicles. The loading platform is 27.4 sq m (295 sq ft) – that's about the same size as a baseball diamond. Each Crawler Transporter is 40 m (131 ft) long, 35 m (115 ft) wide, and weighs 2,721,000 kg (5,998,778 lb). When loaded with a space vehicle, the crawlers move along a special, heavy-duty road, known as a crawlerway, at a top speed of 1.6 km/h (1 mph). The vehicle is powered by 16 electric engines, and the electricity is supplied by an onboard generator run by two diesel engines. Burning fuel at 297 litres per km (126 gal per mile), the Crawler Transporter is a real gas guzzler.

Bus stop

Bollée L'Obeissante
France 1873

Steam chimney

Open cab *for driver*

Engine radiator

LCOG B-type
UK 1911

8.4 m (27.5 ft) long

154
Sutton Green
Wellington W Croydon
Norwood Junction

LONDON TRANSPORT

AEC Regent III RT UK 1938

Open platform *to enter and exit*

Foremost Terra bus
Canada 1986

Be Trendy...Hire a Bendy!

Door powered by compressed air

Volvo B10MA *Bendy Bus* Sweden 1996

The first motorized buses were steam-powered and carried people for short distances in the 19th century. The arrival of the internal combustion engine led to bigger and more powerful buses for commuters, tourists, and school runs.

Driven by twin steam engines, one for each rear wheel, the **Bollée L'Obeissante** could carry 12 passengers at speeds up to 40 km/h (25 mph). Gradually, petrol-engine buses took over. The first mass-produced bus, the **LCOG B-type**, had seats for 16 passengers inside and 18 on the top

Volvo B12M Sweden 2001

Underfloor-mounted engine

Joint covered by flexible rubber seals

The bendy, 28-m- (91.8-ft-) long B12M can seat up to **270 passengers**.

School bus USA 2002

High-mounted driver's cab

Rails for a flexible roof

Roma Cristiana open bus Italy 2003

Fold-down steps

15 m (49.2 ft) long

Wi-fi onboard for using gadgets

xury Seats

Van Hool sleeper bus Belgium 2009

deck. Double-decker buses proved popular, with room for many more people. The **AEC Regent III RT** used to carry up to 64 passengers around London, UK, while today's open-topped buses, such as the **Roma Cristiana**, give tourists brilliant city views. The rugged, single-decker

Foremost Terra Bus transports tourists and workers around ice-bound regions in Canada and Antarctica. The **Volvo B10MA** can bend in the middle to travel around corners, while the **Van Hool sleeper bus's** seats convert into 42 beds for long, overnight journeys.

Tractor

Tractors are a farm's workhorses, used to pull ploughs and other tools in fields, or to carry and lift a range of loads. These machines vary in size, from tiny tractors used in gardens and parks to giant beasts with massive pulling power. The **Massey Ferguson 7618** is a versatile, large tractor that can perform lots of different jobs in the field.

Engine ❯ A large engine burns diesel fuel. This tractor has a top speed of around 50 km/h (31 mph) on the road and 28 km/h (17 mph) on the field.

Engine bonnet

Vertical exhaust

Massey Ferguson 7618

MASSEY FERGUSON

7618

Dyna-6

Radiator grille

Mudguard

Weight frame ❯ Weights can be added to the front of the tractor to balance out the weight of the tools or loads it carries behind it.

Fuel tank

Tyre tread ❯ Deep tread on the rubber tyre helps the tractor grip the soft ground and move forwards or backwards.

Driver's cab

Warning light

Cab light > Fitted on all four corners of the cab, these light up the area around the tractor.

Rear wheel > Huge rear wheels fitted with giant tyres 1.8 m (5.9 ft) in diameter and 58 cm (22.8 in) wide, support the weight of the tractor.

Steps to the cab

Total tractor

Chimney funnel

Clayton & Shuttleworth Dorothy UK 1914

Steering chains turn front wheels

Canopy covered driver and engine

Twin City 40-65
UK 1916

Waterloo Boy
USA 1917

Steel wheels fitted with blades dig into the ground to provide more grip

Caterpillar Sixty
USA 1931

Ferguson TE-20 UK 1946

Rubber tyres with heavy tread for better grip

Big Bud 16V 747 USA 1978

Driver's cab sits high above ground

Each tyre measures 2.4 m (7.8 ft) in diameter

Powered by steam, the first farm tractors were often heavy and slow, but they could pull objects with great force. Over time, diesel and petrol engines replaced steam, while solid steel wheels made way for tracks and wide rubber tyres.

The **Clayton & Shuttleworth Dorothy** steam-powered tractor weighed 10,000 kg (22,046 lb) and had a top speed of 8 km/h (5 mph). In contrast, the 6,900-kg (15,212-lb) **JCB Fastrac 185-65** can reach 80 km/h (50 mph). The **Ferguson TE-20** became so

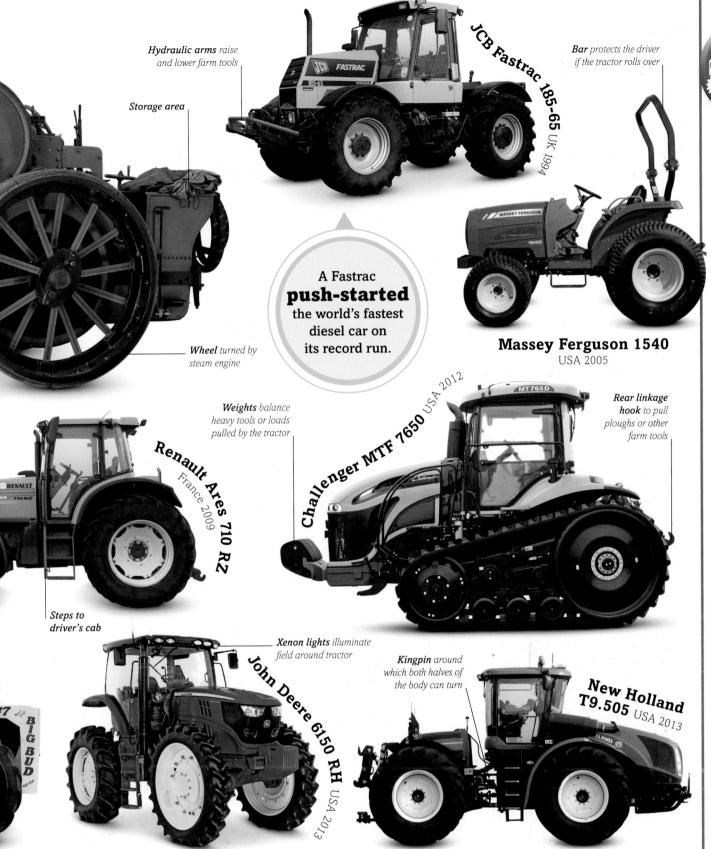

Hydraulic arms raise and lower farm tools

Storage area

Bar protects the driver if the tractor rolls over

JCB Fastrac 185–65 UK 1994

Wheel turned by steam engine

A Fastrac **push-started** the world's fastest diesel car on its record run.

Massey Ferguson 1540
USA 2005

Weights balance heavy tools or loads pulled by the tractor

Challenger MTF 7650 USA 2012

Rear linkage hook to pull ploughs or other farm tools

Renault Ares 710 RZ France 2009

Steps to driver's cab

Xenon lights illuminate field around tractor

Kingpin around which both halves of the body can turn

New Holland T9.505 USA 2013

John Deere 6150 RH USA 2013

BIG BUD

popular that over half a million were built. Some tractors run on a continuous belt called a track, which spreads weight evenly over the ground, giving good stability and grip. The **Caterpillar Sixty** had steel tracks, while the modern **Challenger MTF 7650** has rubber tracks.

Tractors today range greatly in size. The small **Massey Ferguson 1540** is used in parks and gardening, while the **New Holland T9.505** is so long that its body is hinged in the middle. At 8.23 m (27 ft) long, the **Big Bud 16V 747** was used on large American cotton farms.

On the farm

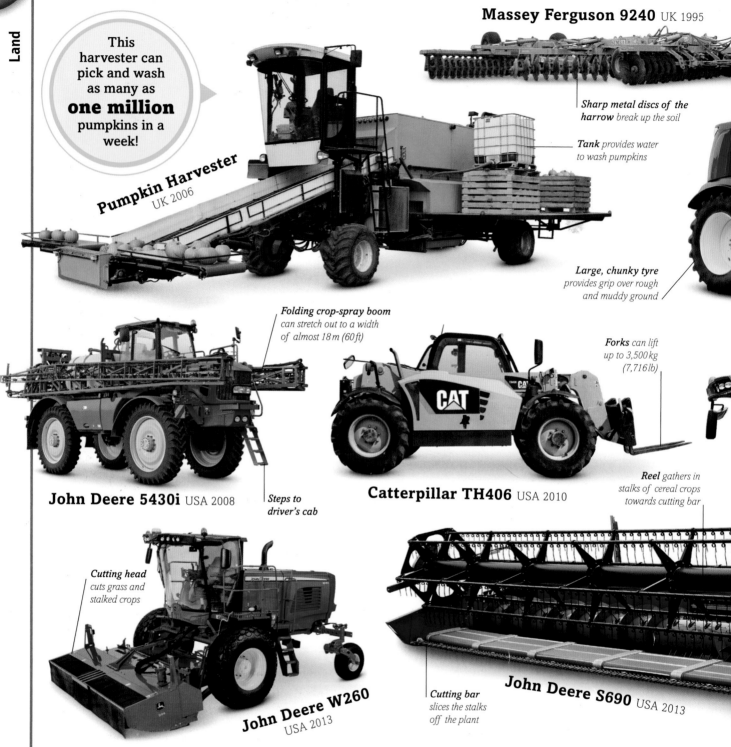

This harvester can pick and wash as many as **one million** pumpkins in a week!

Pumpkin Harvester UK 2006

Massey Ferguson 9240 UK 1995

Sharp metal discs of the harrow break up the soil

Tank provides water to wash pumpkins

Large, chunky tyre provides grip over rough and muddy ground

Folding crop-spray boom can stretch out to a width of almost 18 m (60 ft)

John Deere 5430i USA 2008

Steps to driver's cab

Catterpillar TH406 USA 2010

Forks can lift up to 3,500 kg (7,716 lb)

Reel gathers in stalks of cereal crops towards cutting bar

Cutting head cuts grass and stalked crops

John Deere W260 USA 2013

Cutting bar slices the stalks off the plant

John Deere S690 USA 2013

Farming involves a vast amount of hard work but, fortunately, machines have come to the rescue. Farm machines automate and speed up many tasks, which previously had to be done by hand or by using animals.

Some farm tools like ploughs and disc harrows can be pulled or operated by multi-purpose tractors such as the **Massey Ferguson 9240**. Growing crops are protected by crop-dusting machines, such as the **John Deere 5430i**, whose giant booms spray large areas of fields

Hydraulic-powered grippers can hold and lift hay bales

New Holland 740TL USA 2013

New Holland T6.140
USA 2013

Unloading pipe discharges 135 litres (35.7 gal) of grain per minute

Driver's cab

Grain tank can hold up to 14,100 litres (3,725 gal) of grain

New Holland Braud 960L USA 2013

Cutter head removes flowers from top of corn plant

Narrow wheels fit into gaps between rows of corn crops

Hagie 204SP Detassler USA 2013

with pest-removing chemicals. Come harvest time, different machines speed up the collection of crops, such as the **New Holland Braud 960L**, which travels above rows of vines, harvesting grapes, or the **Pumpkin Harvester**, which picks, washes, and packs pumpkins. Large combine harvesters, such as the **John Deere S690**, cut the stalks of cereal crops, separate the grain, and shoot the remaining straw out the back. This straw is packed into hay bales that can be lifted by forklifts, such as the **Caterpillar TH406**, or held by grippers, as on the **New Holland 740TL**.

MONSTER LEAP
At the Monster Mania festival, in the UK, Ian Batey flies high in his *Lil' Devil* monster truck over a row of old cars. Fuelled by high octane racing methanol in its hefty V8 engine, this powerful vehicle boasts ten times as much power as a regular family car. It weighs more than 4,000 kg (8,818 lb) – guaranteeing a crushing ending for any of the wrecked cars should it land on them.

Ever since Bob Chandler built the original Bigfoot monster truck in 1979 in the USA, these mean machines have been entertaining crowds all over the world with their antics. Events include races over dirt courses in arenas as well as stunts, jumps off ramps, and plenty of car crushing. Many monster trucks begin life as a humble pickup, a Chevrolet Silverado in the case of *Lil' Devil*. Only the body is kept, as the vehicle is tricked out with a tubular steel frame chassis and mighty 1.7-m- (5.6-ft-) high "terra" tyres. These ride on suspension systems capable of absorbing enormous impacts on landing while the driver, held firmly in his seat in a racing harness, focuses on pulling amazing monster truck moves.

Construction and mining

Front roller can be moved left or right to turn the vehicle

Hamm HW90/10 Germany 1987

Arm can move bucket to dig down to depths of more than 4.5 m (14.8 ft)

Steel bucket

Case Poclain 688B USA 1993

The **hopper** can hold **90 tonnes** of rock – as heavy as **20** monster trucks.

Vertical exhaust pipe

Steel loader can lift more than 1,000 kg (2,205 lb) in a single scoop

Hopper can be tipped by hydraulic arms

Caterpillar 950G USA 1998

75570

Tyre is 2.7 m (8.9 ft) tall and weighs more than 1,500 kg (3,307 lb)

BELAZ-75570

9.7 m (31.8 ft) tall

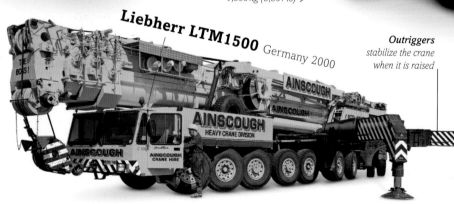

Liebherr LTM1500 Germany 2000

Outriggers stabilize the crane when it is raised

AINSCOUGH

Construction sites and mines have a lot of digging, levelling, and heavy lifting going on, and big, rugged machines do most of the work. They have to be strong to withstand the stresses of the tasks, and reliable to work all day long.

Excavators are digging machines usually fitted with a steel bucket that cuts into the earth. Some, such as the **Case Poclain 688B**, run on wheels, while others, such as the **John Deere 160DL C**, run on continuous tracks, which are ideal for crossing muddy ground. Front-loaders, such as

Drum *mixes concrete for building purposes*

Mercedes-Benz Germany 2007

John Deere 160DL C USA 2007

Diesel engine *turns the tracks to move digger*

Excavator *can dig up to a depth of 6.5 m (21.3 ft)*

BelAZ-75570 Belarus 2008

75570

90 ТОНН

Backhoe bucket *to dig holes or trenches for pipelines*

Front-loader *can carry and push large amounts of soil and other materials*

JCB 3CX UK 2009

The **Dancing Diggers** are a team of JCBs that perform routines to music.

Long blade *levels materials for a smooth surface*

Caterpillar 12M2 USA 2011

John Deere 650K XLT USA 2012

the **Caterpillar 950G**, feature a large front-scoop, and backhoe loaders, such as the **JCB 3CX**, have both, a front-loader and a rear bucket-digger. The **John Deere 650K XLT** is a bulldozer fitted with a long, strong blade to push materials along the ground, while compactors, such as the **Hamm** HW90/10, use heavy rollers to press down and make a firm surface. Giant cranes lift materials when building tall structures and some, such as the **Liebherr LTM1500**, are mobile, with an arm that telescopes out and up to a distance of 84 m (276 ft) – longer than a Boeing 747 jumbo jet.

Tanks and tracks

Stabilizer prevents tank from tipping over backwards

Renault FT-17 France 1917

Mark V UK 1918

Turret hatch, below which tank commander sits

Gun originally used in ships and coastal forts

Continuous metal tracks around side of body

M4A1 Sherman USA 1941

Panzerkampfwagen IV Germany 1936

Turret holds three of the five crew members

T-34/85
Soviet Union 1941

Large gun can fire shells over 5 km (3 miles)

Tough armour made of ceramics and metals

CHALLENGER 1 MBT

3 m (9.8 ft) tall

Tanks are heavily armoured vehicles that run on tracks so they can cross muddy ground and other difficult terrain. They are usually equipped with a powerful, shell-firing artillery gun. The first tanks saw service in World War I.

The **Mark V** had an eight-man crew and a top speed of 8 km/h (5 mph), the same as the two-man **Renault FT-17** – the first tank with a rotating gun turret. The **Panzerkampfwagen IV's** powerful gun could pierce the armour of other tanks. It had a top speed of 39 km/h (24 mph) and

Land

M4 Sherman V
Crab USA 1943

Heavy, spinning chains pound the ground to set off landmines

Amphibious landing craft

M-29C Weasel tank transported inside

Landing Vehicle Tracked Mk IV Buffalo USA 1943

With a top speed of 92 km/h (57 mph), this was the **fastest tank** of World War II.

M18 Hellcat USA 1944

4.9-m- (16-ft-) long aluminium body holds a crew of three

Alvis FV107 Scimitar UK 1971

Smoke-grenade launchers generate smokescreen for defence

Tracks can travel through 1.8-m- (6-ft-) deep water

Challenger 1 MBT UK 1983

FV104 Samaritan UK 1978

Leopard C2 Germany 2000

Armoured skirt protects upper tracks

a range of 200 km (125 miles). The **T-34/85**, one of its opponents, could travel twice as far. Other military vehicles are also armoured and tracked but perform different tasks. The **FV104 Samaritan** is a battlefield ambulance, carrying up to six patients on stretchers, while the **Sherman** *Crab* has flailing chains to clear paths through minefields. Main battle tanks, such as the 62-tonne (68-US-ton) **Challenger 1 MBT**, are large and fitted with powerful weapons. In contrast, the **Alvis FV107 Scimitar** weighs less than 8 tonnes (9 US tons) and can travel at 80 km/h (50 mph).

Steam train

Steam trains have engines that burn fuel in their firebox. The heat boils water to produce steam, which is fed into cylinders where it expands to drive the pistons. The movement of the pistons turns the wheels with the help of a rod and a crank, moving the train. This American locomotive from 1863, called **Thatcher Perkins**, weighs 41 tonnes and could haul several wagons or carriages at 80 km/h (50 mph).

B&O Class B No. 147
Thatcher Perkins

Steam-powered whistle

Cab

B. & O. R. R.

Tender ❯ On many trains, this stored both water and fuel, often in the form of coal or, on this train, wood, to power the engine.

Wheel brakes ❯ To slow down the train, the driver pulls a lever, which presses brake shoes directly onto the driving wheels.

Driving wheel

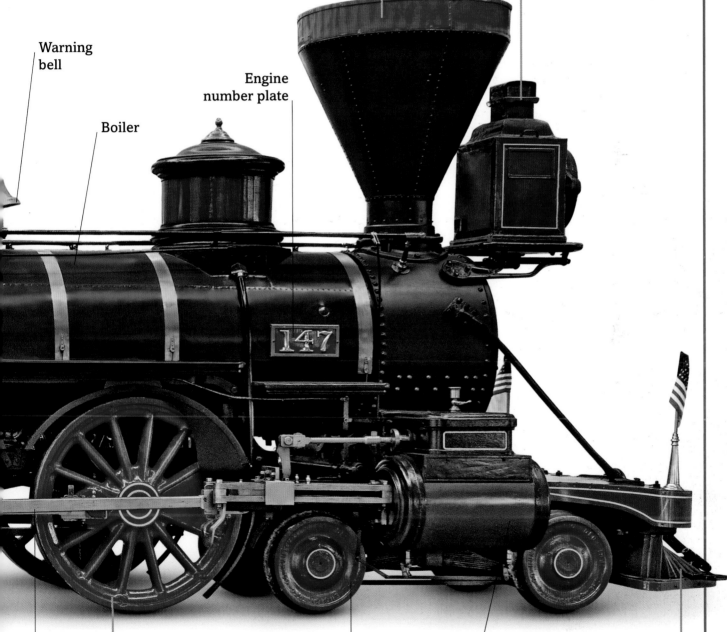

Chimney ❯ The smoke from the burning fuel in the firebox is channelled up and out through the chimney. This one is fitted with layers of mesh to stop dangerous sparks from escaping.

Headlamp ❯ A large lamp burned oil to light up the tracks ahead.

Warning bell

Boiler

Engine number plate

147

Coupling rod

Wheel arrangement ❯ Steam engines are defined by the number of wheels they have. This one has four leading wheels and six driving wheels.

Leading wheel

Engine cylinder

Pilot ❯ Also known as the cowcatcher, this brushes aside obstacles, such as tree branches, from the locomotive's path.

125

Early steam

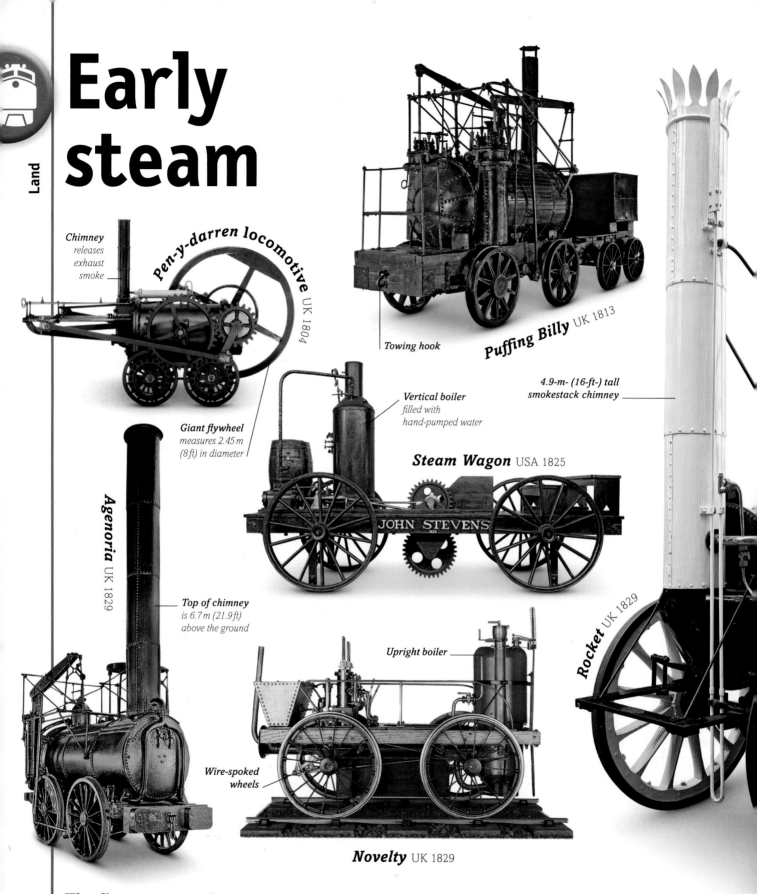

Chimney
releases
exhaust
smoke

Pen-y-darren locomotive UK 1804

Puffing Billy UK 1813

Towing hook

Giant flywheel
measures 2.45 m
(8 ft) in diameter

Vertical boiler
filled with
hand-pumped water

*4.9-m- (16-ft-) tall
smokestack chimney*

Steam Wagon USA 1825

JOHN STEVENS

Agenoria UK 1829

Top of chimney
is 6.7 m (21.9 ft)
above the ground

Upright boiler

Rocket UK 1829

*Wire-spoked
wheels*

Novelty UK 1829

The first steam engines were used in factories to run machines, or in mines to pump out water. Richard Trevithick, an English mining engineer, was one of the first to use steam to power a moving locomotive, sparking a transport revolution.

In Wales in 1804, Trevithick's **Pen-y-darren** made the first railway journey at less than 4 km/h (2 mph), hauling 11 tonnes of cargo and 70 people over 14.4 km (8.9 miles). Other steam engines, such as the **Puffing Billy** and **Agenoria**, quickly followed, ferrying coal or goods from factories.

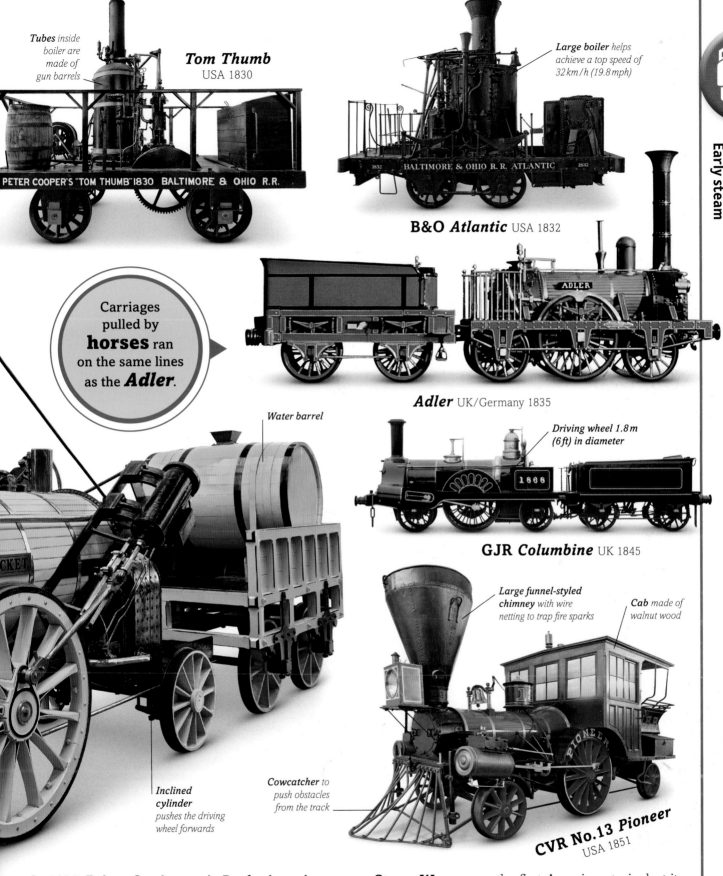

Tubes *inside boiler are made of gun barrels*

Tom Thumb
USA 1830

PETER COOPER'S "TOM THUMB" 1830 BALTIMORE & OHIO R.R.

Large boiler helps achieve a top speed of 32 km/h (19.8 mph)

1832 BALTIMORE & OHIO R.R. ATLANTIC 1832

B&O *Atlantic* USA 1832

Carriages pulled by **horses** ran on the same lines as the ***Adler***.

ADLER

Adler UK/Germany 1835

Driving wheel 1.8 m (6 ft) in diameter

1868

GJR *Columbine* UK 1845

Water barrel

Inclined cylinder pushes the driving wheel forwards

Large funnel-styled chimney with wire netting to trap fire sparks

Cab made of walnut wood

PIONEER

Cowcatcher to push obstacles from the track

CVR No.13 *Pioneer*
USA 1851

In 1829, Robert Stephenson's **Rocket** beat the **Novelty** at the Rainhill Trials in the UK, where engines competed to run on the Liverpool and Manchester Railway – the world's first inter-city line. Stephenson's company later built the **Adler**, the first German commercial train. John Steven's

Steam Wagon was the first American train, but it ran on a small circular track. The first engine used on regular service in the USA was **Tom Thumb** on the Baltimore & Ohio Railroad (B&O). By 1840, the country had over 4,500 km (2,796 miles) of track, more than found in the whole of Europe.

Mainstream steam

SNB *Limmat*
Germany/Switzerland 1847

Wooden-clad cylinder

Engine named after the river it travelled alongside

Fairy Queen was given **national treasure** status by India in 1972.

Headlight

B&O L Class No. 57 Memnon USA 1848

Crown-shaped chimney opening

Hinged door to access smokebox

Headlight

Driver's cab

EIR 22

L N

EIR No. 22 Fairy Queen UK/India 1855

Steam railways boomed in the later half of the 19th century, opening up new territories and connecting towns and cities. Locomotives developed rapidly, to become faster, more reliable, and able to pull more carriages or cargo wagons.

The **SNB *Limmat*** ran on the first railway line in Switzerland, while the **EIR No. 22 *Fairy Queen*** operated in India for 54 years. The **DHR Class B**, also from India, had a short wheelbase, which helped it grip the track of the Darjeeling Mountain Railway that rose 2,000 m (6,560 ft) in

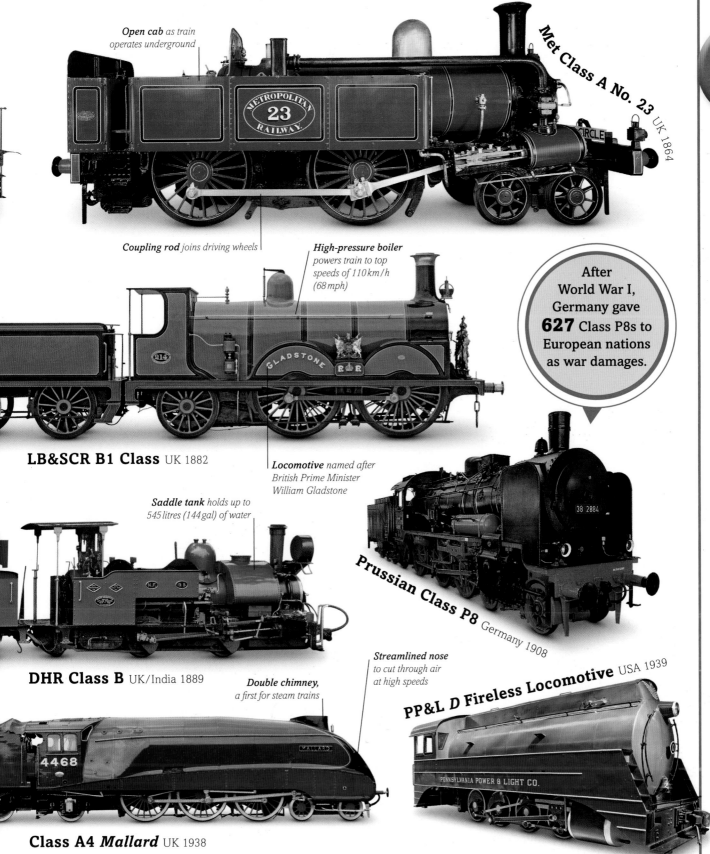

Open cab as train operates underground

Met Class A No. 23 UK 1864

Coupling rod joins driving wheels

High-pressure boiler powers train to top speeds of 110 km/h (68 mph)

After World War I, Germany gave **627** Class P8s to European nations as war damages.

LB&SCR B1 Class UK 1882

Locomotive named after British Prime Minister William Gladstone

Saddle tank holds up to 545 litres (144 gal) of water

Prussian Class P8 Germany 1908

DHR Class B UK/India 1889

Double chimney, a first for steam trains

Streamlined nose to cut through air at high speeds

PP&L *D* Fireless Locomotive USA 1939

PENNSYLVANIA POWER & LIGHT CO.

Class A4 *Mallard* UK 1938

altitude. In contrast, the **Met Class A** ran on the world's first underground train line, the Metropolitan Railway in central London. Steam trains were built well into the 20th century. More than 3,700 **Prussian Class P8** engines were built and used in Romania, Poland, France, and elsewhere. Innovations included the **PP&L *D* Fireless**, which stored steam in its boiler so it could work in places where flammable fuel was a hazard. Steam engines were also streamlined for extra speed. The **Class A4 *Mallard*** was the fastest, with a top speed of 202 km/h (125 mph).

FLYING SCOTSMAN
The No. 4472 *Flying Scotsman* powers along the tracks of the Carlisle to Settle line in the north-west of England, a service known as the "Cumbrian Mountain Express". The 21.7-m- (71.2-ft-) long locomotive weighed over 97.5 tonnes, but generated enormous pulling power. In 1934, it became the first steam locomotive officially recorded to exceed 160 km/h (100 mph).

The *Flying Scotsman* was designed by the British engineer Sir Nigel Gresley, who had joined the railways as a 17-year-old apprentice. The locomotive was built in 1923, and soon after was painted in its famous apple green livery. During World War II, however, it was painted black. After 40 years of faithful service, the *Flying Scotsman* was retired by British Rail in 1963, but the engine's travels weren't over. It was saved from being scrapped by enthusiast Alvin Pegler and, after restoration, underwent a five-year tour of the USA, before being taken to Australia, where she set a new world record for the longest non-stop locomotive run, travelling 679 km (422 miles) on the Alice Springs to Melbourne route.

Diesel train

Diesel trains contain one or more large internal combustion engines that generate hauling power. This power is transferred to the wheels by different transmission systems. Locomotives using the diesel-mechanical system, such as this **BR Class 05**, transfer the power directly to the wheels by means of shafts and cranks. In a diesel-electric system, the power is converted into electricity in a generator, which drives the motors that turn the locomotive's wheels.

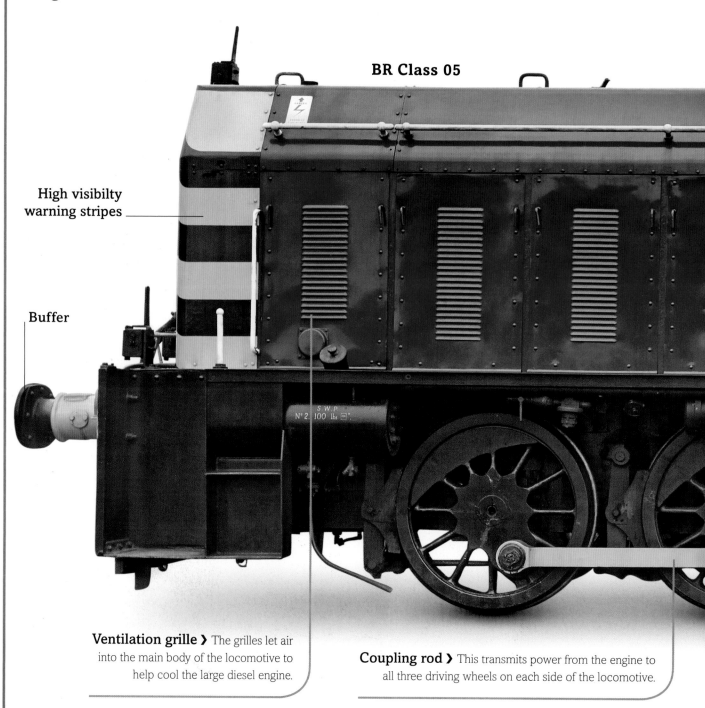

BR Class 05

High visibilty warning stripes

Buffer

Ventilation grille ❯ The grilles let air into the main body of the locomotive to help cool the large diesel engine.

Coupling rod ❯ This transmits power from the engine to all three driving wheels on each side of the locomotive.

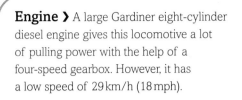

Engine ❯ A large Gardiner eight-cylinder diesel engine gives this locomotive a lot of pulling power with the help of a four-speed gearbox. However, it has a low speed of 29 km/h (18 mph).

Cab ❯ The 3.5-m- (11.5-ft-) high cab gives a good view down the long bonnet, while twin rear windows allow the driver to see what is going on behind. Inside, a series of dials gives the driver details of the engine's speed, temperature, and status.

Signalling horns

Narrow cab door

D 2595

Hand rail

Driving wheel is 1.02 m (3.3 ft) in diameter

Counterweight ❯ This helps to balance the force of the coupling rod.

Steps to driver's cab

Dawn of diesel

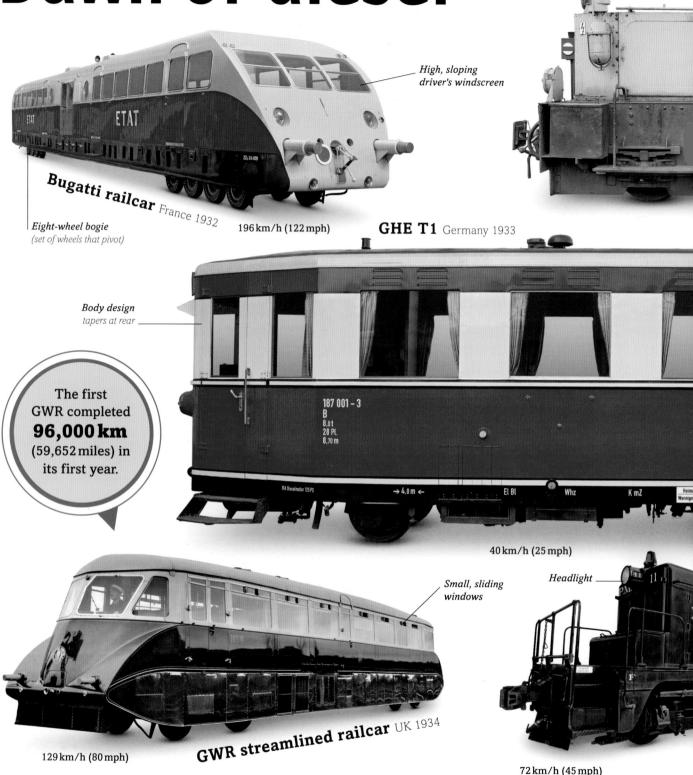

High, sloping driver's windscreen

Bugatti railcar France 1932

Eight-wheel bogie (set of wheels that pivot)

196 km/h (122 mph)

GHE T1 Germany 1933

Body design tapers at rear

The first GWR completed **96,000 km** (59,652 miles) in its first year.

187 001-3
B
8,0 t
28 Pl.
8,70 m

IFA Dieselmotor 125 PS   → 4,0 m ←   El Bl   Whz   K mZ   Heima Wernige

40 km/h (25 mph)

Small, sliding windows

Headlight

GWR streamlined railcar UK 1934

129 km/h (80 mph)

72 km/h (45 mph)

As engine technology developed in the early 20th century, some engineers turned away from steam in favour of locomotives that ran on diesel fuel. Diesel-engined trains entered service in numbers from 1930s onwards.

Diesel engines required less maintenance than steam locomotives and could be operated without extra crew to stoke the boiler. This made some, such as the **VC Porter No.3** and **DR Class Kö**, ideal as low-speed shunters. Many early diesel trains used their engines to drive the wheels

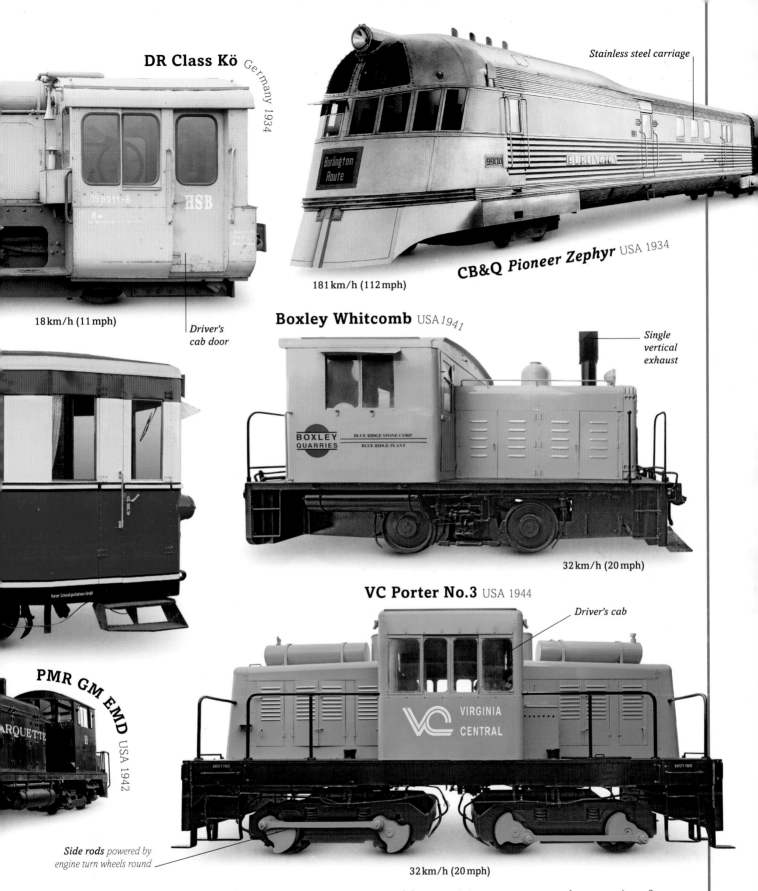

DR Class Kö *Germany 1934*

HSB

199011-8

18 km/h (11 mph)

Driver's cab door

CB&Q *Pioneer Zephyr* USA 1934

Stainless steel carriage

Burlington Route

9900

BURLINGTON

181 km/h (112 mph)

Boxley Whitcomb USA *1941*

Single vertical exhaust

BOXLEY QUARRIES

BLUE RIDGE STONE CORP.

BLUE RIDGE PLANT

32 km/h (20 mph)

VC Porter No.3 USA 1944

Driver's cab

VC VIRGINIA CENTRAL

SAFETY FIRST

32 km/h (20 mph)

PMR GM EMD USA 1942

ARQUETTE

Side rods powered by engine turn wheels round

mechanically, but not the **PMR GM EMD**. A diesel-electric locomotive, its diesel engine powered a generator that supplied electricity to its four electric motors. Diesel engines were also used to power railcars – train passenger carriages with motors fitted below. The **GHE T1** railcar could carry 34 passengers and ran on just four wheels. The **GWR streamlined railcar** had a top speed of 129 km/h (80 mph), while the **Bugatti railcar** was even faster. This sleek machine broke the record for high-speed trains in 1934 with a top speed of 196 km/h (122 mph).

135

Mainstream diesel

171 km/h (106 mph)

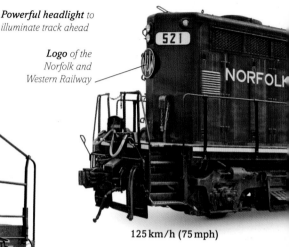

Powerful headlight to illuminate track ahead

Logo of the Norfolk and Western Railway

Baldwin Class DS-4-4-660 USA 1946

CHESAPEAKE WESTERN

96 km/h (60 mph)

125 km/h (75 mph)

Stainless steel body is 25.91 m (85 ft) long

BALTIMORE AND OHIO

Budd RDC railcar USA 1949

137 km/h (85 mph)

Two **jet aircraft** engines were fitted to the roof of a Budd to set a speed record in 1966.

B&O F7 Class USA 1949

MARC 7100

Ladder to driver's cab

80–193 km/h (50–120 mph)

Diesel locomotives became common after World War II. Although they were often more expensive to build, many were much cheaper and easier to operate than steam locomotives, and spent less time in repair shops as well.

Baldwin Class DS-4-4-660 shunters were used to move carriages and wagons in railway yards. With their 660-horsepower diesel engines, some 139 were built. The rugged and reliable **N&W EMD GP9 Class** served all over the USA and Canada as a shunter, with more than 4,000

English Electric DP1 *Deltic* UK 1955

Spacious cab provided at either end of the locomotive

N&W EMD GP9 Class USA 1955

Driver's cab mounted on the roof

DB VT11.5 Germany 1957

160 km/h (100 mph)

UP GM EMD Class SD60 USA 1984

Radiator cooling fans

Rounded fuel tanks

105 km/h (65 mph)

Sliding double doors

Upper deck connected to lower by two spiral staircases

BR GM EMD Class 66 UK/USA 1998

100 km/h (62 mph)

DWA Class 670 railcar
Germany 1996

121 km/h (75 mph)

produced. The **DB VT11.5** hauled first class passengers at speeds of up to 160 km/h (100 mph) on the famed Trans-Europ Express services, which linked 130 cities throughout Europe. Diesel-powered railcars, such as the **Budd RDC**, proved very versatile. On small lines, each railcar could operate by itself to carry a limited number of passengers, or they could be linked together for greater capacity. Another option was a double-decker, such as the **DWA Class 670 railcar**, which could hold up to 110 people on two decks.

Rail workhorses

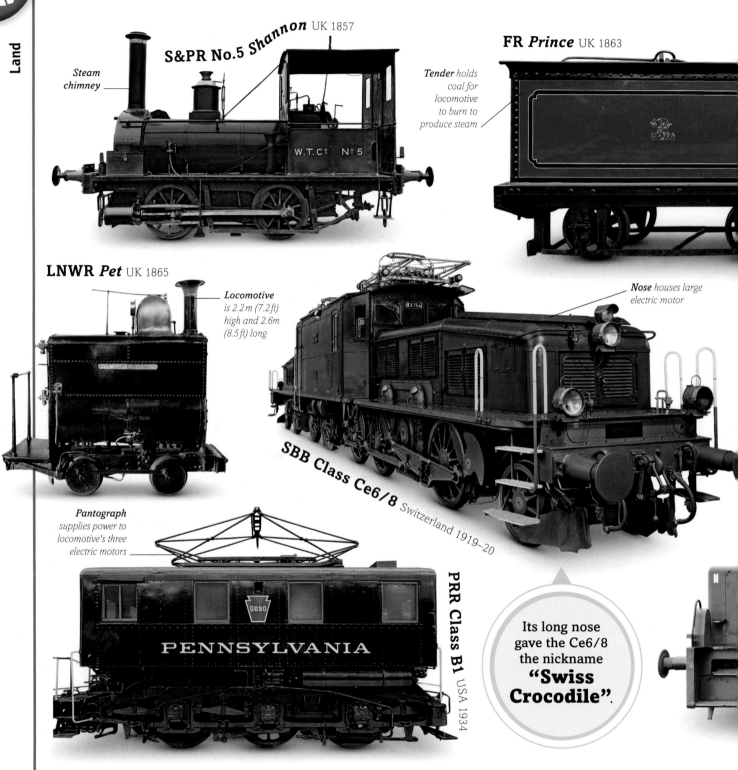

S&PR No.5 *Shannon* UK 1857

Steam chimney

FR *Prince* UK 1863

Tender holds coal for locomotive to burn to produce steam

LNWR *Pet* UK 1865

Locomotive is 2.2 m (7.2 ft) high and 2.6 m (8.5 ft) long

Nose houses large electric motor

SBB Class Ce6/8 Switzerland 1919–20

Pantograph supplies power to locomotive's three electric motors

PENNSYLVANIA

PRR Class B1 USA 1934

Its long nose gave the Ce6/8 the nickname **"Swiss Crocodile"**.

While passenger trains grab all the attention, thousands of other trains are busy at work every day. These rail workhorses haul vast amounts of freight, and move other trains and carriages around railway yards.

Freight trains often use diesel engines, such as the **DR V100**, more than 1,100 of which have served across the world. The electric **SBB Class Ce6/8**, similar in design to the DR V100, has a central cab with a protruding nose at each end. The engine was hinged so that it could turn on

Steam dome helps to control steam pressure

Chimney joined to smokebox channels smoke out of train

PRINCE

Driver's cab

Sandbox contains sand, which can be rubbed on rails for better grip during bad weather

Front coupling

50

BALTIMORE & ANNAPOLIS R.R.

B&A GE 70-ton switcher USA 1946

604

PHANTOM

BR Class 08 *Phantom* UK 1953

Central driver's cab gives excellent visibility in all directions

DR V100 Germany 1966

112 331-4

Driver's cab

Deutsche Reichsbahn

101 691-4

DR V15 Germany 1959

tight tracks in the Swiss mountains. Not all freight is carried cross-country. Many trains move goods and equipment on lines serving docks, mines, and factories, such as the **FR Prince**, which hauled slate from Welsh mines. Many small locomotives are also used to move around carriages, wagons, and larger locomotives, to assemble and disassemble train services. These shunters, such as the **DR V15** and the **BR Class 08**, had to be robust and reliable. More than 100 Class 08s are still in service more than 50 years on.

Going electric

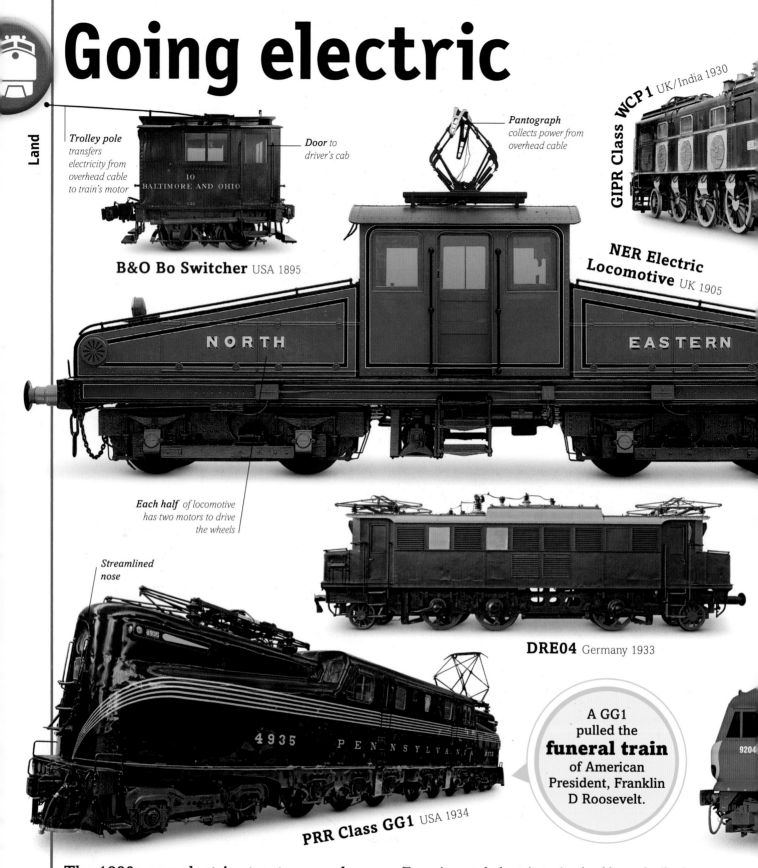

Trolley pole transfers electricity from overhead cable to train's motor

Door to driver's cab

B&O Bo Switcher USA 1895

Pantograph collects power from overhead cable

GIPR Class WCP1 UK/India 1930

NER Electric Locomotive UK 1905

NORTH EASTERN

Each half of locomotive has two motors to drive the wheels

Streamlined nose

DRE04 Germany 1933

4935 PENNSYLVANIA

PRR Class GG1 USA 1934

A GG1 pulled the **funeral train** of American President, Franklin D Roosevelt.

The 1880s saw electric streetcars and trams rattling around cities and it was not long before electric trains appeared. They offered advantages over smoke-belching steam trains, but needed electrified railway lines on which to run.

Experimental electric trains had been built since the 1830s but the first main line electric service was in Baltimore, USA, in the 1890s. The **B&O Bo Switcher** operated in Baltimore's docklands at a top speed of 16 km/h (9 mph). Electric trains get their power supply either from overhead

SNCF Class BB9000 France 1954

Pilot pushes obstructions from the track

Single pantograph connects with overhead power lines of 11,000 volts

Penn Central/Budd Metroliner USA 1969

DR Class 243 Germany 1982

The BR Class 92 was built to run in the **Channel Tunnel** linking England and France.

Locomotive weighs 126 tonnes

BR Class 92 UK 1993

DB SCHENKER

cables or via a third rail running along the track. The **NER** used both systems. After World War I, many countries began the electrification of some of their lines. The **GIPR Class WCP 1s** were the first electric engines to run in India. The 24.2-m- (79.3-ft-) long **PRR Class GG1** was designed to travel around tight bends on American tracks. Electric railcars, such as the **Budd Metroliner**, also ran on American railways. Electric trains proved to be reliable workhorses and more than 600 **DR Class 243s** were built for East German railroads to haul freight and passengers.

High-speed electric trains

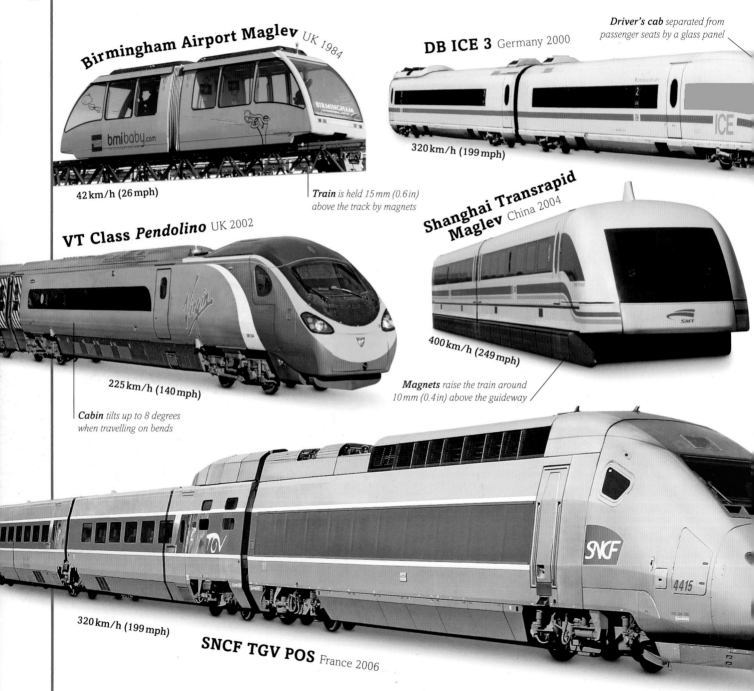

Birmingham Airport Maglev UK 1984

42 km/h (26 mph)

Train is held 15 mm (0.6 in) above the track by magnets

DB ICE 3 Germany 2000

320 km/h (199 mph)

Driver's cab separated from passenger seats by a glass panel

VT Class *Pendolino* UK 2002

225 km/h (140 mph)

Cabin tilts up to 8 degrees when travelling on bends

Shanghai Transrapid Maglev China 2004

400 km/h (249 mph)

Magnets raise the train around 10 mm (0.4 in) above the guideway

SNCF TGV POS France 2006

320 km/h (199 mph)

The need for speed has never been greater, as high-speed trains take on aircraft and road traffic to get passengers from one point to another in the quickest possible time. Meet some of the most rapid railway vehicles of all time.

The superfast **JRN700 Shinkansen** train can accelerate from 0 to 270 km/h (168 mph) in three minutes and can tilt slightly to keep its speed when moving around bends. While most high-speed electric trains, such as the **Hyundai Rotem KTX**, have powerful wheel-turning

JRN700 Shinkansen Japan 2007

Long, streamlined nose cuts through the air smoothly

300 km/h (186 mph)

Aluminium body

LSER Class 395 *Javelin* UK 2009

Nose cone contains horn and coupler

225 km/h (140 mph)

Automatic sliding doors

Hyundai Rotem KTX South Korea 2010

Train's wheels are powered by eight electric motors

SNCF TGV *Euroduplex* France 2012

305 km/h (190 mph)

NTV AGV ETR 575 Italy 2012

320 km/h (199 mph)

Train can seat 560 passengers

300 km/h (186 mph)

Nose cone contains coupler to link train to other locomotives

L0 Series Shinkansen Japan Under Development

In 2007, a modified TGV set a world speed record of **575 km/h** (357 mph).

Track-side electromagnets propel train to high speeds

600 km/h (373 mph)

electric motors housed in a power unit at the front of the train, the **DB ICE 3** has its motors spread out over the entire length of the train to distribute the weight. The **SNCF TGV Euroduplex** is a rare example of a high-speed double decker train. Some trains use powerful electromagnets to raise them above their track and move them along. This is called magnetic levitation (maglev). The first public passenger maglev train was the **Birmingham Airport Maglev** in the UK, while the fastest is the **Shanghai Transrapid Maglev**, in China.

BULLET TRAIN
Sleek, streamlined, and super-fast, a Japanese Shinkansen high-speed "bullet train" speeds across Honshu Island past snow-capped Mount Fuji. In 2014, Japan celebrated 50 years since Shinkansen trains ran for the very first time, just before the 1964 Tokyo Olympic Games. Today, Japan's high-speed rail network has carried more than 11 thousand million passengers.

The first Shinkansen trains ran at speeds of up to 210 km/h (130 mph). The latest classes of trains take their power from 25,000 volt overhead electricity lines, and can reach a top speed of 320 km/h (200 mph). The trains run on their own lines, separate from slower rail traffic – a total of 2,387 km (1,483 miles) of high-speed track crosses Japan. As many as

13 bullet trains per hour fly between Japan's two biggest urban areas, Tokyo and Osaka, providing an unrivalled high-speed service. Before they were introduced, the journey time between the two cities was around 6 hours, 40 minutes. The fastest services today complete the route in just 2 hours, 22 minutes.

Urban railways

Single, large wiper cleans entire windscreen

SIEMENS

Transilien

Mud Island Monorail USA/Switzerland 1982

Mud Island River Park

Suspended car can hold up to 180 passengers

Gatwick Adtranz C-100 UK/Canada 1987

Gatwick

Gatwick

Train runs on wheels fitted with rubber tyres

SMRT North-South Line C151 Singapore 1987

SMRT

Train travels at speeds up to 80 km/h (50 mph)

U55 Hauptbahnhof

poleor

be Berlin

2659

Berlin U-Bahn Germany 1992

Trains on the Berlin U-Bahn carry over **508 million** passengers every year.

Articulated joints between short carriages

Rail services in towns and cities ferry millions of people every day. Some travel for work or for school, others for fun and leisure. There are urban railways that link airports with towns, while others help reduce congestion on city roads.

Rapid transit systems, such as the **Matra Taipei Metro**, offer quick and reliable transport between city stations separated by short distances. To avoid cluttering up the streets, many train lines run underground. The **Berlin U-Bahn** has 80 per cent of its 146 km (90 miles)

Siemens Avanto Germany 1995

Matra Taipei Metro Taiwan/France 1996

Rail supplies
750-volt electricity to power train's motors

Hollow box girder contains cable along which train's wheels run

Bombardier MOVIA Canada/Singapore 2000s

Düsseldorf H-Bahn Skytrain Germany 2002

Large windscreen on driver's cab

Moscow Monorail Russia 2004

Driverless train has a maximum speed of 90 km/h (56 mph)

Automatic coupler, to link with other trains

Vossloh Wuppertal Schwebebahn Germany 2015

of lines running below the surface of the city. Monorails are trains that run on a single rail. Many, such as the **Moscow Monorail**, have their trains running on top of the rail, while some, such as the **Mud Island Monorail**, are suspended below the rails. While many urban trains are controlled by a human driver, some systems run automatically. The **Gatwick Adtranz**, the **Düsseldorf H-Bahn Skytrain**, and the popular **Bombardier MOVIA**, which runs in Singapore and China among other countries, are driverless vehicles.

147

Trams and trolleybuses

Great Orme Tramway UK 1902

Tram pulled uphill by cable moved by electric motors

Hand-operated double doors

Electric tram Czech Republic 1907

Pantograph connects tram with overhead electricity supply

W2 Class Melbourne tram Australia 1927

This W2 Class has been converted into a restaurant on wheels

Wheels powered by four electric motors

English Electric Balloon
UK 1934

Several **Balloon** trams still run in Blackpool, **80 years** after they were built.

Hong Kong Tramways
China 1980s

Trams run on tracks and are powered by electricity supplied by overhead cables. They are also known as streetcars, as they share space on roads with other vehicles. Trolleybuses are also electrically powered, but they run on tyres instead of tracks.

Britain's first electric tramway was built in Blackpool in 1885. The double-decker **English Electric Balloon**, which could hold up to 94 passengers, ran along at speeds of up to 70 km/h (43 mph). The **Hong Kong Tramways** is an all-double decker service – the only one in the

Flexity Swift M5000 Canada/Germany 2009

Bury

3002B

Metrolink

3002

Some **CAF** trams run an average distance of **95,000 km** (59,030 miles) per year.

Five articulated segments allow tram to travel around bends

CAF Urbos 3 Spain 2009

Seats up to 66 passengers

Low floor sits 35 cm (13.8 in) above the track

Aluminium body panels

Trolley pole channels electricity from overhead wire to trolleybus

Solaris Trollino 15 Poland 2001

LISTAS
Ferencas
(1811–1886)
Ferenz Liszt
VENGRIJOS SŪNUS. PIANISTAS VIRTUOZAS IR KOMPOZITORIUS ROMANTIKAS.

San Francisco Trolleybus USA 2003

Belkommunmash 42003A Belarus 2007

world – and uses narrow trams, only 1.98 m (6.5 ft) wide. Modern trams such as the **Flexity Swift** are found in Manchester, Istanbul, and Cologne, while the **CAF Urbos 3** runs on tramways all over the world, from Australia and Brazil to Taiwan and Spain. Trolleybuses, such as

the **San Francisco Trolleybus** and the **Solaris Trollino 15**, run on regular roads and need only a series of roadside poles from which their overhead power line is suspended. The Trollino is quieter and generates much less pollution than buses powered by petrol or diesel engines.

149

HOLD ON TIGHT!
Followers of the Hindu religion crowd a train on its way to the northern Indian town of Govardhan, to take part in the Guru Purnima festival. Indian locomotives and carriages are not normally as crowded as this, but the country does run one of the largest and busiest railway systems in the world, with enough track – some 115,000 km (71,500 miles) in total – to circle the Earth almost three times.

This WDM-3A class locomotive is just one of 5,345 diesel engines that runs along the tracks of Indian Railways. The company also operates 4,568 electric locomotives and 43 steam engines. These haul more than 62,000 passenger coaches and 239,000 freight wagons, stopping at more than 7,200 stations throughout India. Some services also travel over the border, into the neighbouring countries of Pakistan, Nepal, and Bangladesh. In India the cost of train fares is low, and the number of car owners relatively small, so rail travel is incredibly popular. In 2014, more than 8.5 billion passengers took the train, giving Indian Railways' 1.3 million employees plenty of work to do.

WATER

Taking to the water

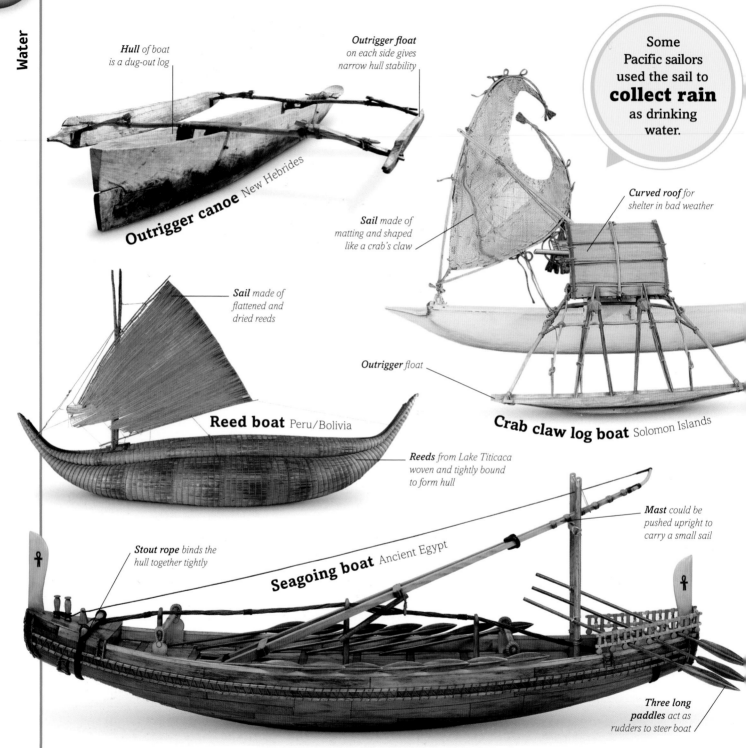

Hull of boat is a dug-out log

Outrigger float on each side gives narrow hull stability

Outrigger canoe New Hebrides

Some Pacific sailors used the sail to **collect rain** as drinking water.

Sail made of matting and shaped like a crab's claw

Curved roof for shelter in bad weather

Sail made of flattened and dried reeds

Reed boat Peru/Bolivia

Outrigger float

Crab claw log boat Solomon Islands

Reeds from Lake Titicaca woven and tightly bound to form hull

Stout rope binds the hull together tightly

Mast could be pushed upright to carry a small sail

Seagoing boat Ancient Egypt

Three long paddles act as rudders to steer boat

No one knows the name of the first sailor, or the craft that he or she used. They may have sat astride a log, or on bundles of reeds, lashed together. What we do know is that people have travelled or fished in boats for more than 10,000 years.

Some of the earliest boats were large tree trunks, hollowed out to form simple **dugout canoes**. Ancient people throughout the Pacific learned how to build **outrigger canoes**, with a second, smaller hull floating on the water to provide stability, while the native American people built

Dugout canoe Haiti

Prow (front) of boat shaped to a point to cut through water

Panels of birch bark, waterproofed with resin from spruce trees, sewn together

Bark canoe North America

Frame made from branches of willow

Simple oar made from ash wood

Currach Ireland

Currachs are still used for **fishing and fun races** in Ireland and Scotland.

Quffa Iraq

Hull made from woven reeds and rope, sometimes covered in bitumen (tar)

Thung-chai Vietnam

Rim of boat is made of bamboo

Sides lashed to bottom of hull with flax fibre and decorated with bird feathers

Stern covered with ceremonial designs

Maori war canoe New Zealand

bark canoes out of a wooden frame covered in tree bark. Reeds, which grow in abundance at the edges of many rivers and lakes, were dried, bound, and woven to form **reed boats**. Reeds could also be woven to form circular boats for fishing. Known as **Thung-chai** in Vietnam, and coracles in UK, a similar form of boat called a **Quffa** existed in Iraq for at least 5,000 years. The ancient Egyptians built reed boats to sail the River Nile, but around 5,500 years ago built larger, wooden **seagoing boats** to venture beyond the Nile and into the Mediterranean Sea.

World of watercraft

Square sail hanging from horizontal yardarm

Kayak outer surface made of tanned sealskin

Seal bladder float – when a seal or large fish is caught, the float is attached so it can be towed

The Inuit used kayaks to hunt sea mammals such as **seals** and **whales**.

Compartment to store live fish

Sampan China

Cargo vessel Japan

Whaling boat Indonesia

Sail of matted palm leaves

Long, sharp harpoon for attacking a whale

Stout rope from mast to bow of ship called a forestay

Short wooden mast

Triangular lateen sails can be rigged so that boat can sail in different winds

Pearling dhow Kuwait

Flat, square-ended stern (back) of hull made of hardwood

Fishing dory Portugal

Long oars carved from wood

Simple anchor to prevent drifting when in good fishing waters

An astonishing variety of vessels have been built to travel on water. Across the world, people have used ingenuity, and the local materials available, to build boats, rafts, canoes, and other watercraft, for fishing, transport, war, and pleasure.

Amongst the simplest boats are **fishing rafts**, often just a bundle of tree branches lashed together to form a platform. The raft-like **Jangada**, however, is able to sail over reefs on the Brazilian coast to fish for hake and mackerel, often spending 2 to 3 days at sea. Throughout

Built-in tray *holds harpoon rope made of leather*

Harpoon

Inuit kayak Arctic

Large triangular sail *helps vessel travel at speeds between 20–28 km/h (12–17 mph)*

Battle canoes could be more than 30m (100ft) long, and hold up to **200 warriors**.

Battle canoe Fiji

Support *for canopy, erected in bad weather*

Open stern *where outboard motor can be fitted*

Bamboo punting pole

Woven cord rigging

Rounded roof shelter *used for sleeping in*

Each of the two hulls *was covered in gum and mulberry bark, to help make it watertight*

Seating *for two passengers, side-by-side*

Steel bow, *weighing 10–20 kg (22–44 lb), helps balance weight of gondolier at the back*

Gondola Italy

Single oar *used for steering and propulsion by standing gondolier*

Hull *made of six logs from the lightweight piúva tree, lashed together*

Sides *added to raft to prevent catch being washed overboard*

Jangada Brazil

Daggerboard *helps stop raft drifting sideways*

Fishing raft West Africa

Southeast Asia, another flat-bottomed boat, the **sampan**, is used by people to fish, travel, and even live in. In the Arctic, single- and two-person **Inuit kayaks** were used to hunt for mammals and fish, while in Indonesia, brave hunters chased after sperm whales, often two or three times longer than their flimsy **whaling boats**. On the Pacific island of Fiji, people built larger **battle canoes**, featuring a platform laid over a double hull. And in Italy, slender **gondolas** travel the canals that criss-cross the city of Venice, acting as water taxis.

OVER THE TOP A kayaker takes a terrifying plunge, hurtling over the highest of the five cascading waterfalls on the Agua Azul river in the Mexican state of Chiapas. He's one of six top professional kayakers who tackled the river and its waterfalls for the short adventure movie, *Beyond The Drop*. For a safe landing, the kayaker must keep inside the flow of water, and land in the cushion of air and water at the foot of the waterfall.

It is likely that the first canoes and kayaks took to the water thousands of years ago, and that most were built of wood. But the appeal of paddling your own personal watercraft still holds today, even if modern canoes and kayaks are usually built from plastics, fibreglass, or, in the case of the most advanced, Kevlar and carbon fibre. Thousands of amateur kayakers enjoy paddling on rivers, lakes, or the sea, at weekends or on holiday. A handful of the very best kayakers compete in competitions, either in speed races on flatwater, or on very technical whitewater slalom courses. Extreme kayaking is an adventure sport for the crazy few who enjoy paddling down racing rivers, including giant waterfalls!

Sailing ship

Sailing ships rely on the force of the wind catching their sails to propel them through the water. By changing the number of sails, and their positions, an experienced crew can adjust the speed and direction of the ship. HMS *Endeavour* left Plymouth, UK, in 1768, skippered by Captain James Cook, and sailed round the world on a three-year, 48,000-km (30,000-mile) voyage of exploration. The former collier (coal ship) became the first European vessel to explore the east coast of Australia.

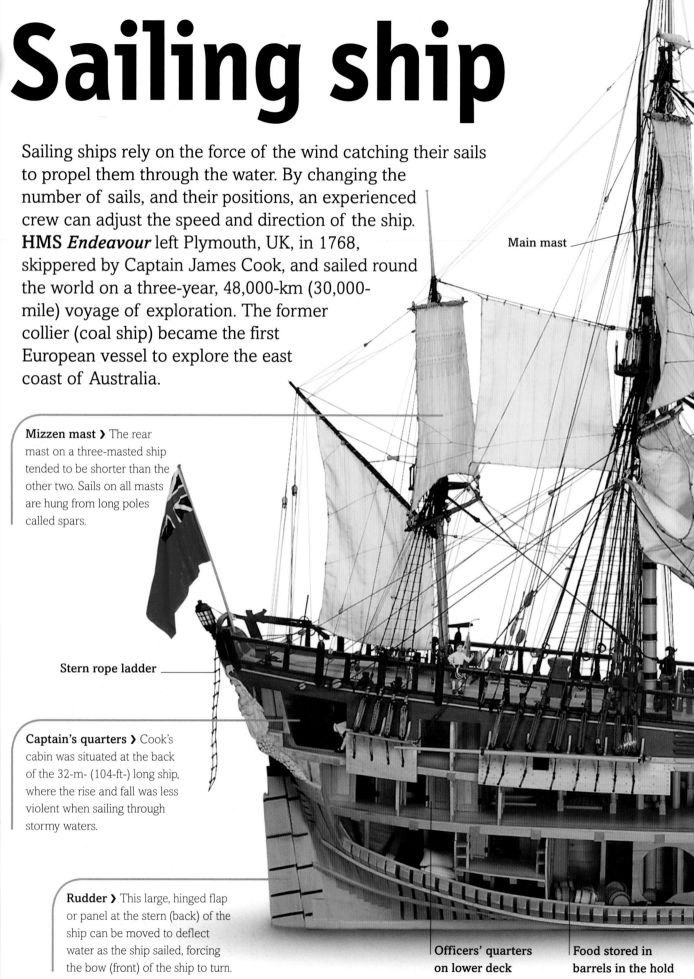

Main mast

Mizzen mast ❯ The rear mast on a three-masted ship tended to be shorter than the other two. Sails on all masts are hung from long poles called spars.

Stern rope ladder

Captain's quarters ❯ Cook's cabin was situated at the back of the 32-m- (104-ft-) long ship, where the rise and fall was less violent when sailing through stormy waters.

Rudder ❯ This large, hinged flap or panel at the stern (back) of the ship can be moved to deflect water as the ship sailed, forcing the bow (front) of the ship to turn.

Officers' quarters on lower deck

Food stored in barrels in the hold

Foremast ❯ This is the front mast on a three-masted ship. On the *Endeavour*, the foremast was built of pine and fir wood, and towered some 34 m (112 ft) above the ship's deck.

Jib sail ❯ Skilled sailors were able to use jib sails to steer the ship, by altering their positions. When fully rigged, with all of its sails on all of its masts, the *Endeavour* had more than 2,700 square m (29,000 square ft) of sail.

HMS Endeavour

Bowsprit ❯ The long pole rising from the bow of the ship to which the rigging for the bottom of the jib sails was attached.

Hull ❯ For many centuries, the body of a sailing ship was crafted out of planks of wood. *Endeavour*'s hull was made mostly of white oak, and was flat-bottomed, for sailing in shallow waters. It was divided into different sections, including below-deck living quarters for 90 sailors.

One of 22 cannons protecting the ship

Rowing boat

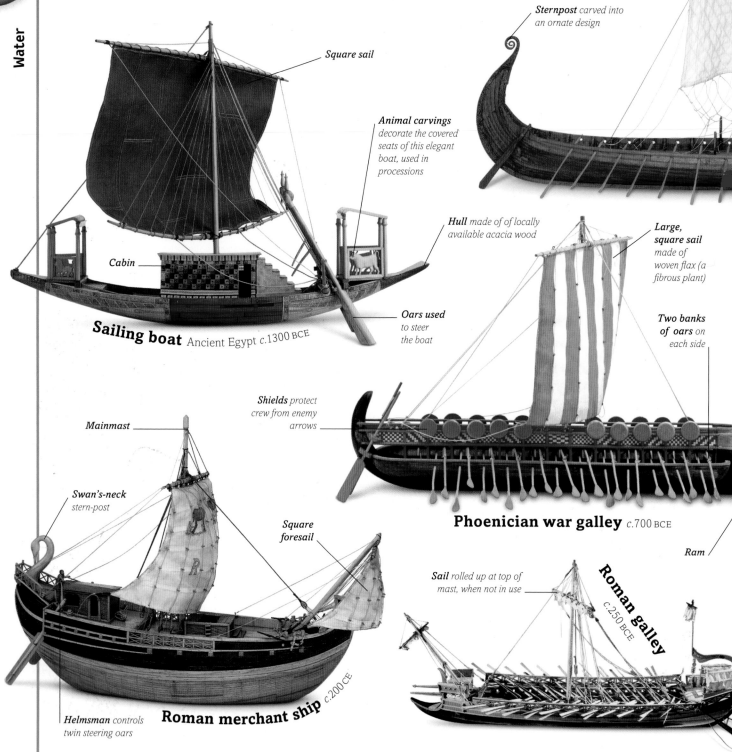

Sail power

Square sail

Sternpost *carved into an ornate design*

Animal carvings *decorate the covered seats of this elegant boat, used in processions*

Hull *made of of locally available acacia wood*

Cabin

Sailing boat Ancient Egypt *c.*1300 BCE

Oars used *to steer the boat*

Large, square sail *made of woven flax (a fibrous plant)*

Two banks of oars *on each side*

Mainmast

Shields *protect crew from enemy arrows*

Swan's-neck *stern-post*

Square foresail

Phoenician war galley *c.*700 BCE

Ram

Sail *rolled up at top of mast, when not in use*

Roman galley *c.*250 BCE

Roman merchant ship *c.*200 CE

Helmsman *controls twin steering oars*

Thousands of years ago, people learned to harness the power of the wind to push their craft through the water. Sails made of cloth, reeds, or matting, and hung from a mast, caught the wind to move boats faster than people could row or paddle.

Some of the earliest-known **sailing boats** were found on the River Nile in Egypt, more than 5,000 years ago. They used a large, square sail made of cloth, which worked best when sailing downwind (with wind coming from behind the boat). Square sails were also invented independently in parts of

Large single sail hung from a single spar, called a yard, or yardarm

Hull built of overlapping wooden planks fixed to a frame

The dragon head on the prow of this dromon fired **burning flames** at the enemy.

Lookout position at the top of the main mast, for spotting approaching ships or land

Rigging enabled crew to climb up and unfurl sails

Viking longship
Norway *c.*800 CE

Oars for use when there is no wind

Oars were manned by as many as 100 crew

Yardarm

Foresail

Dromon Eastern Roman Empire *c.*650 CE

During the Ming Dynasty, China had a navy with more than **3,000 war junks**.

Junk China *c.*1840

Fighting junk fitted with guns

Lantern

Wooden rudder

Gunport

Cocca Italy *c.*1500

South America, and also in China, where they were often fitted to the **junks** that sailed the Pacific and Indian oceans. Many ancient sailing ships, such as **Phoenician war galleys**, **Roman galleys**, and **Viking longships**, were fitted with rows of oars, for when there was no wind. Viking longships were designed with shallow hulls so they could sail right up to the shore to attack and raid settlements. The Vikings were skilled sailors who travelled right across Europe and, around 1000 CE, crossed the Atlantic, reaching Newfoundland in Canada.

Trade and exploration

Wooden hull *is approximately 17.7 m (58 ft) long*

Main mast top castle *manned by crew member searching for land*

Santa Maria
Spain 1460

When the *Santa Maria* was finally **broken up**, the wood was used to build a **fort**.

Lateen sails *used when winds blew towards the side of the ship*

Caravel
Portugal 1490s

Hull *is approximately 27.5 m (90 ft) long*

Mayflower England 1600s

Short, deep wooden hull *could carry plenty of cargo below decks*

HMS Bounty England 1784

Mizzen mast *added to ship when it was converted from a warship to a survey vessel*

HMS Beagle England 1820

Hull *converted to transport breadfruit plants from Tahiti to the Caribbean*

Ship *carried 74 people on a 5 year survey voyage*

From the 15th century onwards, European sailing ships travelled the world. Many were trading vessels, carrying cargoes as varied as slaves, food, and spices. Others explored new lands, on epic voyages of discovery.

Portugal was a major sea trading nation in the 15th century, and **caravels** sailed along the coasts of Europe and Africa. Two accompanied the *Santa Maria* on Christopher Columbus' famous 1492 voyage across the Atlantic. Many European ships would later head west for trade, to conquer,

Masts carried sails, but ship was also powered by a diesel engine

Fram Norway 1892

Square hull to keep ship small, as ships were taxed based on their size

Fluyt Netherlands 1700s

Square topsail

Hull was specially strengthened against the pressure of ice freezing around it

The *Fram* had a **windmill** on board which ran a generator to power electric lights.

Bowsprit

Cutty Sark UK 1869

Skysail is the highest sail on the mast

Wooden hull 64.8 m (212.6 ft) long

Hull, made from iron plates riveted together, carried guano (animal dung), wheat, and coal

Wendur Scotland 1884

or establish colonies, such as the **Mayflower**, which carried pilgrims to settle in North America. As European explorers found new lands, more merchant ships engaged in trade. The **fluyt** was a common Dutch design with a very narrow deck. Fast ships called clippers, such as the **Cutty Sark**, sailed between Asia and Europe. One of the most epic trips of all was made by **Fram**, which sailed more than 100,000 km (60,000 miles) around the Arctic, before carrying Norwegian explorer Roald Amundsen to Antarctica, where he became the first person to reach the South Pole.

War at sea

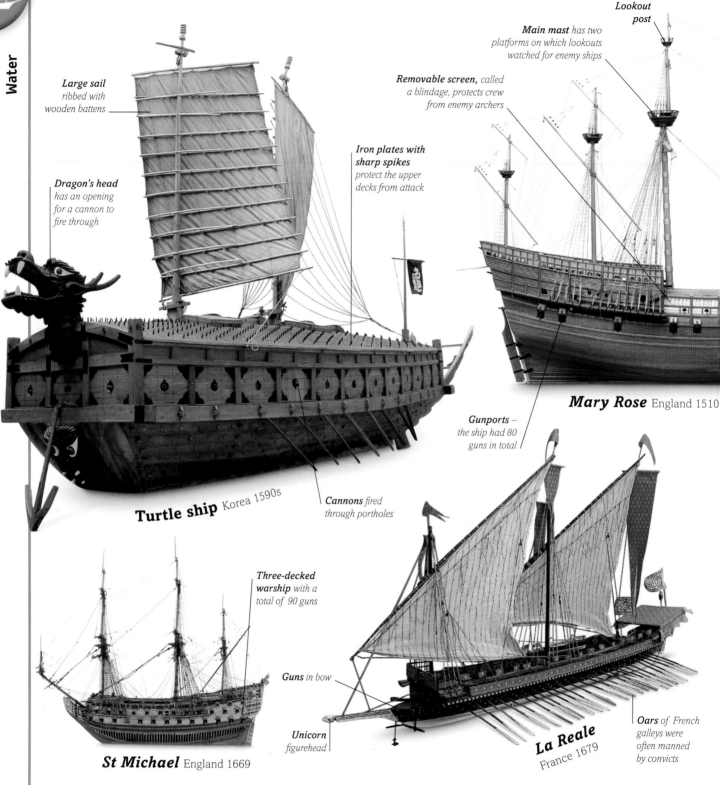

Large sail ribbed with wooden battens

Dragon's head has an opening for a cannon to fire through

Turtle ship Korea 1590s

Cannons fired through portholes

Iron plates with sharp spikes protect the upper decks from attack

Lookout post

Main mast has two platforms on which lookouts watched for enemy ships

Removable screen, called a blindage, protects crew from enemy archers

Mary Rose England 1510

Gunports – the ship had 80 guns in total

Three-decked warship with a total of 90 guns

St Michael England 1669

Guns in bow

Unicorn figurehead

La Reale France 1679

Oars of French galleys were often manned by convicts

For almost as long as there have been ships, the sea has been a battlefield for rival nations planning invasion, or for control of shipping routes and trade. From the 16th century, warships bristled with guns and battles at sea became even more deadly.

Before naval artillery, battles at sea were mostly close hand, with fire, rams, or arrows used in attack. The Korean **turtle ship** protected itself against archers, and from being boarded, with its hefty, spiked deck armour. Big guns allowed ships to fight more at a distance. The **Mary Rose's** iron

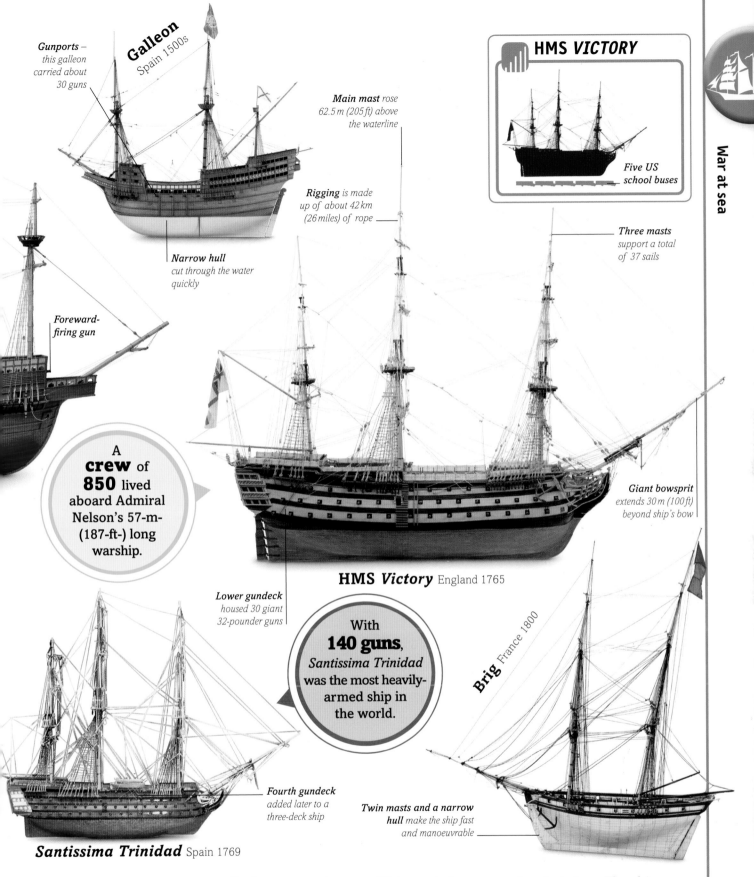

Galleon Spain 1500s

Gunports – this galleon carried about 30 guns

Main mast rose 62.5 m (205 ft) above the waterline

Rigging is made up of about 42 km (26 miles) of rope

Narrow hull cut through the water quickly

Foreward-firing gun

HMS VICTORY

Five US school buses

Three masts support a total of 37 sails

A **crew** of **850** lived aboard Admiral Nelson's 57-m- (187-ft-) long warship.

Giant bowsprit extends 30 m (100 ft) beyond ship's bow

HMS *Victory* England 1765

Lower gundeck housed 30 giant 32-pounder guns

With **140 guns**, *Santissima Trinidad* was the most heavily-armed ship in the world.

Brig France 1800

Fourth gundeck added later to a three-deck ship

Twin masts and a narrow hull make the ship fast and manoeuvrable

Santissima Trinidad Spain 1769

cannons fired through flaps called gunports, in the hull. To boost firepower, some ships were built with extra decks of guns. This led to three-decker warships, such as the ***St Michael***, which fought in the Caribbean, and the ***Santissima Trinidad***, which later received a fourth deck of heavy guns.

This made her menacing, but slow. Flagships, such as the French navy's ***La Reale***, were home to a fleet's commander. **HMS *Victory*** was the flagship under British admiral Lord Nelson at the battle of Trafalgar. With 104 guns, she was a formidable, as well as fast, fighting machine.

RIDING THE WIND
The BMW Oracle Racing Team 90 (BOR90) trimaran (three-hulled boat) lifts up into the air during a training run. The 34.5-m- (113-ft-) long, 27.4-m- (90-ft-) wide giant is about the same size as two basketball courts and was built to win the America's Cup, sailing's most prestigious competition, which it did in 2010. The picture shows how racing sailors sometimes need a real head for heights!

Trimaran BOR90 (later renamed USA–17) needed more than nine months of careful construction in Washington State, USA, before it could be let loose on the water for testing, crew training, and modifications. Its body is made mostly of carbon fibre and weighs 16 tonnes (18 US tons). The main sail is not made of fabric, but is solid and made of carbon fibre and Kevlar, a material found in bulletproof armour. The result was a 58-m- (190-ft-) tall monster sail. At 3,524 kg (7,770 lb), it was so heavy that powerful hydraulic systems were needed to move it, rather than regular rigging, but it boosted the trimaran's speed to more than 50 km/h (31 mph) during parts of its triumphant America's Cup run.

Steamship

Steamships burned coal or oil to heat water and create steam to power an engine. This either drove a paddle wheel or turned a screw propeller, as found on the *SS Great Britain*. When launched in 1843, SS *Great Britain* was the largest ship in the world, and the first iron-hulled steamship powered by a screw propeller. Two years later, it became the first propeller-powered steamship to cross the Atlantic Ocean, a journey that took 14 days.

Hull ❯ The 98-m- (322-ft-) long hull is fashioned out of overlapping iron plates riveted together to form a watertight outer body.

Main mast ❯ The tallest mast on a ship. On the SS *Great Britain*, this is the only mast to carry large, square sails.

Bowsprit

SS Great Britain

Funnel

Decks ❯ The SS *Great Britain* has three decks. The bottom one is used for cargo, supplies, and accommodation.

Steerage ❯ Second-class accommodation, known as steerage, is at the bottom of the ship.

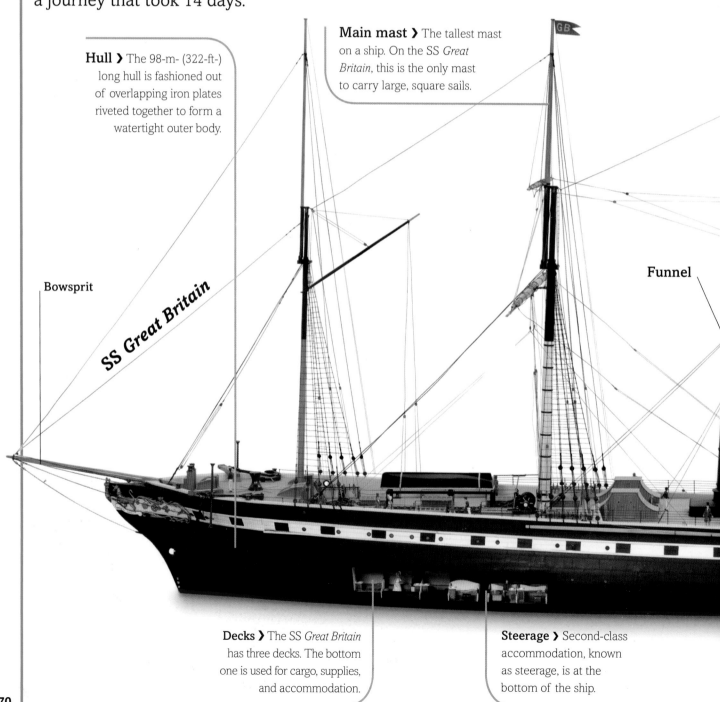

Rigging ❯ On the SS *Great Britain*, the rigging is made of iron cable rather than rope. This is to reduce drag.

Mast ❯ Five of the ship's masts can be folded down on deck to reduce air resistance when the ship is solely under steam power.

Spar ❯ Sails are hung from these long poles attached to masts.

Helm

Lifeboat ❯ There are seven lifeboats for 252 passengers and 130 crew.

First-class dining saloon and cabins

Propeller screw ❯ The giant propeller has six blades and measures 4.9 m (16 ft) in diameter. As it turns, the propeller pushes water back, moving the ship forward.

Steam meets steel

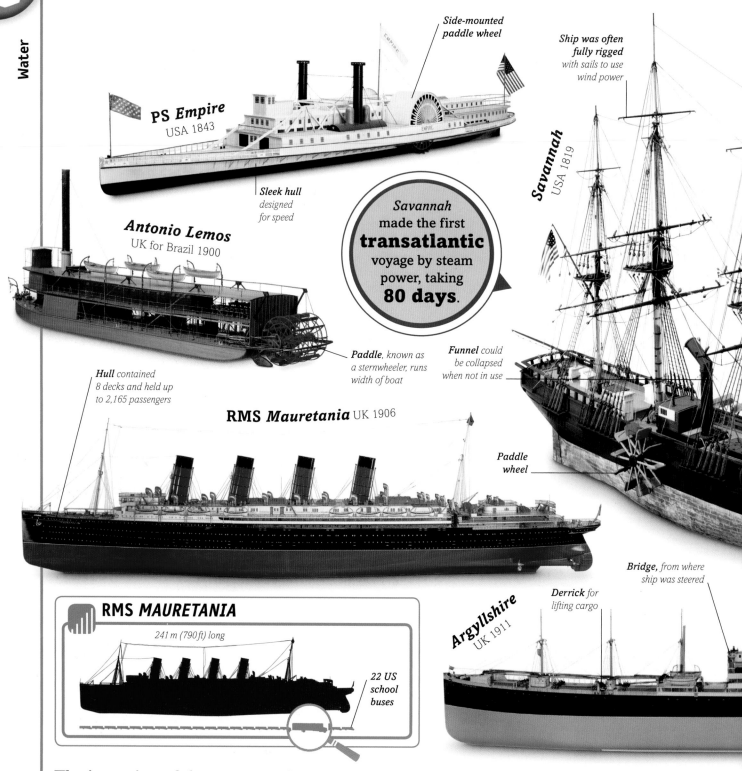

PS Empire
USA 1843

Side-mounted paddle wheel

Sleek hull designed for speed

Ship was often fully rigged *with sails to use wind power*

Savannah USA 1819

Antonio Lemos
UK for Brazil 1900

Savannah made the first **transatlantic** voyage by steam power, taking **80 days**.

Paddle, *known as a sternwheeler, runs width of boat*

Funnel *could be collapsed when not in use*

Hull *contained 8 decks and held up to 2,165 passengers*

RMS *Mauretania* UK 1906

Paddle wheel

Bridge, *from where ship was steered*

Derrick *for lifting cargo*

Argyllshire UK 1911

RMS *MAURETANIA*

241 m (790 ft) long

22 US school buses

The invention of the steam engine meant that ships no longer had to rely on the wind. When steam power was used to drive steel ships, the result was large, sturdy vessels that could travel greater distances faster than ever before.

Early steamships could not hold much cargo because of the vast amounts of coal they needed to carry as fuel. The **SS *Agamemnon***, however, could run on just 20 tonnes of coal a day, allowing it to sail economically between Europe and the Far East. Powerful steam liners

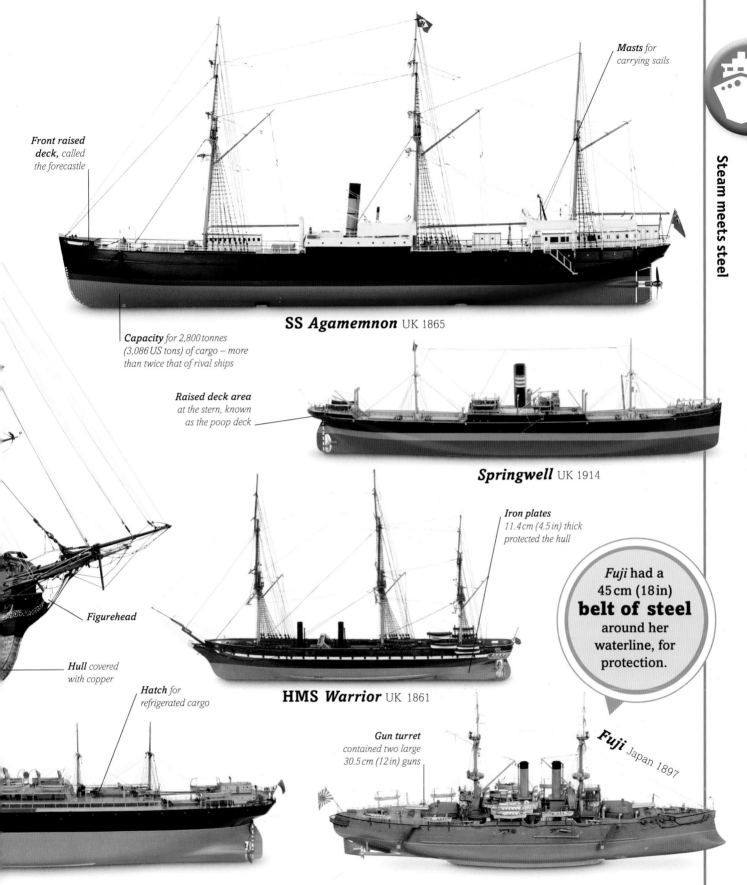

Masts for carrying sails

Front raised deck, called the forecastle

SS *Agamemnon* UK 1865

Capacity for 2,800 tonnes (3,086 US tons) of cargo – more than twice that of rival ships

Raised deck area at the stern, known as the poop deck

Springwell UK 1914

Iron plates 11.4 cm (4.5 in) thick protected the hull

Figurehead

Hull covered with copper

Hatch for refrigerated cargo

HMS *Warrior* UK 1861

Fuji had a **45 cm (18 in) belt of steel** around her waterline, for protection.

Gun turret contained two large 30.5 cm (12 in) guns

Fuji Japan 1897

such as the **RMS *Mauretania***, were now able to cross the Atlantic in as little as four or five days. Early steamships, such as the **PS *Empire***, were mostly made of wood, but iron and steel hulls became more common. Steel made it possible to build refrigerated ships, such the ***Argyllshire***, which transported meat from South America and Australasia to Europe. Steel and steam were also adopted by navies. **HMS *Warrior*** was amongst the first Royal Navy ships to come with an iron hull and steel armour. It carried a crew of 706 as well as 40 giant artillery guns.

Working ships

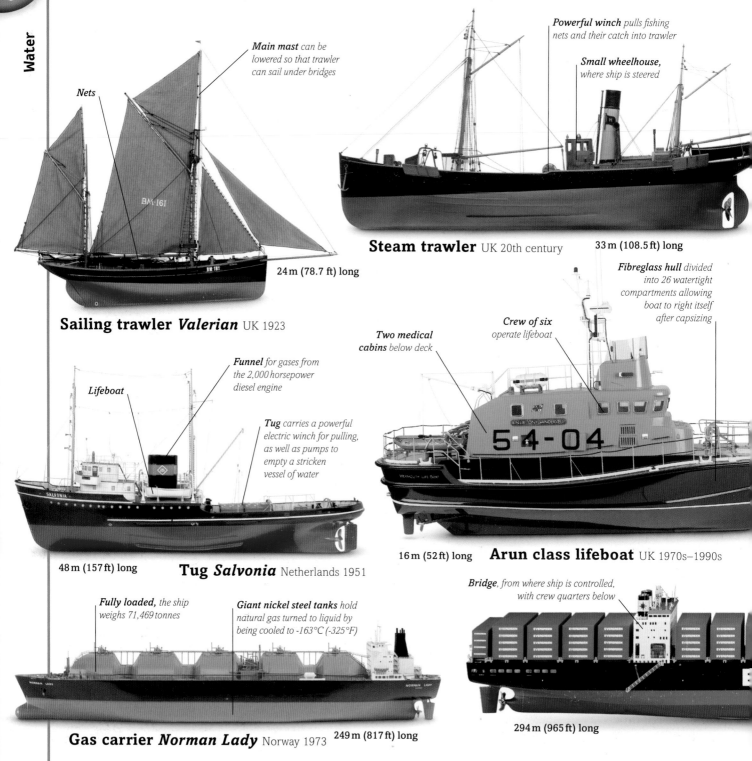

Main mast *can be lowered so that trawler can sail under bridges*

Nets

Powerful winch *pulls fishing nets and their catch into trawler*

Small wheelhouse, *where ship is steered*

Steam trawler UK 20th century   33 m (108.5 ft) long

24 m (78.7 ft) long

Sailing trawler *Valerian* UK 1923

Fibreglass hull *divided into 26 watertight compartments allowing boat to right itself after capsizing*

Crew of six *operate lifeboat*

Two medical cabins *below deck*

Funnel *for gases from the 2,000 horsepower diesel engine*

Lifeboat

Tug *carries a powerful electric winch for pulling, as well as pumps to empty a stricken vessel of water*

54-04

48 m (157 ft) long

Tug *Salvonia* Netherlands 1951

16 m (52 ft) long   **Arun class lifeboat** UK 1970s–1990s

Bridge, *from where ship is controlled, with crew quarters below*

Fully loaded, *the ship weighs 71,469 tonnes*

Giant nickel steel tanks *hold natural gas turned to liquid by being cooled to -163°C (-325°F)*

Gas carrier *Norman Lady* Norway 1973   249 m (817 ft) long

294 m (965 ft) long

Every day, thousands of ships are at work in a variety of different ways. Many carry billions of tonnes of goods, fuel, and material across the waters of the world. Others save lives, assist other ships, and catch food from the seas and oceans.

Tankers carry liquids, such as oil or, in the case of *Norman Lady*, liquefied natural gas. The *Shin Aitoku Maru* is an oil tanker with a difference. Its computer-controlled sails help it save fuel, which is used to power its diesel engines. The *Ever Royal* carries goods and

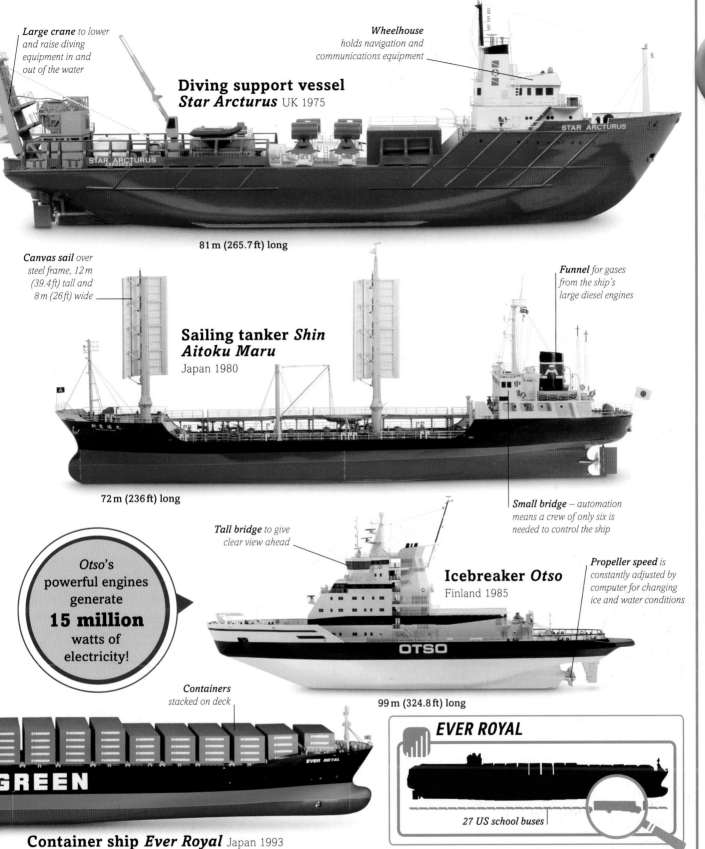

Large crane to lower and raise diving equipment in and out of the water

Wheelhouse holds navigation and communications equipment

Diving support vessel
Star Arcturus UK 1975

81 m (265.7 ft) long

Canvas sail over steel frame, 12 m (39.4 ft) tall and 8 m (26 ft) wide

Sailing tanker *Shin Aitoku Maru*
Japan 1980

Funnel for gases from the ship's large diesel engines

72 m (236 ft) long

Small bridge – automation means a crew of only six is needed to control the ship

Tall bridge to give clear view ahead

Otso's powerful engines generate **15 million** watts of electricity!

Icebreaker *Otso*
Finland 1985

Propeller speed is constantly adjusted by computer for changing ice and water conditions

99 m (324.8 ft) long

Containers stacked on deck

GREEN

EVER ROYAL

27 US school buses

Container ship *Ever Royal* Japan 1993

materials stored in up to 4,200 standard 6-m-(20-ft-) long containers, designed to be easily unloaded onto trucks. Some working ships help serve others. Icebreakers, such as **Otso**, can plough through ice many metres thick to clear a path to let ships through. Other vessels act as

tugs, such as the ocean-going **Salvonia**, which can tow a stricken ship out of danger and home for repairs. Coastguards, and other maritime rescue services, operate boats like the **Arun class lifeboat**, which can travel through the stormiest of waters to rescue people at sea.

Passenger carriers

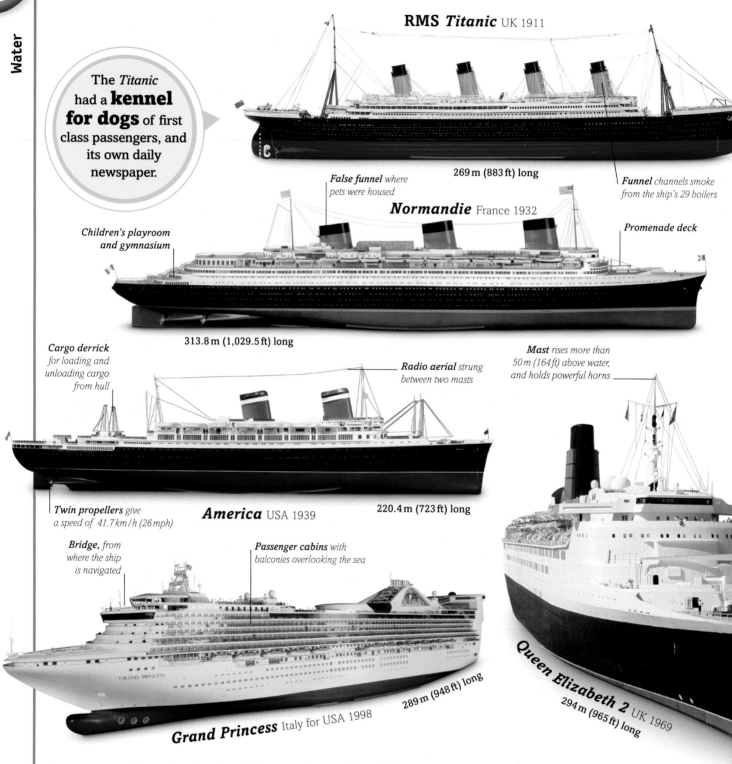

The *Titanic* had a **kennel for dogs** of first class passengers, and its own daily newspaper.

RMS *Titanic* UK 1911

269 m (883 ft) long

False funnel where pets were housed

Funnel channels smoke from the ship's 29 boilers

Normandie France 1932

Children's playroom and gymnasium

Promenade deck

313.8 m (1,029.5 ft) long

Cargo derrick for loading and unloading cargo from hull

Radio aerial strung between two masts

Mast rises more than 50 m (164 ft) above water, and holds powerful horns

Twin propellers give a speed of 41.7 km/h (26 mph)

America USA 1939

220.4 m (723 ft) long

Bridge, from where the ship is navigated

Passenger cabins with balconies overlooking the sea

Grand Princess Italy for USA 1998

289 m (948 ft) long

Queen Elizabeth 2 UK 1969

294 m (965 ft) long

Every year, hundreds of millions of people travel on ships for work or pleasure. Many use ferry services, linking places separated by water. Others holiday aboard large passenger liners, cruising the seas and oceans of the world.

Water taxis, such as Tokyo's **Himiko** water bus, transport people short distances, while larger ferries like the **Arcturus** move people and their vehicles across lakes and seas. The **MDV 1200 Class ferry** has capacity for 175 cars and more than 600 passengers. The **America** liner held

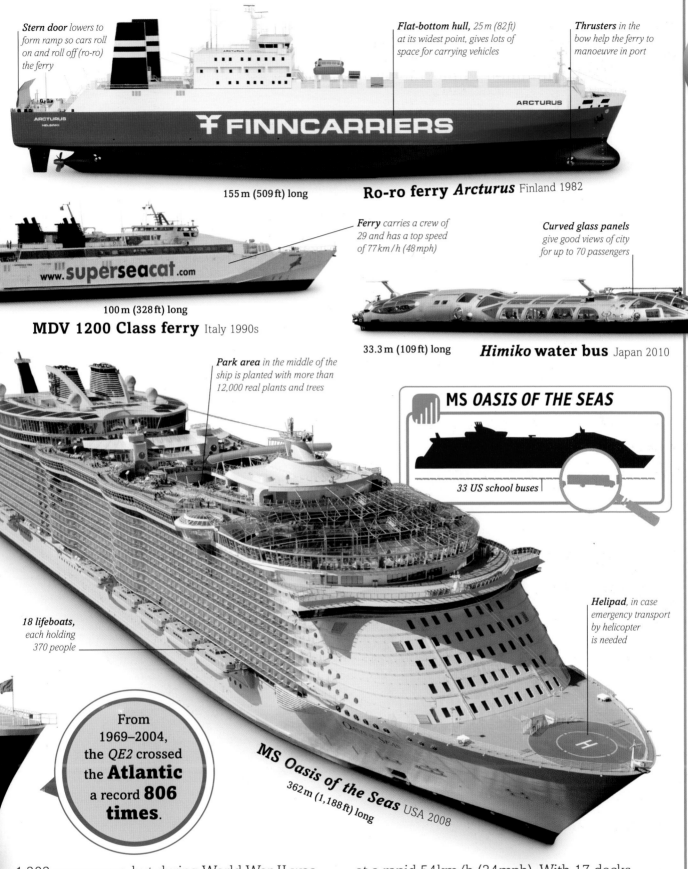

Stern door lowers to form ramp so cars roll on and roll off (ro-ro) the ferry

Flat-bottom hull, 25 m (82 ft) at its widest point, gives lots of space for carrying vehicles

Thrusters in the bow help the ferry to manoeuvre in port

155 m (509 ft) long

Ro-ro ferry *Arcturus* Finland 1982

Ferry carries a crew of 29 and has a top speed of 77 km/h (48 mph)

Curved glass panels give good views of city for up to 70 passengers

100 m (328 ft) long

MDV 1200 Class ferry Italy 1990s

33.3 m (109 ft) long

***Himiko* water bus** Japan 2010

Park area in the middle of the ship is planted with more than 12,000 real plants and trees

MS *OASIS OF THE SEAS*

33 US school buses

18 lifeboats, each holding 370 people

Helipad, in case emergency transport by helicopter is needed

From 1969–2004, the *QE2* crossed the **Atlantic** a record **806 times**.

MS Oasis of the Seas USA 2008
362 m (1,188 ft) long

1,202 passengers, but during World War II was converted into a troop ship carrying 7,678 soldiers. Over the years, even bigger passenger liners were launched, including the **RMS *Titanic***, which sank on its maiden voyage in 1912, and the ***Normandie***, which could carry 1,972 passengers at a rapid 54 km/h (34 mph). With 17 decks carrying up to 3,600 passengers, the ***Grand Princess*** became the world's largest liner, until overtaken by the gigantic **MS *Oasis of the Seas***, which, at 225,282 tonnes (248,330 US tons), weighs almost five times as much as the *Titanic*.

CITY ON THE SEA
The world's biggest cruise ship, Royal Caribbean International's *Allure of the Seas,* enters her home harbour of Port Everglades, Florida, USA, in 2010. This gigantic,16-deck floating hotel is almost as long as four football fields, and houses up to 6,318 guests who are looked after by a crew of 2,384 people. It's almost as if a small floating city has taken to the water.

Built in Finland between 2008 and 2010, this gigantic vessel is 362 m (1,188 ft) long. She rises to 72 m (236 ft) above the waterline, but her funnels can telescope down for passing under low bridges. The liner's many attractions include 25 restaurants, a 1,380-seat theatre, a full-sized basketball court, a rock climbing wall, 21 swimming pools and jacuzzis, and wave machines that pump out more than 220,000 litres (58,000 gal) of water a minute, so people can surf as they cruise! There's even a 680-m- (2,230-ft-) long running track, and a park area with thousands of real plants and trees. The 225,282-tonne (248,330-US ton) ship cruises the Caribbean or Mediterranean Sea at the stately speed of 42 km/h (26 mph).

World War ships

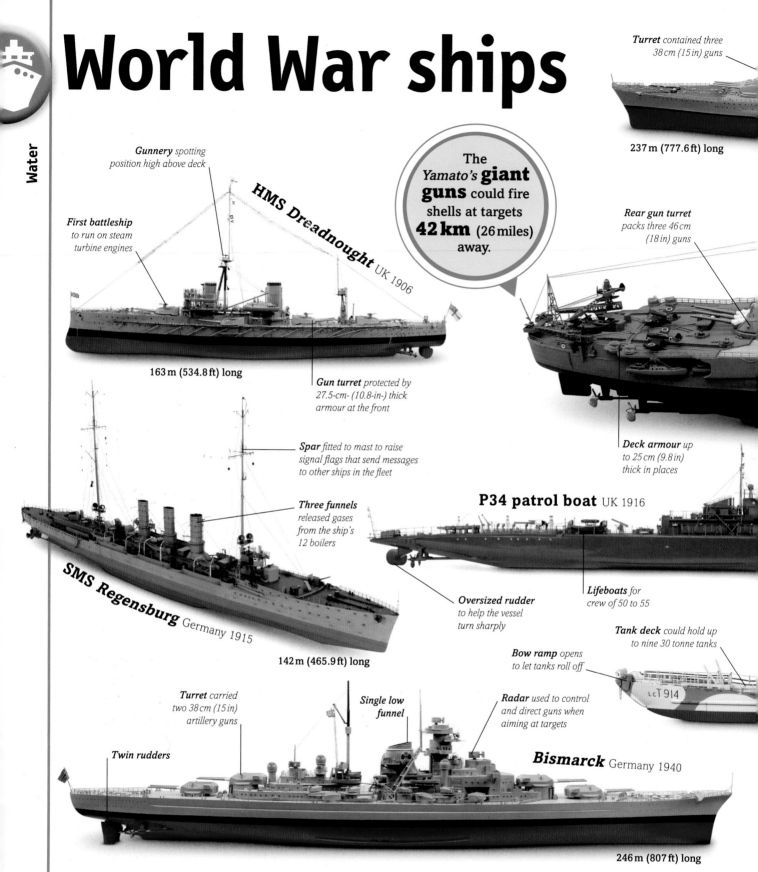

Turret contained three 38 cm (15 in) guns

237 m (777.6 ft) long

Gunnery spotting position high above deck

HMS *Dreadnought* UK 1906

First battleship to run on steam turbine engines

The *Yamato's* **giant guns** could fire shells at targets **42 km** (26 miles) away.

Rear gun turret packs three 46 cm (18 in) guns

163 m (534.8 ft) long

Gun turret protected by 27.5-cm- (10.8-in-) thick armour at the front

Spar fitted to mast to raise signal flags that send messages to other ships in the fleet

Three funnels released gases from the ship's 12 boilers

Deck armour up to 25 cm (9.8 in) thick in places

P34 patrol boat UK 1916

SMS *Regensburg* Germany 1915

Oversized rudder to help the vessel turn sharply

Lifeboats for crew of 50 to 55

142 m (465.9 ft) long

Tank deck could hold up to nine 30 tonne tanks

Bow ramp opens to let tanks roll off

Turret carried two 38 cm (15 in) artillery guns

Single low funnel

Radar used to control and direct guns when aiming at targets

Bismarck Germany 1940

Twin rudders

246 m (807 ft) long

Shipping played a crucial part in both World War I and World War II. As well as fighting in battles, warships were used to disrupt enemy supply convoys, protect their own navies, and transport troops and equipment to invade enemy territory.

HMS *Dreadnought* was faster and more heavily armed than previous battleships and started an arms race between the major naval powers before World War I. Smaller ships, such as the cruiser SMS *Regensburg* and the **P34 patrol boat**, saw active service during WWI. P34 was

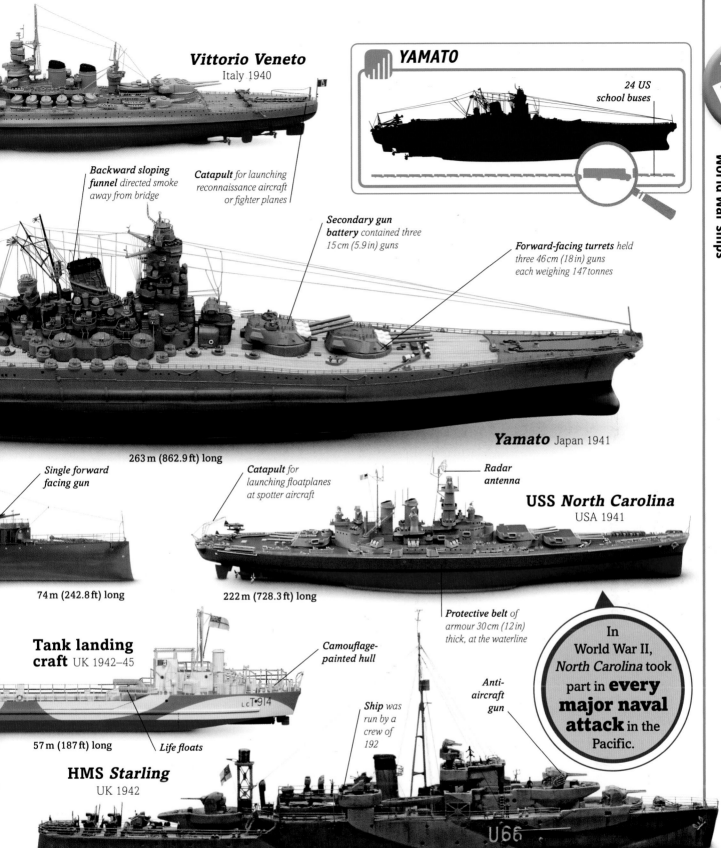

Vittorio Veneto
Italy 1940

YAMATO

24 US school buses

Backward sloping funnel directed smoke away from bridge

Catapult for launching reconnaissance aircraft or fighter planes

Secondary gun battery contained three 15 cm (5.9 in) guns

Forward-facing turrets held three 46 cm (18 in) guns each weighing 147 tonnes

Yamato Japan 1941

263 m (862.9 ft) long

Single forward facing gun

74 m (242.8 ft) long

Catapult for launching floatplanes at spotter aircraft

Radar antenna

USS North Carolina
USA 1941

222 m (728.3 ft) long

Protective belt of armour 30 cm (12 in) thick, at the waterline

In World War II, *North Carolina* took part in **every major naval attack** in the Pacific.

Tank landing craft UK 1942–45

Camouflage-painted hull

LCT•914

57 m (187 ft) long

Life floats

Ship was run by a crew of 192

Anti-aircraft gun

HMS Starling
UK 1942

U66

91 m (298.5 ft) long

one of the first dedicated anti-submarine vessels. **HMS Starling** performed a similar role during World War II, sinking 14 German U-boats. The *Bismarck* was Germany's biggest battleship, until it was sunk in 1941. Biggest of all was the *Yamato*, at over 70,000 tonnes. It was heavily armed, with nine giant guns, dozens of smaller artillery weapons, and 162 anti-aircraft guns. It cruised the Pacific with a range of 13,300 km (8,264 miles). **Tank landing craft** had a tenth of that range, but were crucial in ferrying tanks during the Normandy landings.

Aircraft carriers

Elevator *raises planes stored below onto flight deck*

Up to 36 biplanes *could be carried*

Gases from funnel *could create difficult air currents for landing aircraft*

239.7 m (786.4 ft) long

HMS Furious UK 1917

Hangar *for aircraft storage*

Nuclear reactors can keep USS *George Washington* running for **18 years**, with no need to refuel!

Akagi Japan 1927

260.7 m (855.3 ft) long

Hangar deck *on two levels*

Bulges in hull *makes the ship more stable and adds protection against torpedoes*

Quick-firing anti-aircraft guns

Four propellers *move the carrier at speeds up to 56 km/h (35 mph)*

Twin 20 cm (8 in) guns in turret *can aim shells at targets more than 27 km (17 miles) away*

Ship can hold more than 2,700 personnel

USS Saratoga USA 1927

270.7 m (888 ft) long

Anti-aircraft guns

Radio masts *for communication between ship and aircraft*

Hangers *can hold more than 60 aircraft*

Aircraft *parked on armoured flight deck*

HMS Illustrious UK 1940

243.8 m (799.9 ft) long

HMS Ark Royal UK 1938

Flight deck *ended in "round down" to reduce air turbulence for planes taking off*

229 m (751.3 ft) long

As aircraft became important military weapons, ships that could act as floating airbases were designed. These aircraft carriers are huge vessels with a large, flat flight deck, from which helicopters and planes can take off and land.

Many early aircraft carriers, including the **USS Saratoga**, **HMS Furious** and the **Akagi,** were initially designed as battlecruisers before being converted. The *Akagi* carried up to 66 aircraft, which took off from three flight decks, while the *Saratoga* could carry up to 78 planes. Purpose-

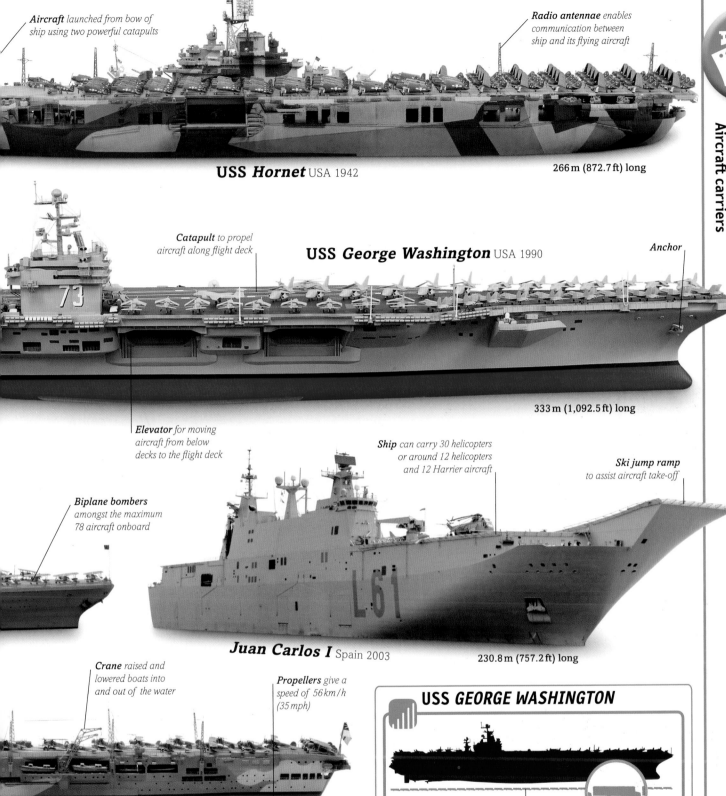

Aircraft *launched from bow of ship using two powerful catapults*

Radio antennae *enables communication between ship and its flying aircraft*

USS Hornet USA 1942

266 m (872.7 ft) long

Catapult *to propel aircraft along flight deck*

USS George Washington USA 1990

Anchor

73

333 m (1,092.5 ft) long

Elevator *for moving aircraft from below decks to the flight deck*

Biplane bombers *amongst the maximum 78 aircraft onboard*

Ship *can carry 30 helicopters or around 12 helicopters and 12 Harrier aircraft*

Ski jump ramp *to assist aircraft take-off*

Juan Carlos I Spain 2003

L-61

230.8 m (757.2 ft) long

Crane *raised and lowered boats into and out of the water*

Propellers *give a speed of 56 km/h (35 mph)*

USS GEORGE WASHINGTON

30 US school buses

built aircraft carriers, such as **HMS Illustrious** and the **USS Hornet**, featured catapults powered by hydraulics or steam to propel the aircraft on take-off, as well as hangers below the flight deck to store inactive planes. Aircraft carriers have large crews – 1,580 in the case of **HMS Ark**

Royal. However, this figure is dwarfed by the more than 6,000 who serve aboard the Nimitz Class carrier, **USS George Washington**. This 88,000-tonne (97,003-US-ton) ship holds up to 90 aircraft of varying types, from reconnaissance planes and helicopters to fighters and bombers.

Modern warships

Merlin helicopter

Turret with two 113 mm (4.5 in) guns with a range of up to 18 km (11 miles)

HMS *Diamond* UK 1952

Twin propellers

D35

119 m (390 ft) long

Crane for deploying equipment or recovering mines

46 m (151 ft) long

M1157

HMS *Kirkliston*
UK 1954

Twin propellers powered by diesel engine

The ship's Tomahawk missiles have a range of more than **1,300 km** (800 miles).

Tracking antenna can receive data sent from satellites or rockets

Ship staffed by a crew of 120 as well as up to 100 technical experts

A601

***Monge* A601** France 1990   225 m (738 ft) long

USS *Arleigh Burke*
USA 1991

51

Tomahawk cruise missiles can launch vertically from this launch grid

Sikorsky SH-60 Seahawk helicopter on helipad

154 m (505 ft) long

Aircraft carriers and nuclear submarines have taken over from battleships as the biggest and most lethal craft in a navy's fleet. Yet, there remains plenty of work for smaller ships, which are built to perform a wide variety of important roles.

Frigates like **HMS *Lancaster*** and **HMCS *Vancouver*** are multi-purpose, able to protect and escort other ships, perform coastal patrols, intercept suspicious ships, and engage in anti-submarine warfare. The **USS *Arleigh Burke*** destroyer also tackles submarines, as well as

Funnel

Radar and electronics mast

Anti-aircraft missile system – ship is also armed with anti-ship missiles and anti-submarine torpedoes

F229

HMS *Lancaster* UK 1992   133 m (436 ft) long

Sea King helicopter carried on the stern

Radar antenna

134 m (440 ft) long   **HMCS *Vancouver***
Canada 1993

Helipad *on stern can bring in doctors or evacuate injured personnel*

Crane *for loading and unloading a maximum of 24 containers of supplies*

A 511

101 m (331.3 ft) long   **Elbe class** Germany 1993

151 m (495 ft) long

Murasame class destroyers Japan 1994

Flight deck supports 6–8 Harrier II jet aircraft

Landing craft well *can hold 40 amphibious assault vehicles*

USS *Iwo Jima* USA 2000   257 m (843 ft) long

Camouflaged hull

Twin diesel engines *power four waterjets, to propel the boat forward*

USS *IWO JIMA*

23 US school buses

Type 022 missile boat China 2004   42 m (138 ft) long

attacking other targets at sea or on land, using guided missiles. Some warships have highly specialized roles. **HMS *Kirkliston*** swept for mines laid in shallow coastal waters. The ***Monge* A601** monitors the skies, using its 14 antennae and other electronic systems to track missiles and space missions. The **Type 022 missile boat** can creep under enemy warning systems to launch attacks on shipping, whilst the **USS *Iwo Jima*** supports missions onshore, carrying just short of 1,900 marines, up to 30 helicopters, and large numbers of amphibious landing craft.

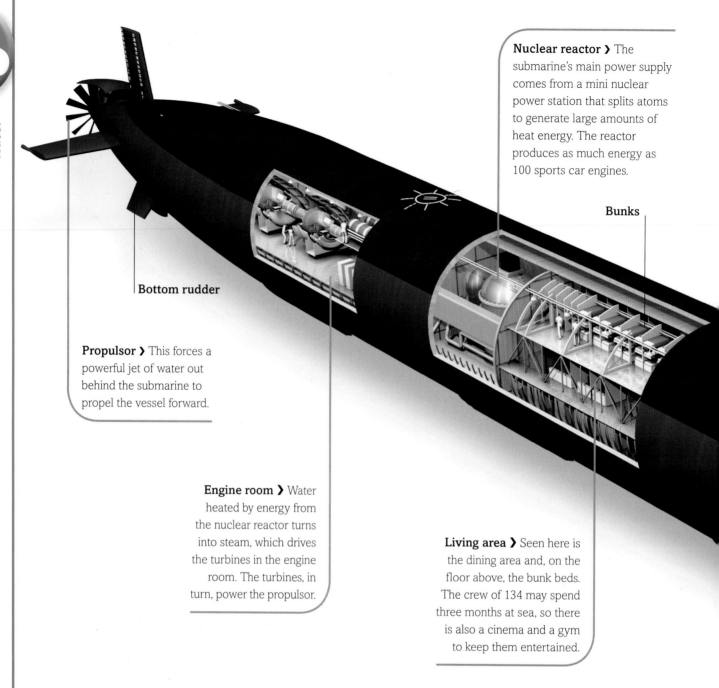

Nuclear reactor ❯ The submarine's main power supply comes from a mini nuclear power station that splits atoms to generate large amounts of heat energy. The reactor produces as much energy as 100 sports car engines.

Bunks

Bottom rudder

Propulsor ❯ This forces a powerful jet of water out behind the submarine to propel the vessel forward.

Engine room ❯ Water heated by energy from the nuclear reactor turns into steam, which drives the turbines in the engine room. The turbines, in turn, power the propulsor.

Living area ❯ Seen here is the dining area and, on the floor above, the bunk beds. The crew of 134 may spend three months at sea, so there is also a cinema and a gym to keep them entertained.

Submarine

Submarines can adjust their buoyancy (how much they can float or sink) using large ballast tanks that can be filled with air or seawater. These tanks allow submarines to dive deep below sea level, cruise stealthily underwater, or rise to the surface. The 115-m- (377-ft-) long **Virginia class submarine** serves in the US Navy. Packed with advanced systems, each submarine took around nine million working hours to build.

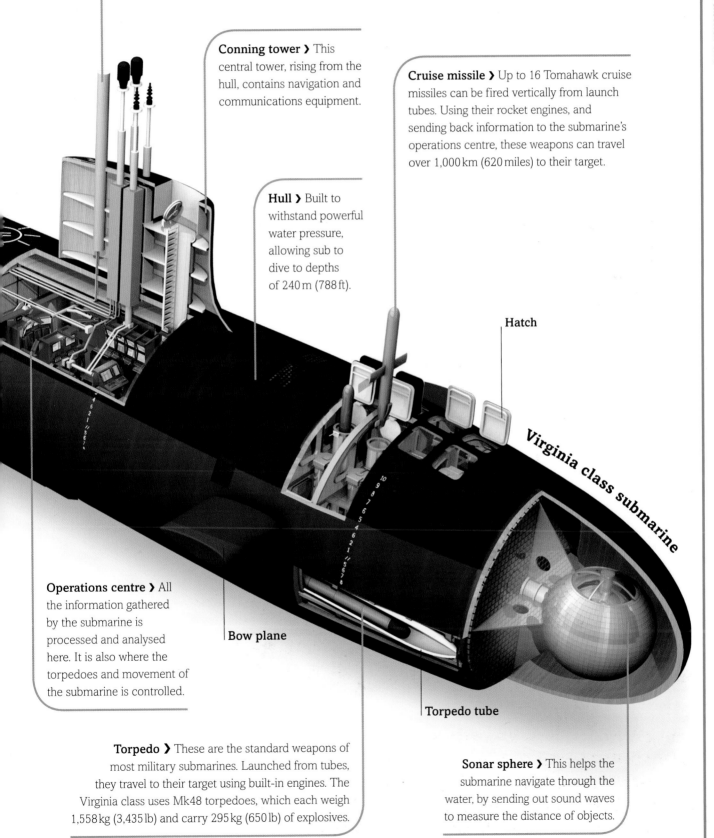

Masts ❯ These carry radio and global positioning antennae, and a mast that allows the crew to see above the surface using night vision and a zoom lens.

Conning tower ❯ This central tower, rising from the hull, contains navigation and communications equipment.

Cruise missile ❯ Up to 16 Tomahawk cruise missiles can be fired vertically from launch tubes. Using their rocket engines, and sending back information to the submarine's operations centre, these weapons can travel over 1,000 km (620 miles) to their target.

Hull ❯ Built to withstand powerful water pressure, allowing sub to dive to depths of 240 m (788 ft).

Hatch

Operations centre ❯ All the information gathered by the submarine is processed and analysed here. It is also where the torpedoes and movement of the submarine is controlled.

Bow plane

Virginia class submarine

Torpedo tube

Torpedo ❯ These are the standard weapons of most military submarines. Launched from tubes, they travel to their target using built-in engines. The Virginia class uses Mk48 torpedoes, which each weigh 1,558 kg (3,435 lb) and carry 295 kg (650 lb) of explosives.

Sonar sphere ❯ This helps the submarine navigate through the water, by sending out sound waves to measure the distance of objects.

Dive, dive, dive

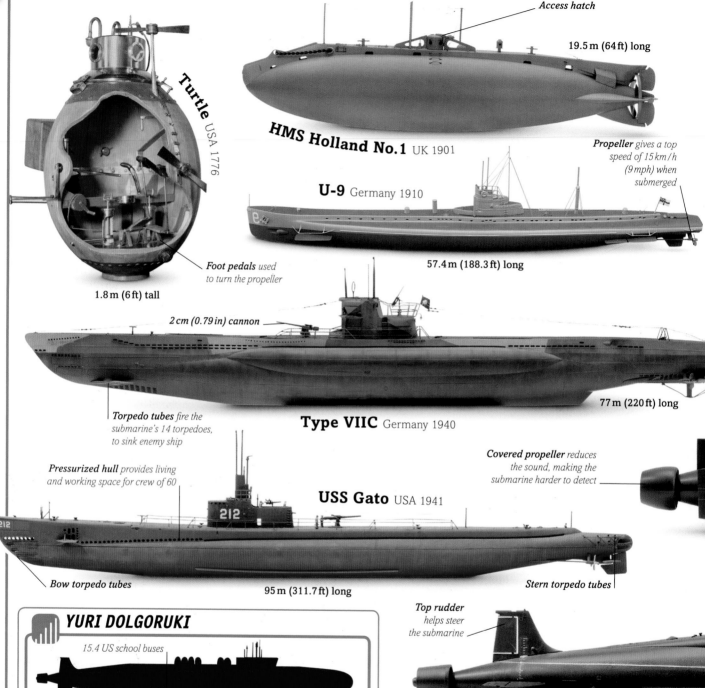

Three Aichi M6A stored in, and launched, from this submarine

Access hatch

19.5 m (64 ft) long

Turtle USA 1776

HMS Holland No.1 UK 1901

U-9 Germany 1910

Propeller gives a top speed of 15 km/h (9 mph) when submerged

57.4 m (188.3 ft) long

Foot pedals used to turn the propeller

1.8 m (6 ft) tall

2 cm (0.79 in) cannon

77 m (220 ft) long

Torpedo tubes fire the submarine's 14 torpedoes, to sink enemy ship

Type VIIC Germany 1940

Pressurized hull provides living and working space for crew of 60

Covered propeller reduces the sound, making the submarine harder to detect

USS Gato USA 1941

Bow torpedo tubes

95 m (311.7 ft) long

Stern torpedo tubes

YURI DOLGORUKI

15.4 US school buses

Top rudder helps steer the submarine

170 m (558 ft) long

With their ability to lurk beneath the waves for weeks at a time, submarines are a potentially deadly underwater weapon. Submersibles are much smaller vessels, used for underwater scientific research, and rescue and salvage work.

The **Turtle** was the first sub to see action, when it attempted to place explosives on the hulls of enemy ships during the American Civil War. It was not until World War 1 that subs became effective in warfare. The German **U-9** sank 16 ships, and the **Type VIIC** U-boat reached depths

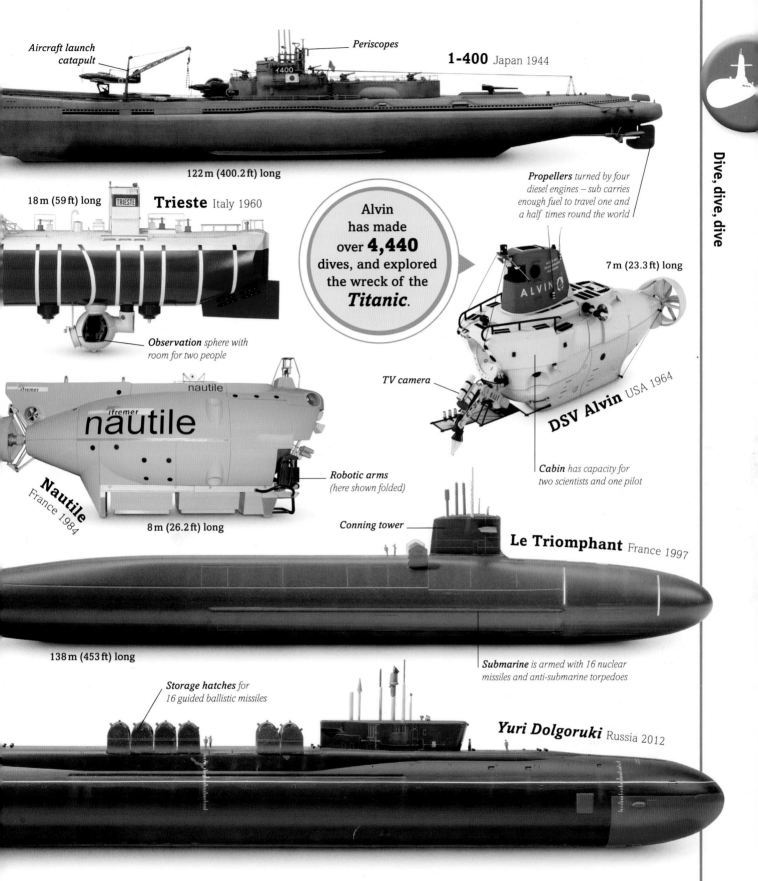

1-400 Japan 1944

Aircraft launch catapult

Periscopes

122 m (400.2 ft) long

Propellers turned by four diesel engines – sub carries enough fuel to travel one and a half times round the world

18 m (59 ft) long **Trieste** Italy 1960

Alvin has made over **4,440** dives, and explored the wreck of the *Titanic*.

7 m (23.3 ft) long

Observation sphere with room for two people

TV camera

DSV Alvin USA 1964

Nautile France 1984

8 m (26.2 ft) long

Robotic arms (here shown folded)

Cabin has capacity for two scientists and one pilot

Conning tower

Le Triomphant France 1997

138 m (453 ft) long

Submarine is armed with 16 nuclear missiles and anti-submarine torpedoes

Storage hatches for 16 guided ballistic missiles

Yuri Dolgoruki Russia 2012

of 150 m (492 ft). The **USS Gato** could travel up to 20,000 km (12,427 miles) on patrols, while **1-400** class submarines, the largest of World War II, could launch aircraft from their decks. Nuclear energy gave modern submarines like **Le Triomphant** and ***Yuri Dolgoruki*** limitless power, allowing them to patrol for months at a time. Small research submersibles have limited range, but can perform amazing feats. **DSV Alvin** can dive to 6,400 m (21,000 ft), while **Trieste** carried people to the deepest part of the Pacific Ocean, 10,911 m (35,797 ft) below sea level.

Need for speed

Navigation and communications antennae

BHC AP1-88 Hovercraft
UK 1990s

Large cabin can hold 190 – 243 passengers

Rubber skirt is filled with air by fans under the body of the hovercraft

This craft is used by the Canadian Coastguard

Capacity for up to 30 cars, which enter craft using a ramp at the back

Railings for observers on the roof of the cabin

Voskhod 352 Eurofoil
Russia 1973

SR.N4 Mk.I Hovercraft UK 1968

Six-bladed fan propels craft at speeds up to 70 km/h (43 mph)

Windshield of cockpit that seats 3 to 4

Skirt, made up of 68 sections, keeps the craft on a cushion of air

Military *Zubr*-class hovercraft are the world's **biggest**, and can carry up to **500 troops**.

BHC Coastal Pro Hovercraft UK 2015

Some vessels don't travel through water, they skim the surface so that most of their hull, or body, rides above it. This means they can travel faster. Surface-skimming craft, such as hovercrafts and hydrofoils, are certainly fast movers!

A hovercraft rides on a cushion of air generated by lift fans under their bodies, which enables it to whizz over both land and water. The **SR.N4 Mk.I Hovercraft** could hold 254 passengers and cruise at more than 100 km/h (62 mph), while the **BHC AP1-88 Hovercraft** was used by

Handlebars contain levers for throttle and brake

Bridge from where the craft is controlled and steered

Sea-Doo® Spark™ Canada 2013

Boeing 929 Jetfoil USA 1974

Perspex canopy covers cockpit

Smooth aluminium body fitted over a steel frame

Handlebars contain sound system and speakers

The K7 set a world water speed record of **444km/h** (276mph) in 1964.

Bluebird K7 UK 1955

Kawasaki Ultra 310LX Japan 2015

V-shaped hull allows craft to travel smoothly through choppy water

Rear view mirror

S. SUTTIPUN

7

ptt Lubricants

Singha Drinking Water

Sleek, streamlined body design fashioned out of light but strong carbon fibre

F1 Powerboat USA 2014

Catamaran hull design with two floating hulls

the Canadian Coastguard for rescue missions. Hydrofoils, such as the **Voskhod 352 Eurofoil**, use wing-like foils under the hull, which lift the boat out of the water as it travels forward. Jetfoils are hydrofoils that use water jets to provide their forward thrust, such as the **Boeing 929 Jetfoil**, which has a top speed of 80km/h (50mph). Personal watercraft, like the **Sea-Doo® Spark™** and the **Kawasaki Ultra 310LX,** also use water thrusters, while the fastest boats of all, **F1 Powerboats**, use propellers driven by powerful engines to race at over 200km/h (124mph).

Fun and games

Inboard motor at the back of the boat spins propeller to move boat forwards

Motorboat USA 1950s

Inflatable body, 2.2 m (7.2 ft) long, takes less than 90 seconds to inflate

Wilderness raft USA

Safety helmets must be worn as well as life jackets

Whitewater dinghy USA

Mooring ring

Flexible cover can be removed in good weather

1,200 inflatable dinghies paddled down the River Aar in Switzerland in 2011.

Twin hulls make this a catamaran-style cabin cruiser

Cabin cruiser USA

Chimney

Old tyres cushion sides of boat when moored

Narrowboat UK 1960s

There is nothing like messing about on the water! Plenty of different boats and watercraft, of all shapes and sizes, allow people to have fun on rivers, lakes, and seas, to explore wildernesses, and take part in races and competitions.

A **wilderness raft** is a type of inflatable dinghy that is small and light enough to be carried in a backpack, before it is filled with air. Rugged **whitewater dinghies** are larger and ride down rapids and fast-flowing water. Paddles are used in **canoes** and **kayaks**, while a **rowing boat**

Large fan, inside a safety cage, is spun by the engine to push the boat forwards

In 2013, an airboat reached a **top speed** of **163.5 km/h** (102 mph)!

Large sail made of cotton rigged to mast

Sailing dinghy RNSA 14 UK 1920s

Shallow hull for travelling through swamplands

Airboat USA 2010s

Hull made of overlapping wood panels over a wood frame

Tiller

Rowing boat Boy Albert UK 1920s

Oars fitted into rowlocks

Metal rudder is controlled by turning tiller

Boom is gripped for stability and to adjust sail angle to wind

Twin-bladed paddle allows kayaker to paddle continuously without switching sides

Kayaker sits in an enclosed seat

Kayak UK 1980s

Rope handles for lifting boat out of water

Single-bladed paddle used to push the water backwards

Mast fits into joint on the board

Windsurfer USA 1990s

Canoe UK 1980s

has oars, which pivot in fittings, called rowlocks, as they are rowed back and forth. **Sailing dinghies** are used to teach people how to sail, while **airboats** offer thrilling rides, speeding along with the help of large fans spun by car or aircraft engines. **Narrowboats** were once used to haul coal, cotton, and other goods along canals before there were train and road networks. Today, they are fitted with beds and kitchens, and used for pleasure cruising. You can live aboard **cabin cruisers**, too, which travel on open water as well as canals.

A FLYING SUCCESS

Guido Cappellini's F1 Powerboat flies across the surface of Doha Bay during the Qatar F1 Powerboat Grand Prix in 2009. This racing catamaran is tearing along at over 200 km/h (124 mph) around a course marked out by floating buoys. As many as 24 F1 powerboats take part in each race, battling for position as points earned count towards the coveted World Championship title.

F1 Powerboats are the ultimate speed machines on water. Equipped with monstrous 425 horsepower engines, they weigh around 500 kg (1,102 lb) and can accelerate from a standing start to 160 km/h (100 mph) in only four seconds, quickly hitting top speeds of around 225 km/h (140 mph). Inside its sleek carbon fibre body, the driver is firmly strapped in, and protected by a crash cabin, as he pushes his powerboat to the limit. There are no gears and no brakes. It is edge-of-the-seat racing, with boats taking tight corners at 100–150 km/h (62–93 mph). Cappellini won this and four other races in the 2009 season, to be crowned world champion for a record tenth time.

AIR

Aeroplane

Aeroplanes are heavier than air, so they need to overcome the force of gravity, which pulls them towards the ground. They do this with the help of curved wings, which produce an upward force, called lift, as the plane moves through the air. Most aircraft today are monoplanes, which means they have a single set of wings. This **de Havilland DH60 Gipsy Moth** is a biplane, with two pairs of wings and an open cockpit with two seats.

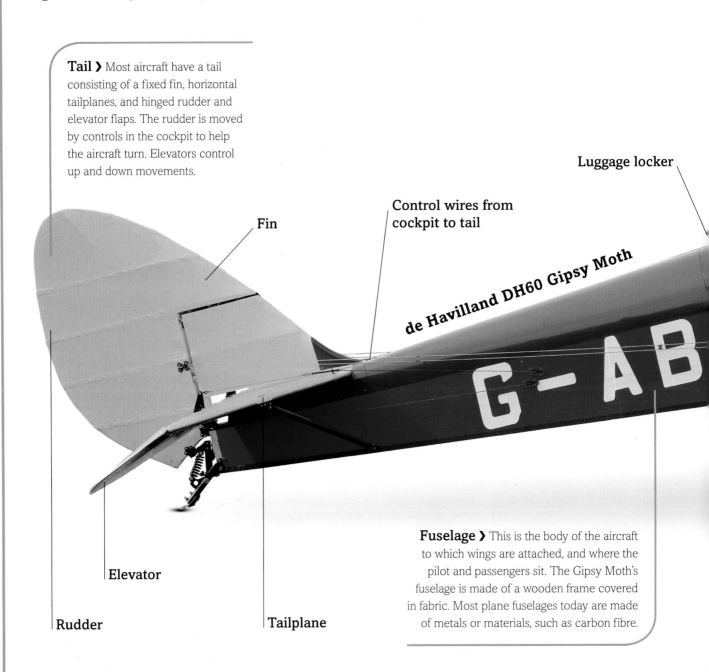

Tail ❯ Most aircraft have a tail consisting of a fixed fin, horizontal tailplanes, and hinged rudder and elevator flaps. The rudder is moved by controls in the cockpit to help the aircraft turn. Elevators control up and down movements.

Luggage locker

Control wires from cockpit to tail

Fin

de Havilland DH60 Gipsy Moth

G-AB

Elevator

Rudder

Tailplane

Fuselage ❯ This is the body of the aircraft to which wings are attached, and where the pilot and passengers sit. The Gipsy Moth's fuselage is made of a wooden frame covered in fabric. Most plane fuselages today are made of metals or materials, such as carbon fibre.

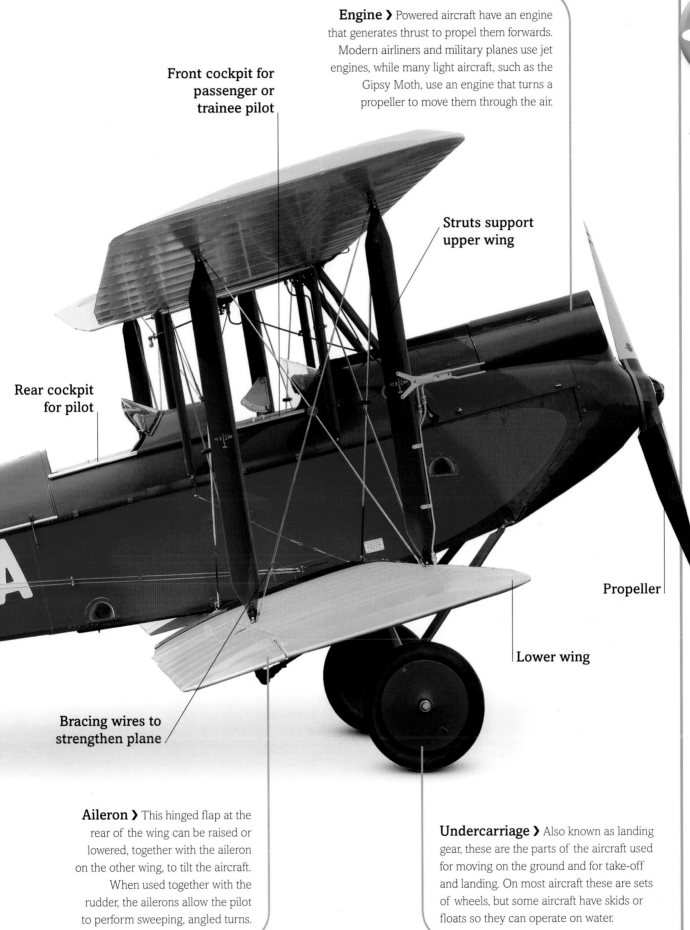

Front cockpit for passenger or trainee pilot

Engine ❯ Powered aircraft have an engine that generates thrust to propel them forwards. Modern airliners and military planes use jet engines, while many light aircraft, such as the Gipsy Moth, use an engine that turns a propeller to move them through the air.

Struts support upper wing

Rear cockpit for pilot

Propeller

Lower wing

Bracing wires to strengthen plane

Aileron ❯ This hinged flap at the rear of the wing can be raised or lowered, together with the aileron on the other wing, to tilt the aircraft. When used together with the rudder, the ailerons allow the pilot to perform sweeping, angled turns.

Undercarriage ❯ Also known as landing gear, these are the parts of the aircraft used for moving on the ground and for take-off and landing. On most aircraft these are sets of wheels, but some aircraft have skids or floats so they can operate on water.

Taking to the skies

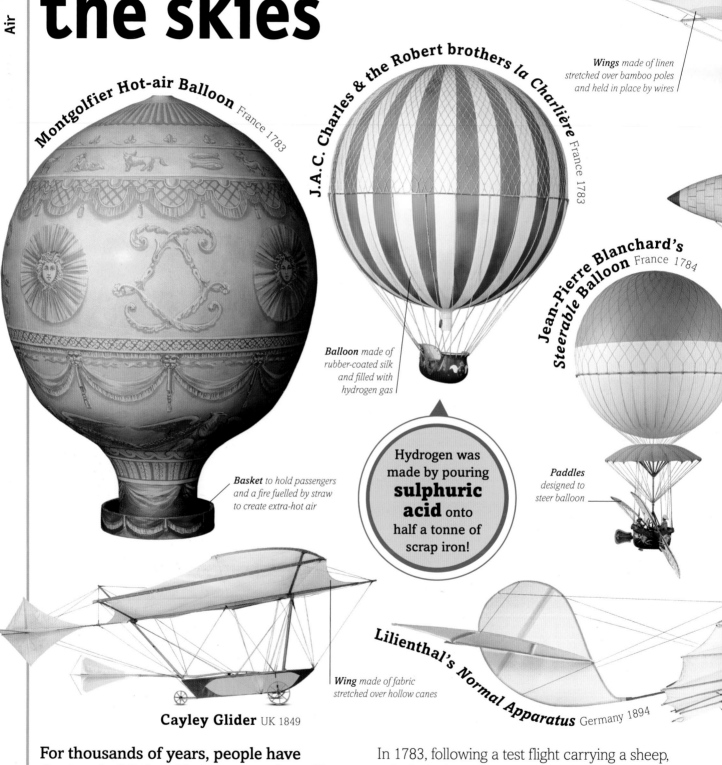

Montgolfier Hot-air Balloon France 1783

J.A.C. Charles & the Robert brothers la Charlière France 1783

Wings made of linen stretched over bamboo poles and held in place by wires

Jean-Pierre Blanchard's Steerable Balloon France 1784

Balloon made of rubber-coated silk and filled with hydrogen gas

Basket to hold passengers and a fire fuelled by straw to create extra-hot air

Hydrogen was made by pouring **sulphuric acid** onto half a tonne of scrap iron!

Paddles designed to steer balloon

Wing made of fabric stretched over hollow canes

Cayley Glider UK 1849

Lilienthal's Normal Apparatus Germany 1894

For thousands of years, people have dreamed of flying. However, getting off the ground successfully proved impossible until the invention of lighter-than-air craft, such as balloons and airships, and research into the principles of flight using gliders.

In 1783, following a test flight carrying a sheep, a duck, and a rooster, the **Montgolfier Hot-air Balloon** took off in Paris, France, with two human passengers. Paris was the centre of the new balloon age. Just ten days later the city saw the launch of the first hydrogen-filled balloon, the

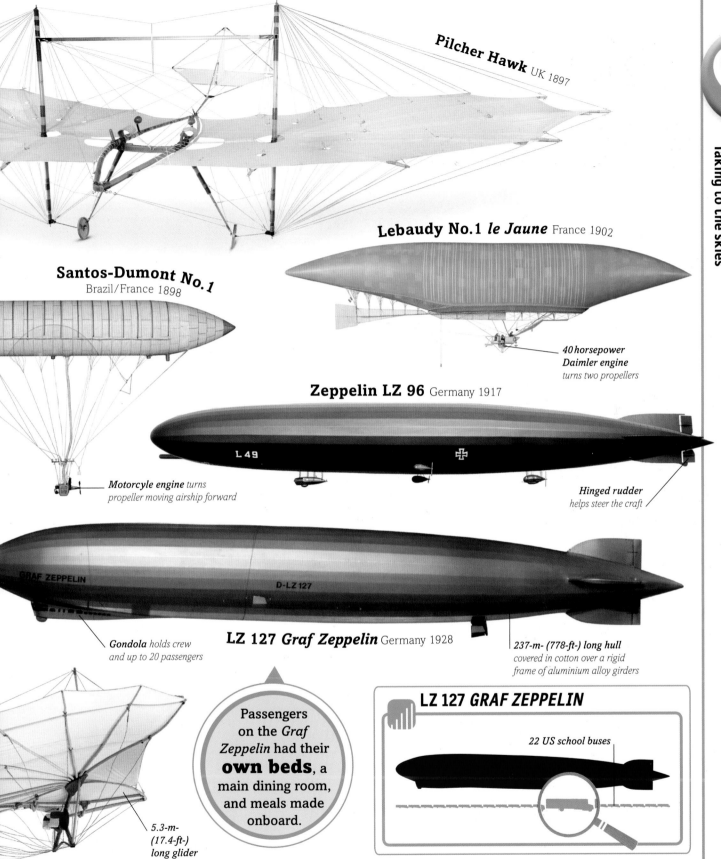

Pilcher Hawk UK 1897

Lebaudy No.1 _le Jaune_ France 1902

40 horsepower Daimler engine turns two propellers

Santos-Dumont No.1
Brazil/France 1898

Zeppelin LZ 96 Germany 1917

L 49

Motorcyle engine turns propeller moving airship forward

Hinged rudder
helps steer the craft

GRAF ZEPPELIN

D-LZ 127

LZ 127 _Graf Zeppelin_ Germany 1928

Gondola holds crew
and up to 20 passengers

237-m- (778-ft-) long hull
covered in cotton over a rigid
frame of aluminium alloy girders

Passengers
on the _Graf
Zeppelin_ had their
own beds, a
main dining room,
and meals made
onboard.

LZ 127 _GRAF ZEPPELIN_

22 US school buses

_5.3-m-
(17.4-ft-)
long glider_

la Charlière, and, in 1898, the first flight of the airship **Santos-Dumont No.1**. In Germany, large airships, such as the **Zeppelin LZ 96**, scouted and bombed during World War I, while post-war airships, such as the _Graf Zeppelin_, offered long-distance transport to the wealthy.

Other inventors, however, believed that winged gliders were the way up. In the 1890s, German engineer Otto Lilienthal made many successful flights in gliders such as the _Normal Apparatus_. His work inspired other glider designs, as well as the Wright Brothers' work on a powered aircraft.

First planes

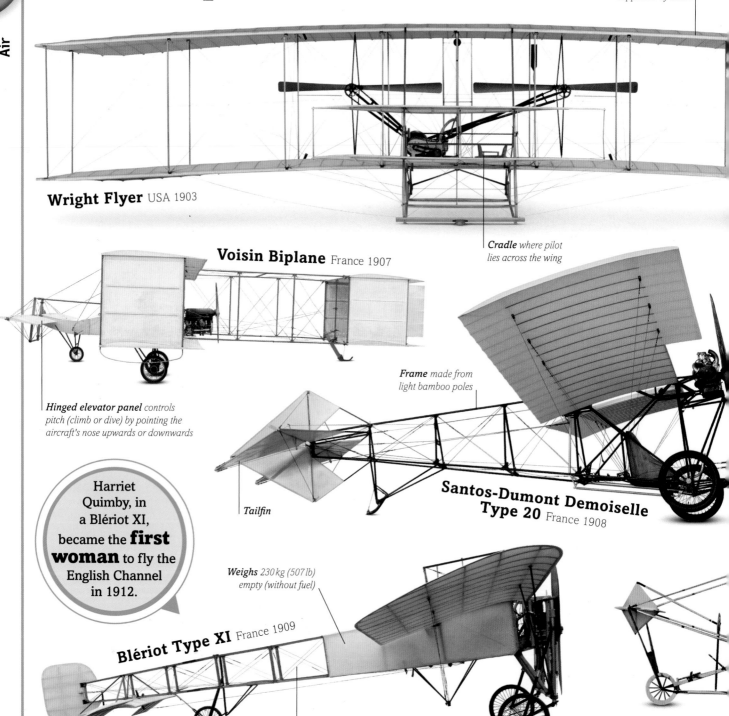

Wings stretch to 12.3 m (40.4 ft) and are supported by struts

Wright Flyer USA 1903

Cradle where pilot lies across the wing

Voisin Biplane France 1907

Frame made from light bamboo poles

Hinged elevator panel controls pitch (climb or dive) by pointing the aircraft's nose upwards or downwards

Tailfin

Santos-Dumont Demoiselle Type 20 France 1908

Harriet Quimby, in a Blériot XI, became the **first woman** to fly the English Channel in 1912.

Weighs 230 kg (507 lb) empty (without fuel)

Blériot Type XI France 1909

Bracing wires make wooden frame fuselage stiffer

On 17 December 1903, American bicycle-maker Orville Wright lifted off into the air in a powered aircraft. This first flight lasted only 12 seconds, and covered less than the length of a modern airliner, but it marked the beginning of a new age.

Built by two brothers, the **Wright Flyer** was a biplane, with two sets of wings, and two propellers spinning behind them. The **Voisin Biplane** and **Shorts S27** copied this pusher-propeller design, but other aircraft, such as the **Santos-Dumont Demoiselle**, mounted their

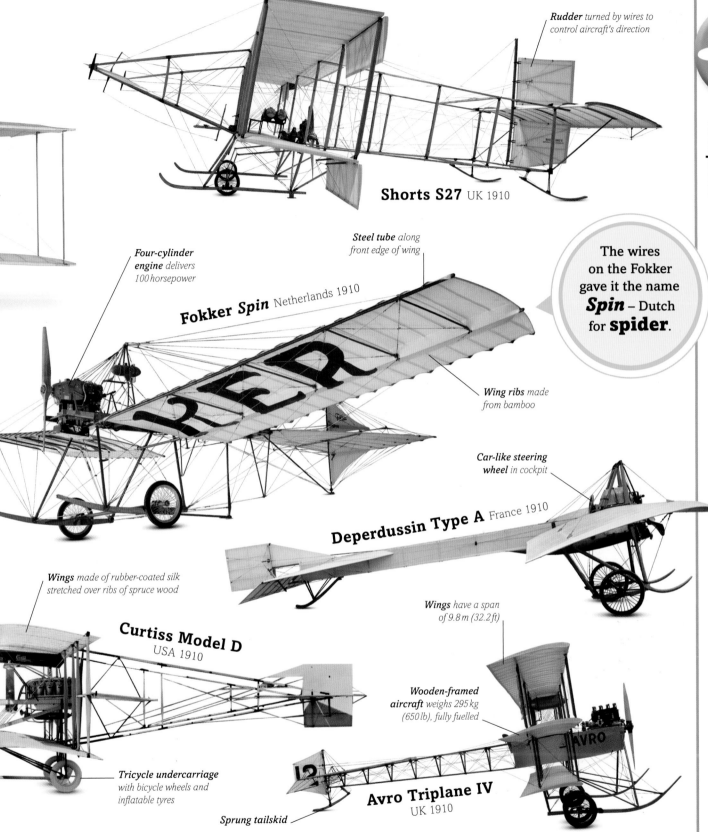

Rudder turned by wires to control aircraft's direction

Shorts S27 UK 1910

Steel tube along front edge of wing

Four-cylinder engine delivers 100 horsepower

Fokker *Spin* Netherlands 1910

Wing ribs made from bamboo

The wires on the Fokker gave it the name ***Spin*** – Dutch for **spider**.

Car-like steering wheel in cockpit

Deperdussin Type A France 1910

Wings made of rubber-coated silk stretched over ribs of spruce wood

Curtiss Model D USA 1910

Wings have a span of 9.8 m (32.2 ft)

Wooden-framed aircraft weighs 295 kg (650 lb), fully fuelled

Avro Triplane IV UK 1910

Tricycle undercarriage with bicycle wheels and inflatable tyres

Sprung tailskid

engine and propeller at the front, or were monoplanes, with a single pair of wings. Early aircraft were built light, using wood, cloth-covered wings, and wires to brace and stiffen their structures. The **Blériot XI** carried French aviator Louis Blériot on the successful first flight from France to England across the English Channel in 1909. The **Deperdussin Type A** flew 100 km (62 miles) at a record speed of 99 km/h (62 mph) in 1911, carrying two people. This, and other record breakers, helped to prove that planes could be a practical form of transport.

203

THE GIRL OF NERVE
Daredevil wingwalker Lilian Boyer hangs from the wingtip of a Curtiss JN-4 Jenny biplane without a safety harness. Flying was new to the public in the 1920s and a ride in a biplane could be an unnerving experience for some, even when safely strapped into their seat. So, large crowds were thrilled by the exploits of barnstormers who performed amazing feats of daring in the sky.

In 1921, Boyer, a 20-year-old restaurant waitress, proved fearless when on her second flight in an aircraft, she stepped out of her seat and onto the wing. Later that year, she teamed up with former World War I pilot, Billy Brock. The pair performed 352 shows across North America throughout the 1920s, dazzling crowds with their exploits. Boyer would stand on the wing of the aircraft as it performed a loop the loop, or dangle from the wing hanging by one hand, or even by a cord she gripped with her teeth! She also mastered jumping from a speeding car to a plane – a stunt she pulled on 143 occasions before bans on low flying came into place in 1929. Miraculously, Boyer lived to the grand age of 88.

Fighter planes

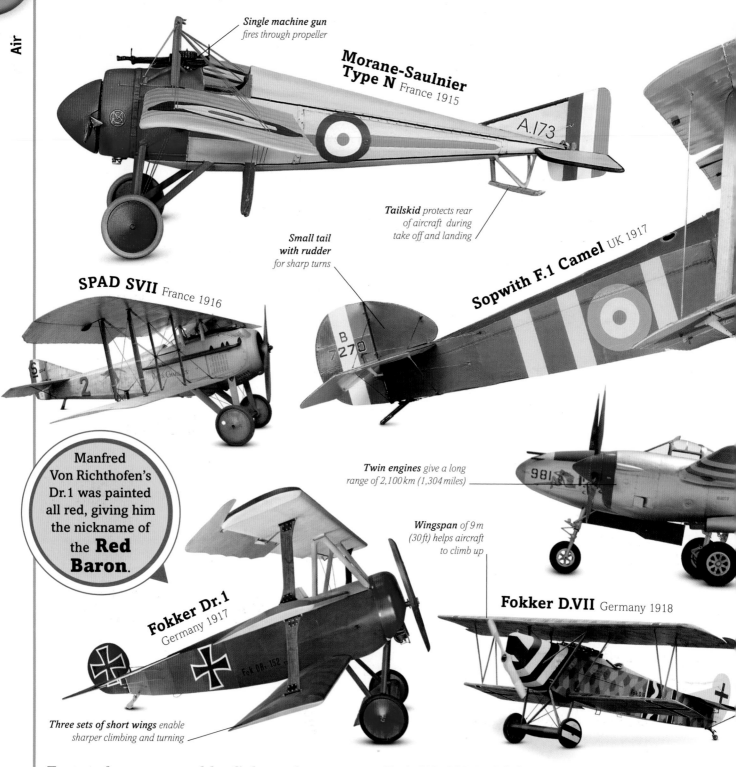

Single machine gun *fires through propeller*

Morane-Saulnier Type N France 1915

A.173

Tailskid *protects rear of aircraft during take off and landing*

Small tail with rudder *for sharp turns*

Sopwith F.1 Camel UK 1917

B 7270

SPAD SVII France 1916

Manfred Von Richthofen's Dr.1 was painted all red, giving him the nickname of the **Red Baron**.

Twin engines *give a long range of 2,100 km (1,304 miles)*

981

Wingspan *of 9 m (30 ft) helps aircraft to climb up*

Fokker D.VII Germany 1918

Fokker Dr.1 Germany 1917

Three sets of short wings *enable sharper climbing and turning*

Fast and manoeuvrable, fighter planes were an air force's hunter-killers during World Wars I and II. Their forward-firing weapons, such as cannons and machine guns, were mounted on the nose or the wings to shoot down other aircraft.

Early World War I fighters, such as the **Morane-Saulnier Type N**, preyed on slow, often unarmed, bombers and reconnaissance aircraft. They were soon outpaced by faster fliers, such as the **Sopwith Camel** and **Fokker D.VII**, which engaged in furious dogfights against each other.

Eight browning machine guns *mounted in wings*

Hawker Hurricane Mk1 UK 1936

Powerful Daimler engine *generates top speed of about 570 km/h (354 mph)*

The Bf 109 was the most produced fighter plane – **33,984** were built between 1936 and 1945.

Messerschmitt Bf 109E Germany 1938

Twin Vickers machine guns

Fiat CR.42 Falco Italy 1940

Top wing *spans 9.7 m (31.8 ft)*

Bottom wing *spans 6.5 m (21.3 ft)*

Wheels *do not retract into the craft*

Mitsubishi A6M5 Zero Japan 1943

Twin booms *extend from body to rear tailplanes*

Cannon *mounted in the wing*

Lockhead P-38 Lightning USA 1941

Front windscreen *made of bulletproof glass*

Rolls Royce Merlin 77 engine *gives top speed of 671 km/h (417 mph)*

Supermarine Spitfire PR MkX UK 1944

Wheels *retract into the wing during flight*

The famous German fighter ace, Baron Manfred von Richthofen, made 19 of his 80 "kills" in his **Fokker Dr.1** triplane. Fighter designs mostly moved from biplanes (with two pairs of wings) to monoplanes (with a single pair of wings) after World War I, and aircraft such as the **Hawker Hurricane Mk1** and the **Messerschmitt Bf 109E** battled in the sky. Some fighters, such as the **Mitsubishi A6M5 Zero**, also served as bombers, while the **Supermarine Spitfire PR MkX** relied on its speed to avoid other fighters as it took photos over enemy lines.

Strike force

Avro 504 UK 1913

Wooden wing frame covered in canvas

Tailskid helps slow aircraft down while landing

Three-bladed propeller

Junkers Ju87 Stuka Germany 1935

Electronics in tail to confuse enemy radar and detect incoming missiles

Tail with rudder

Chin turret manned by bombardier who also aims the bombs

Boeing B-17G Flying Fortress USA 1935

Heinkel He111
Germany 1940

Top speed of 434 km/h (270 mph)

Exhausts to release gases from the Rolls Royce Merlin engine

Fuel tanks in wings and body

de Havilland DH98 Mosquito UK 1940

The B-2 *Spirit* is the world's most expensive aircraft, costing **£1.39 billion** ($2.1 billion) each!

Strike aircraft attack ground targets using bombs or missiles. The first bombers were regular planes from which small bombs were dropped by hand. Specialist bombers were developed at the end of World War I, and saw major action in World War II.

Some World War II bombers, such as the **Junkers Ju87 Stuka**, would dive low to bomb enemy forces on the ground. Others operated from high altitude, as much as 9,000 m (29,528 ft) in the case of the **Boeing B-17G Flying Fortress**. The **Avro Lancaster** had over double the bomb-carrying

Cockpit seats four of the seven man crew with fifth in the nose

Mid gun turret armed with twin machine guns

Avro Lancaster UK 1941

B-29A Superfortress USA 1944

Rolls Royce Merlin engines give top speed of 454 km/h (282 mph)

Boeing B-52H Stratofortress USA 1961

Twin turbofan engines give top speed of 2,300 km/h (1,429 mph)

Tupolev Tu-22M3 Russia 1978

Could carry up to 31,500 kg (69,446 lb) of weapons

Could carry 10 missiles or 15,000 kg (33,069 lb) of bombs

Nose houses radar system to detect enemy fighters from up to 100 km (62 miles) away

Mikoyan-Gurevich MiG-29 Russia 1982

Northrop Grumman B-2 *Spirit* USA 1990

Rocket pods make this a multi-role aircraft

Elevons help aircraft turn, climb, and descend

BOEING B-52H STRATOFORTRESS

48.5 m (159.1 ft) long, equivalent to four US school buses

capacity of the B-17G and more than 7,000 were built. Both were heavily armed, with machine gunners in turrets. Made out of wood, the **de Havilland DH98 *Mosquito*** relied on its speed and agility to evade enemies. Fifty years later, the **Northrop Grumman B-2 *Spirit*** uses stealth technology to strike its targets undetected. Some jet-powered bombers could travel long distances, such as the **Tupolev Tu-22M3**, with a range of 6,800 km (4,225 miles), and the eight-engine **Boeing B-52H Stratofortress**, which could fly more than 16,000 km (9,941 miles).

Racers and record-breakers

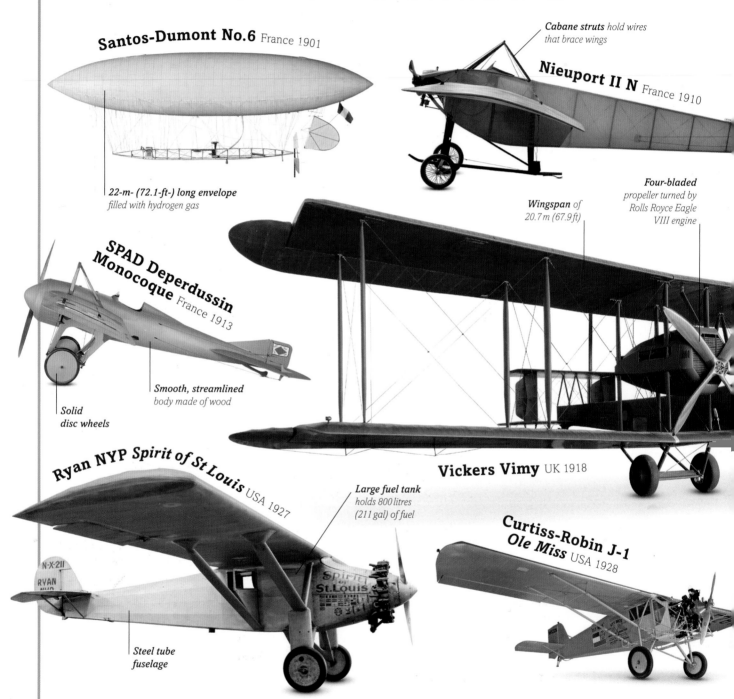

Santos-Dumont No.6 France 1901

22-m- (72.1-ft-) long envelope filled with hydrogen gas

Cabane struts hold wires that brace wings

Nieuport II N France 1910

Four-bladed propeller turned by Rolls Royce Eagle VIII engine

Wingspan of 20.7 m (67.9 ft)

SPAD Deperdussin Monocoque France 1913

Smooth, streamlined body made of wood

Solid disc wheels

Vickers Vimy UK 1918

Ryan NYP Spirit of St Louis USA 1927

Large fuel tank holds 800 litres (211 gal) of fuel

N-X-211 RYAN

Steel tube fuselage

Curtiss-Robin J-1 Ole Miss USA 1928

Getting into the air wasn't enough for some pilots and engineers. They wanted to push their planes to the limit and fly higher, faster, longer than others. Races were held, records set and broken, as aircraft became stronger, more powerful, and reliable.

In 1901, the **Santos-Dumont No.6** airship won one of the first aviation prizes – 100,000 French francs in 1901 for a flight around the Eiffel Tower. In 1919, the **Vickers Vimy** made the first non-stop flight across the Atlantic. American aviator Charles Lindbergh completed a 33½ hour non-

Supermarine S6B UK 1930

Macchi Castoldi M.C.72 Italy 1931

Floats designed to give off heat to cool engine fluids

Gee Bee Model Z Super Sportster USA 1931

Streamlined wheel coverings

Hinged rudder on tail for turning

The fastest propeller-driven seaplane is the M.C.72, with a speed of **709 km/h** (441 mph).

Smooth wings of 12 m (39.4 ft) span to cut through air

Percival P10 Vega Gull UK 1935

Engine gives top speed of 220 km/h (137 mph)

Aircraft only has 7.5 minutes of rocket power to climb into air

Sliding glass canopy reveals seating for pilot and three passengers

Skid for landing as wheels were discarded after take off

Bücker Bü133C Jungmeister Germany 1936

Messerschmitt Me163 Komet Germany 1944

stop solo flight from New York to Paris in 1927 in the *Spirit of St Louis*. In 1935, a **Curtiss-Robin J-1** called *Ole Miss*, aided by inflight refuelling, stayed aloft for 27 days. As aircraft design developed, speed records were frequently broken. The **SPAD Deperdussin Monocoque** set a record of 210 km/h (130 mph), while the **Supermarine S6B** and the **Macchi Castoldi M.C.72** broke the 600 km/h (373 mph) and the 700 km/h (435 mph) barriers. Even faster was the rocket-powered **Messerschmitt Me163 Komet**, which reached 1,005 km/h (624 mph) in 1941.

211

Jet fighters

Messerschmitt Me262 Schwalbe Germany 1942

Wing-mounted turbojet engine gives top speed of 900 km/h (559 mph)

Gloster Meteor UK 1943

Tailplane mounted high up on the tail to be clear of engine exhausts

Wheels retract into body when aircraft is in flight

Republic F-84C Thunderjet USA 1946

Nose contains four machine guns

FS-595

Exhaust channels waste gases from the turbojet engine

Mikoyan-Gurevich MiG-15 Russia 1949

Swept-back tail design matches swept-back wings

U.S. AIR FORCE
8178
FU-178

North American F-86A Sabre USA 1949

The **MiG-15** could climb from sea level to 5,000 m (16,404 ft) in **two minutes**.

Nose contains seven cameras for reconnaissance missions

Saab J35E Draken Sweden 1955

60

Developed during World War II, jet fighters are mostly fast, nimble single-seaters that carry a wide range of weaponry, from cannons to missiles. They attack and see off enemy fighters to establish air superiority over a region.

North American F-86A Sabres and Mikoyan-Gurevich MiG-15s fought each other during the Korean War of 1950. The **Republic F-84C Thunderjet** flew 86,408 missions during the same war, and was the first mass-production jet fighter that could refuel

Dassault Mirage III France 1960

Cockpit seats two persons

Delta wing has maximum span of 8.2 m (27 ft)

Front seat where pilot sits

More F-4 Phantoms were built than any other US supersonic jet – **5,195** in total.

McDonnell Douglas F-4 Phantom II USA 1960

Large external fuel tank

Mikoyan-Gurevich MiG-23 Russia 1970

English Electric Lightning F53 UK 1970

External fuel tank holds more than 1,037 litres (263.9 gal)

Lockheed Martin F-22 Raptor USA 2005

Nose contains six Browning M3 machine guns

Cockpit with ejection seat

Eurofighter Typhoon FGR4 Multinational 2007

midair from a tanker aircraft. The **Mikoyan-Gurevich MiG-23** and the **Dassault Mirage III** could operate as fighter-bombers, carrying ground attack weapons under their bodies and wings. Designed for quick operations, the **Saab J35E Draken**, could be re-armed in just 10 minutes. It could take off from roads as well as runways. Modern warbirds, such as the **Lockheed Martin F-22 Raptor** and the **Eurofighter Typhoon FGR4**, are versatile. They can attack air and ground targets, as well as perform reconnaissance missions.

213

SUPER SPEED An extraordinary sight greets the eyes as a United States Navy Grumman F-14 Tomcat accelerates just 150 m (500 ft) above the Pacific Ocean. A cloud of condensed water vapour forms around the aircraft, known as a shock collar, or vapour cone. The aircraft will shortly go supersonic and travel faster than the speed of sound, an event often accompanied by a loud noise, known as a sonic boom.

When a fast aircraft travels, it generates a series of pressure waves in the air. These waves travel at the speed of sound, approximately 1,225 km/h (761 mph) at sea level, and a little lower at higher altitudes. As the aircraft's speed increases, the waves are forced together to form a single shock wave, which makes a thunder-like boom when released. Most sonic booms last between 0.1 and 0.5 seconds. The first supersonic flight was in 1947. Today, many military jet aircraft regularly travel at supersonic speeds. The F-14 has a top speed of more than 2,400 km/h (1,500 mph) at high altitude. Only two passenger airliners have ever operated at supersonic speeds – the Russian Tupolev Tu-144 and British/French Concorde.

Seaplanes

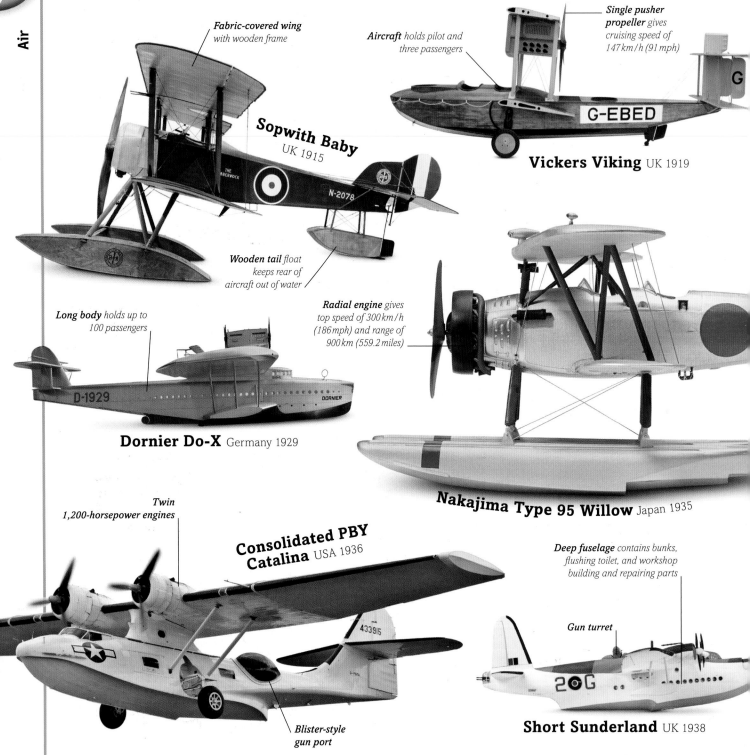

Fabric-covered wing with wooden frame

Aircraft holds pilot and three passengers

Single pusher propeller gives cruising speed of 147 km/h (91 mph)

Sopwith Baby UK 1915

N-2078

G-EBED

Vickers Viking UK 1919

Wooden tail float keeps rear of aircraft out of water

Long body holds up to 100 passengers

Radial engine gives top speed of 300 km/h (186 mph) and range of 900 km (559.2 miles)

D-1929

Dornier Do-X Germany 1929

Nakajima Type 95 Willow Japan 1935

Twin 1,200-horsepower engines

Consolidated PBY Catalina USA 1936

Deep fuselage contains bunks, flushing toilet, and workshop building and repairing parts

Gun turret

433915

2-G

Short Sunderland UK 1938

Blister-style gun port

Planes that can land and take off from water are known as seaplanes. These versatile machines are of two types – floatplanes, which sit on water using pontoons (buoyant floats), and flying boats with a watertight body, like a boat.

Floatplanes saw service in both the World Wars. The **Sopwith Baby** patrolled coasts and spotted airships in WWI. The **Nakajima Type 95 Willow** flew as a light bomber during WWII, while military flying boats, such as the **Short Sunderland** and **Consolidated PBY Catalina**,

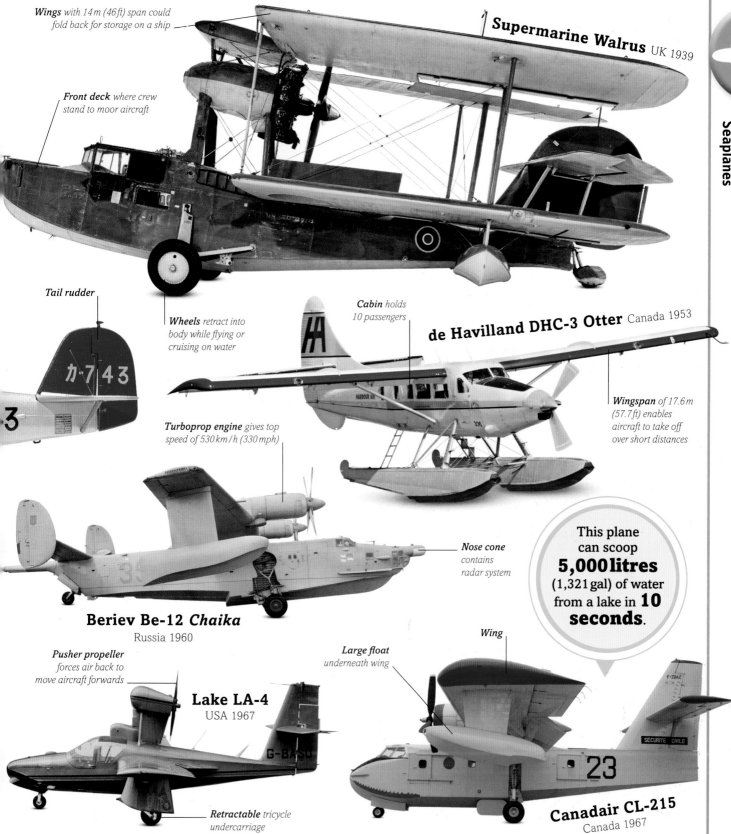

Supermarine Walrus UK 1939

Wings with 14m (46ft) span could fold back for storage on a ship

Front deck where crew stand to moor aircraft

Tail rudder

Wheels retract into body while flying or cruising on water

Cabin holds 10 passengers

de Havilland DHC-3 Otter Canada 1953

Wingspan of 17.6m (57.7ft) enables aircraft to take off over short distances

Turboprop engine gives top speed of 530km/h (330mph)

Nose cone contains radar system

Beriev Be-12 *Chaika*
Russia 1960

This plane can scoop **5,000 litres** (1,321 gal) of water from a lake in **10 seconds**.

Pusher propeller forces air back to move aircraft forwards

Large float underneath wing

Wing

Lake LA-4
USA 1967

Retractable tricycle undercarriage

Canadair CL-215
Canada 1967

performed patrols, hunted submarines, and escorted ships. Other flying boats, such as the 12-engined **Dornier Do-X**, carried passengers across long distances. Some seaplanes are amphibious and can operate from land or water. The **Supermarine Walrus** would take off from a warship, and land on water, and was then returned to the ship by crane. It was used in Canada along with other seaplanes, such as the **de Havilland Otter** and the **Canadair CL-215**. The Canadair is designed to skim a lake or river scooping up large quantities of water to drop on forest fires.

Light aircraft

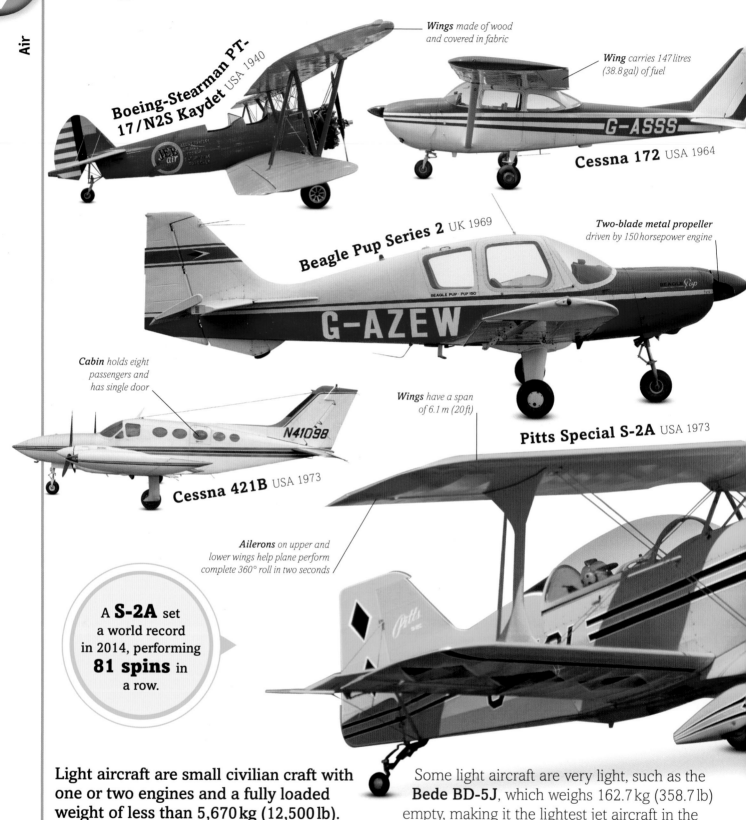

Boeing-Stearman PT-17/N2S Kaydet USA 1940

Wings made of wood and covered in fabric

Wing carries 147 litres (38.8 gal) of fuel

G-ASSS

Cessna 172 USA 1964

Beagle Pup Series 2 UK 1969

Two-blade metal propeller driven by 150 horsepower engine

G-AZEW

Cabin holds eight passengers and has single door

N4109B

Cessna 421B USA 1973

Wings have a span of 6.1 m (20 ft)

Pitts Special S-2A USA 1973

Ailerons on upper and lower wings help plane perform complete 360° roll in two seconds

A **S-2A** set a world record in 2014, performing **81 spins** in a row.

Light aircraft are small civilian craft with one or two engines and a fully loaded weight of less than 5,670 kg (12,500 lb). They are used for travel, learning to fly, aerobatics, and racing, as well as airmail carriers, ambulances, or cropdusters.

Some light aircraft are very light, such as the **Bede BD-5J**, which weighs 162.7 kg (358.7 lb) empty, making it the lightest jet aircraft in the world, and the **Flight Design CTSW**, which weighs 318.4 kg (702 lb) empty and has a parachute system that can carry the entire

Bede BD-5J Microjet USA 1973

Fibreglass body panels fitted over lightweight aluminium frame

Wingspan of just 5.1 m (16.7 ft)

Cockpit seats two side-by-side

Vans RV-6 USA 1986

G-RVVI

Beechcraft A36 Bonanza USA 1987

G-KSHI

Rear cabin seats can fold flat to carry large cargo items

In 2014, Matt Guthmiller, age **19**, became the **youngest** to fly around the world in an A36.

High wing design and pusher propeller gives clear view ahead

Sky Arrow 650 TC Italy 1992

G-BYZR

Three-blade propeller

Wheel fairings

Wings, made mainly of carbon fibre, span 8.5 m (27.8 ft)

Flight Design CTSW Germany 2008

G-CFFJ

101 horsepower engine gives top speed of 230 km/h (143 mph)

aircraft to the ground in an emergency. The **Beagle Pup Series 2** was used for touring and aerobatics, while the two-seater **Pitts Special S-2A**, which can spin, roll, and climb sharply is just used for tricks. Early Pitts planes were offered as kits to be built at home, as was the all-aluminium **Vans RV-6**. In contrast, the **Beechcraft A36 Bonanza** is one of more than 17,000 Bonanzas built in factories. The most manufactured light aircraft of all is the four-seater **Cessna 172** with more than 43,000 produced.

Plane spotting

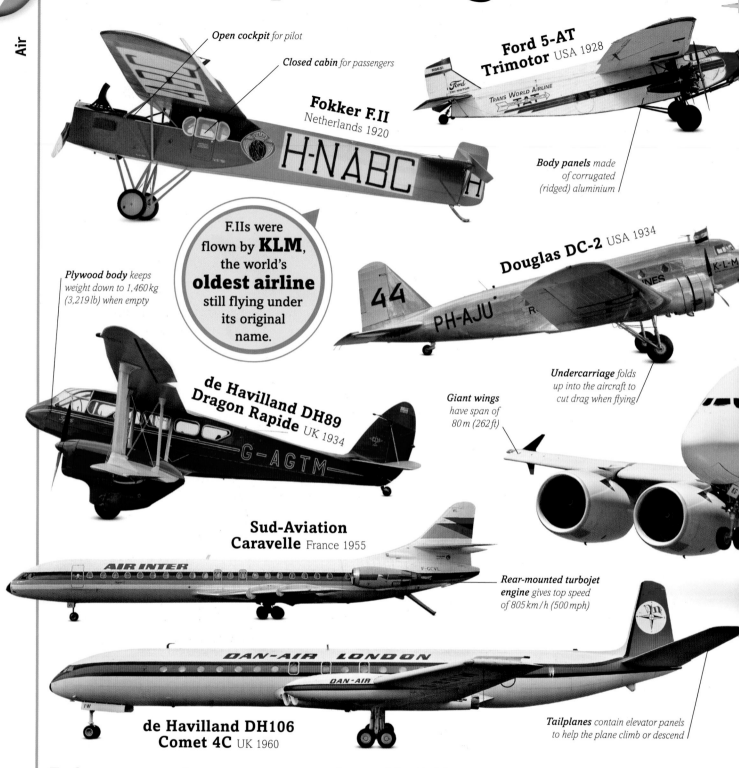

Open cockpit *for pilot*

Closed cabin *for passengers*

Fokker F.II
Netherlands 1920

H·NABC

**Ford 5-AT
Trimotor** USA 1928

Body panels *made
of corrugated
(ridged) aluminium*

F.IIs were
flown by **KLM**,
the world's
oldest airline
still flying under
its original
name.

Plywood body *keeps
weight down to 1,460 kg
(3,219 lb) when empty*

Douglas DC-2 USA 1934

44 PH·AJU

**de Havilland DH89
Dragon Rapide** UK 1934

G-AGTM

Undercarriage *folds
up into the aircraft to
cut drag when flying*

Giant wings
*have span of
80 m (262 ft)*

**Sud-Aviation
Caravelle** France 1955

AIR INTER

Rear-mounted turbojet
engine *gives top speed
of 805 km/h (500 mph)*

**de Havilland DH106
Comet 4C** UK 1960

DAN-AIR LONDON

DAN-AIR

Tailplanes *contain elevator panels
to help the plane climb or descend*

Early passenger planes were converted bombers and other military aircraft. Planes specially built for air travel truly arrived in the 1920s and 1930s. Today, flying has become a fast, convenient, and common form of transport.

The **Fokker F.II** carried just four passengers, while the **Ford 5-AT Trimotor** could hold 13, plus two crew members. The **Douglas DC-2** could carry one passenger more and was flown by more than 30 airlines all around the world, as was the simple but rugged **de Havilland DH89**

Swept-back wings have span of 37.5 m (123 ft)

Turbojet engine, one of three, gives aircraft top speed of 900 km/h (559 mph)

Tupolev Tu-154 Russia 1969

Large tail contains hinged rudder to aid turning

Cockpit contains seats for the pilot and co-pilot

Dornier Do228-101 Germany 1985

Upturned wingtips, called winglets

Airbus A320-214 Multinational 1995

Sharklets - hunting down fuel burn

Airbus A380-800 Multinational 2005

Today, 25,000 passenger planes carry more than **3.4 billion passengers** every year.

Tail rises 24.5 m (80 ft) above the ground

Powerful jet engines give top cruising speed of 945 km/h (587 mph)

Boeing 787-8 Dreamliner USA 2009

Clear cabin windows can be tinted to filter out sunlight

AIRBUS A380-800

The Airbus A380-800 is as long as 6.6 US school buses

72.7 m (238.7 ft) long

Dragon Rapide. Larger airliners powered by jet engines emerged after World War II. The first short-haul jet airliner, the **Sud-Aviation Caravelle**, carried 80 passengers, while the **Tupolev Tu-154** could carry up to 180. Today, the biggest of all is the **Airbus A380-800**, which can carry up to 853 people on two passenger decks. Some modern airliners can travel long distances without landing to refuel. The **Boeing 787-8 Dreamliner** can fly up to 13,000 km (8,078 miles) non-stop – enough to make it from USA to China.

COMING IN LOW
Holidaymakers sunning themselves on the Caribbean island of Saint Martin get their cameras out as an Air Caraibes Airbus A330 airliner comes into land at Princess Juliana International Airport. The stunning sight is repeated over the sands of Maho Beach several times day, as the Caribbean island airport receives more than 58,000 aircraft movements (take-offs or landings) every year.

The airport's 2,300-m- (7,545-ft-) long runway is relatively short by modern standards, and stretches close to the airport's boundary with the beach. An Airbus A330, which can carry more than 200 passengers, needs at least 1,000 m (3,280 ft) and preferably more, to come to a halt once it has touched down. As a result, pilots make their approach over the shimmering waters of the Caribbean as low as they can, in order to get their plane's wheels on the tarmac as quickly as possible. Planes can be just 20 to 30 m (66 to 98 ft) above the ground by the time they fly over the beach. Maho is not the best beach on the island, but draws large crowds of planespotters, keen to get up close to big airliners in flight.

Straight up and supersonic

Bell X-1 USA 1946

Nose shaped like a bullet

Probe measures the distance the plane moves sideways

The Bell X-1 was nicknamed **Glamorous Glennis** after the pilot's wife.

Fairey Delta 2 UK 1954

WG777

McDonnell F-101 Voodoo USA 1957

Happy Hooligans
60312

Two-seater version used as training aircraft

Tailfin contains radio aerial

U.S. AIR FORCE

NASA/ARMY
703
N703NA

Internal fuel tanks hold up to 7,771 litres (2,053 gal)

Lockheed F-104G Starfighter USA 1958

Narrow, circular body with short wings cuts through the air

Fuel tanks mounted on wing tips

The quest for speed led to supersonic aircraft – planes able to fly faster than the speed of sound, 1,235 km/h (767 mph) at sea level. Engineers have also created aircraft that can take off and land vertically, like a helicopter – VTOL planes.

The first supersonic aircraft was the rocket-powered **Bell X-1** piloted by American Charles "Chuck" Yeager. Improvements in jet engines saw startling increases in speeds. The **Fairey Delta 2** was the first to fly faster than 1,609 km/h (1000 mph), the **Lockheed F-104G Starfighter**

Mikoyan-Gurevich MiG-21 Russia 1959

External fuel tank

Exhaust for gases from turbojet engine

Lockheed SR71 Blackbird USA 1964

BAe/Aerospatiale Concorde
Type 1 UK/France 1976

British airways

Fuselage is 2.9 m (9.5 ft) wide, 62 m (203 ft) long and holds 100 passengers

Pilot sits in ejection seat

Outer cockpit windscreen made of quartz can heat up to 300°C (572°F) when flying fast

In 1990, an SR71 flew **coast-to-coast** across the entire USA in under **68 minutes**.

Yakovlev Yak-38 Russia 1971

Nosewheel supports the front of the aircraft

Nose contains laser range finder to measure distances

Hawker Siddeley Harrier GR 3 UK 1973

Blades 7.6 m (24.9 ft) in length spun by turboshaft engine

Engine nozzle moves to direct thrust down or back

Engines tilt upwards for take-off and forwards for level flight

Bell Boeing MV-22B Osprey USA 2007

Instrument boom

Tailfin

Bell XV-15 Tiltrotor USA 1977

Fuselage can hold 32 armed troops

the first to reach 2,000 km/h (1,242 mph), and the **MiG-21** topped 2,380 km/h (1,479 mph). Then, in 1976, the **Lockheed SR71 Blackbird**, a jet spyplane set a record of 3,529 km/h (2,193 mph), which has not been broken since. VTOL aircraft are used in places without long runways. Some, such as the **Hawker Siddeley Harrier GR 3** and **Yakovlev Yak-38**, have engine nozzles that move to direct thrust downwards or behind. Tiltrotor planes, such as the **Bell XV-15**, swivel their entire propeller-spinning engines upwards for take-off and forward for regular flight.

Eyes in the sky

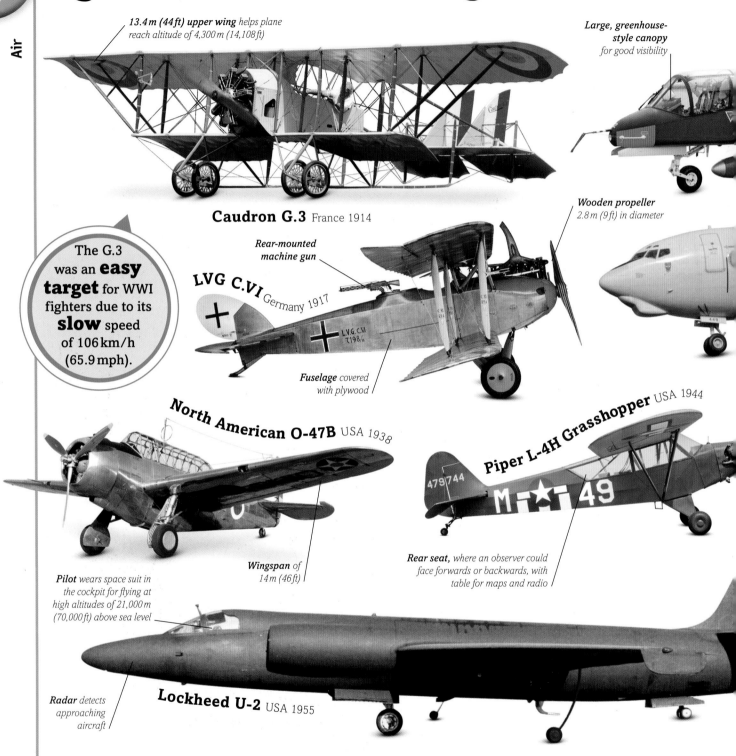

13.4 m (44 ft) upper wing *helps plane reach altitude of 4,300 m (14,108 ft)*

Large, greenhouse-style canopy for good visibility

Caudron G.3 France 1914

The G.3 was an **easy target** for WWI fighters due to its **slow** speed of 106 km/h (65.9 mph).

Rear-mounted machine gun

Wooden propeller 2.8 m (9 ft) in diameter

LVG C.VI Germany 1917

Fuselage *covered with plywood*

North American O-47B USA 1938

Piper L-4H Grasshopper USA 1944

479 744 M 49

Wingspan *of 14 m (46 ft)*

Rear seat, *where an observer could face forwards or backwards, with table for maps and radio*

Pilot *wears space suit in the cockpit for flying at high altitudes of 21,000 m (70,000 ft) above sea level*

Radar *detects approaching aircraft*

Lockheed U-2 USA 1955

Reconnaissance planes scout the land and sea from above. Some go further, acting as spies in the sky using telephoto lenses and other tools to spot troop positions and detect enemy weapons, facilities, or other crucial activity on the ground.

The first spotter planes, such as the **Caudron G.3** and the **LVG C.VI**, were used to detect enemy artillery and troop movements. Later observation aircraft, such as the **OV-10 Bronco** could scout territory and carry weapons. It could also take off from roads or makeshift runways,

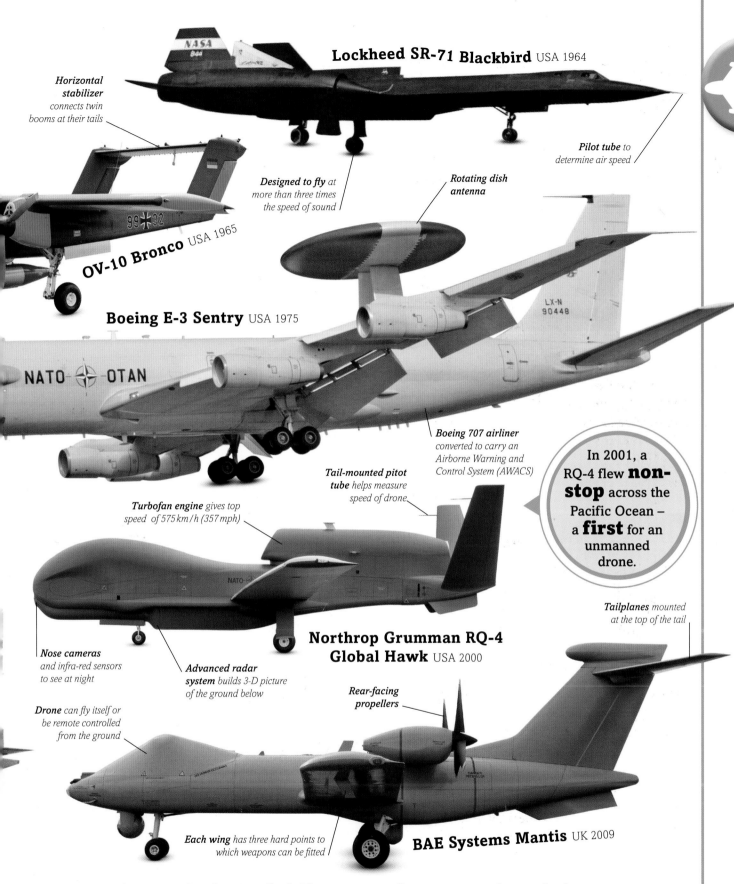

Lockheed SR-71 Blackbird USA 1964

Horizontal stabilizer connects twin booms at their tails

Designed to fly at more than three times the speed of sound

Pilot tube to determine air speed

Rotating dish antenna

OV-10 Bronco USA 1965

99✚32

Boeing E-3 Sentry USA 1975

LX-N 90448

NATO ⊕ OTAN

Boeing 707 airliner converted to carry an Airborne Warning and Control System (AWACS)

Tail-mounted pitot tube helps measure speed of drone

Turbofan engine gives top speed of 575 km/h (357 mph)

In 2001, a RQ-4 flew **non-stop** across the Pacific Ocean – a **first** for an unmanned drone.

Tailplanes mounted at the top of the tail

Northrop Grumman RQ-4 Global Hawk USA 2000

Nose cameras and infra-red sensors to see at night

Advanced radar system builds 3-D picture of the ground below

Rear-facing propellers

Drone can fly itself or be remote controlled from the ground

Each wing has three hard points to which weapons can be fitted

BAE Systems Mantis UK 2009

and fly more than 2,200 km (1,367 miles). The **SR-71 Blackbird** was a dedicated spy plane that operated at high speed and altitude, out of the range of enemy ground-to-air missiles. No Blackbird was ever shot down by enemy forces. Advanced fighters, feature stealth technology that confuses enemy radars and other sensors, in order to spy undetected. Unmanned aerial vehicles (UAVs), or drones, such as the **BAE Systems Mantis**, can fly long missions gathering information without risking pilots' lives. The Mantis can fly for up to 30 hours.

Helicopter

A helicopter's long, thin rotor blades have a curved shape, similar to that of an aircraft's wing. When these blades are spun quickly by the engine, they travel through the air and like an aircraft wing create lift. Their ability to take off and land vertically, and to hover mid-air, make helicopters incredibly useful for military and police work, and search-and-rescue missions, as performed by this **Sea King**.

Rotor head

Westland Sea King HAR.3

Radar dome

Tail rotor blade

Foldable hinged tail boom

Winch crane

Tailplane

ZE370

Tail rotor > This six-bladed rotor spins to balance out the effects of the main rotor blades. By varying the speeds of the tail rotor, the pilot can use it as a rudder to steer.

Sponson > This contains inflatable bags, which can be filled with air to help the helicopter float, should it land on water.

Turbine engine ❭ The helicopter's two Rolls Royce Gnome turboshaft engines spin the rotor head, which can be angled to change the helicopter's direction. The Sea King has a cruising speed of 208 km/h (129 mph), and a maximum range of 1,230 km (764 miles).

Rotor blade ❭ The rotor blades are fitted to the rotor head, which is spun by the engine to generate lift. The Sea King can rise up at speeds of 10 m (33 ft) per second. When the helicopter is stored on a ship, or in a hangar, the blades can be folded up.

Interior ❭ The pilot and the co-pilot fly the helicopter from the cockpit, while two crew members operate the radio and winch system, which can lift people out of the water and into the helicopter. The Sea King can hold up to 18 rescued people or 6 stretchers.

Powerful forward-facing headlight

Hull and avionics ❭ The Sea King's hull-shaped body enables it to float on water. Stored inside its nose are radio and navigation electronics that enable the helicopter to find stricken boats and people at sea.

Undercarriage wheels

Whirlybirds

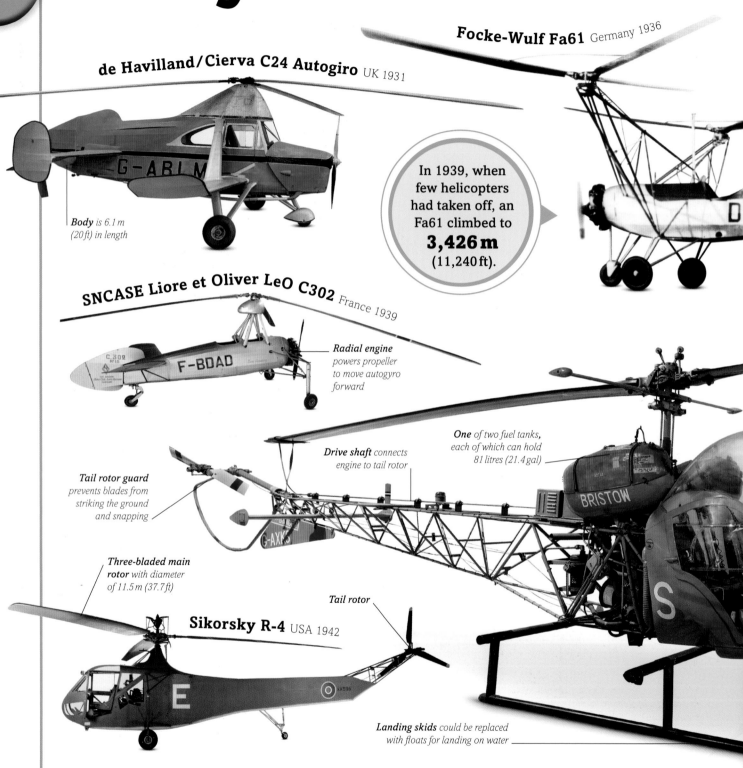

Focke-Wulf Fa61 Germany 1936

de Havilland/Cierva C24 Autogiro UK 1931

G-ABLM

Body is 6.1 m (20 ft) in length

In 1939, when few helicopters had taken off, an Fa61 climbed to **3,426 m** (11,240 ft).

SNCASE Liore et Oliver LeO C302 France 1939

C.302

F-BDAD

Radial engine powers propeller to move autogyro forward

Drive shaft connects engine to tail rotor

One of two fuel tanks, each of which can hold 81 litres (21.4 gal)

Tail rotor guard prevents blades from striking the ground and snapping

G-AXM

BRISTOW

S

Three-bladed main rotor with diameter of 11.5 m (37.7 ft)

Tail rotor

Sikorsky R-4 USA 1942

E

Landing skids could be replaced with floats for landing on water

With long, thin, wing-shaped blades whizzing around, it is no surprise that the first autogyros and helicopters got the nickname "whirlybirds". These versatile craft first came into their own in the 1930s and 1940s.

Autogyros, such as the **Cierva C24**, use a main rotor for lift, but also have a propeller at the front to provide thrust. This gave the C24 a top speed of 177 km/h (110 mph). The experimental **Focke-Wulf Fa61** came with two sets of rotors, to increase lift, but only two were ever made.

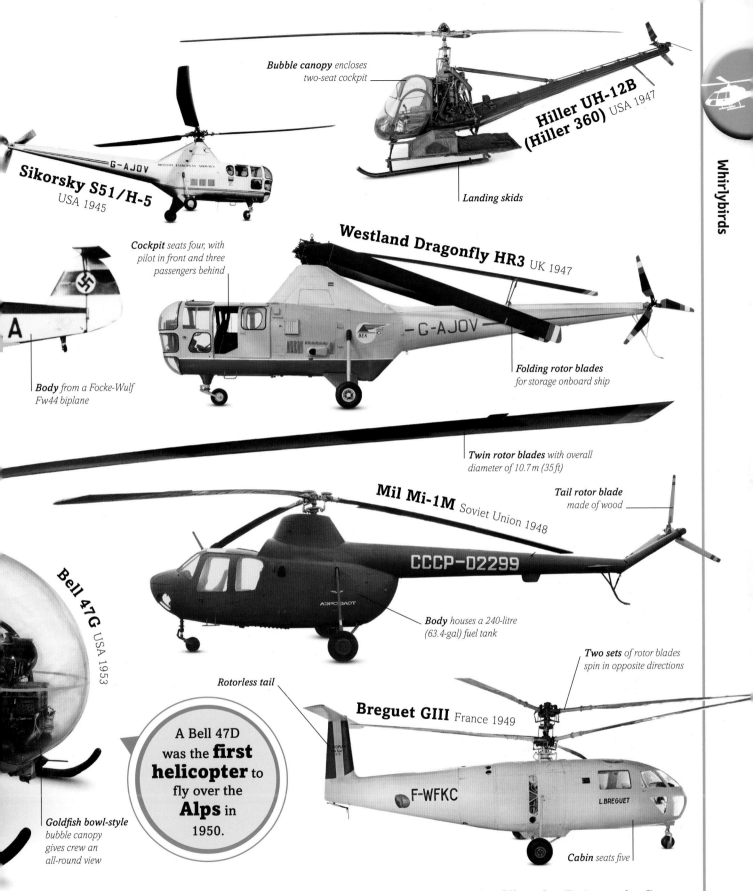

Bubble canopy encloses two-seat cockpit

Hiller UH-12B (Hiller 360) USA 1947

Landing skids

Sikorsky S51/H-5 USA 1945

G-AJOV

Cockpit seats four, with pilot in front and three passengers behind

Westland Dragonfly HR3 UK 1947

-G-AJOV-

A

Body from a Focke-Wulf Fw44 biplane

Folding rotor blades for storage onboard ship

Twin rotor blades with overall diameter of 10.7 m (35 ft)

Mil Mi-1M Soviet Union 1948

Tail rotor blade made of wood

CCCP-02299

Bell 47G USA 1953

Body houses a 240-litre (63.4-gal) fuel tank

Two sets of rotor blades spin in opposite directions

Rotorless tail

Breguet GIII France 1949

A Bell 47D was the **first helicopter** to fly over the **Alps** in 1950.

Goldfish bowl-style bubble canopy gives crew an all-round view

F-WFKC

L.BREGUET

Cabin seats five

In contrast, more than 5,600 Bell 47 helicopters were built between 1946 and 1974. These included the **Bell 47G**, which became famous for medical evacuation, a task also performed by the **Westland Dragonfly HR3,** which flew the world's first scheduled helicopter service from 1950 onwards. The **Sikorsky R-4** was the first helicopter used by the American and the British military, rescuing injured air crash survivors in Asia as early as 1944, while the Soviet Union's first production helicopter was the **Mil Mi-1M**, of which over 2,500 were eventually built.

231

Working choppers

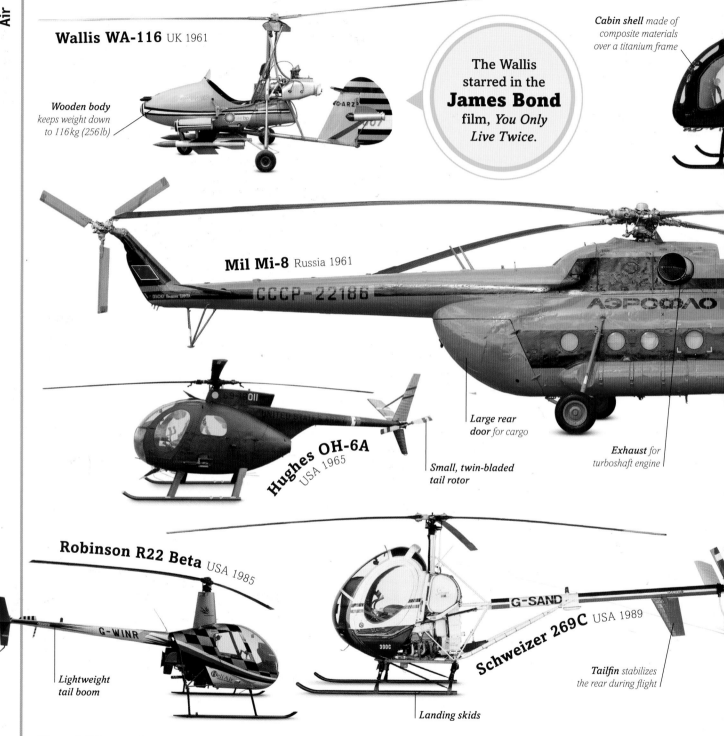

Wallis WA-116 UK 1961

Wooden body keeps weight down to 116 kg (256 lb)

The Wallis starred in the **James Bond** film, *You Only Live Twice*.

Cabin shell made of composite materials over a titanium frame

Mil Mi-8 Russia 1961

Large rear door for cargo

Exhaust for turboshaft engine

Hughes OH-6A USA 1965

Small, twin-bladed tail rotor

Robinson R22 Beta USA 1985

Lightweight tail boom

Schweizer 269C USA 1989

Tailfin stabilizes the rear during flight

Landing skids

The ability to hover in mid-air makes helicopters ideal platforms for aerial photography, search and rescue, and reconnaissance missions. They can also operate from isolated areas and city helipads, ferrying people and supplies.

The 1960s saw the production of both tiny autogyros and giant helicopters. The single-seater **Wallis WA-116** was just 3.4 m (11.2 ft) long, but could fly more than 200 km (124 miles), while the **Mil Mi-8** was 18.2 m (60 ft) long and could carry 27 people or 3,000 kg (6,614 lb) of cargo. Biggest

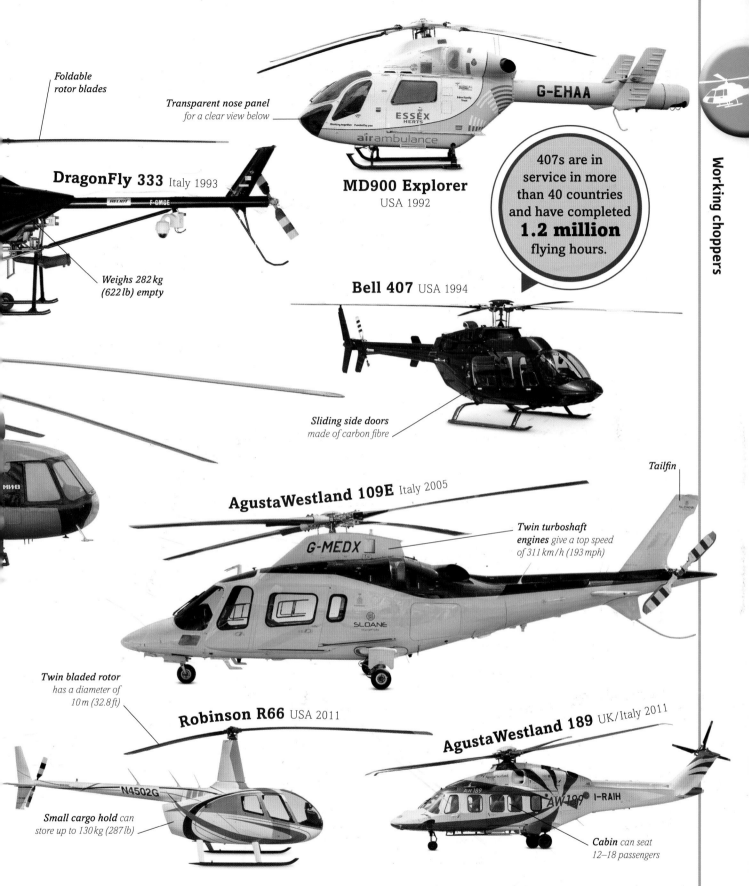

Foldable rotor blades

Transparent nose panel
for a clear view below

DragonFly 333 Italy 1993

HELIDT F-GMGE

MD900 Explorer
USA 1992

ESSEX HERTS
air ambulance

G-EHAA

407s are in service in more than 40 countries and have completed **1.2 million** flying hours.

Weighs 282 kg (622 lb) empty

Bell 407 USA 1994

Sliding side doors
made of carbon fibre

Tailfin

AgustaWestland 109E Italy 2005

G-MEDX

Twin turboshaft engines give a top speed of 311 km/h (193 mph)

SLOANE

Twin bladed rotor
has a diameter of 10 m (32.8 ft)

Robinson R66 USA 2011

AgustaWestland 189 UK/Italy 2011

N4502G

AW189 I-RAIH

Small cargo hold can
store up to 130 kg (287 lb)

Cabin can seat
12–18 passengers

of all is the 40-m- (131-ft-) long Mil Mi-26. The **DragonFly 333** was developed for filmmakers and archaeologists to perform aerial surveys, while the **Robinson R22 Beta** was used to patrol pipelines and to get around large farms or ranches. The **MD900 Explorer** is used by coastguards and

the police forces, and also serves as an air ambulance, a task some **Bell 407** seven-seater helicopters also perform. Other 407s transport workers to and from offshore oil rigs, while variants of the **Schweizer 269C** have been used to train more than 60,000 army helicopter pilots.

Air support

Bell AH-1 Cobra USA 1965

Twin-bladed tail rotor

Movable turret holds either twin machine guns, or grenade launchers

Kamov Ka-25PL Russia 1965

Mil Mi-24A Hind-A Russia 1971

Tough titanium rotor blades

Short wing provides mounting points for weapons, such as cannons

Cockpit seats pilot and co-pilot

SA Gazelle France 1973

Enclosed fenestron (fan in tailfin)

Mil Mi-14 BT Russia 1973

Rotor blades have a diameter of 21.3 m (69.9 ft)

Sponson (storage area)

Rear wheels retract up into sponson allowing helicopter to land on water

Radar equipment housed in fuselage fairing

Military helicopters serve armies, navies, and air forces all over the world. Their ability to land in small spaces, hover in mid-air, and drop supplies accurately make them invaluable on the battlefield, as well as behind the lines.

Many military helicopters, such as the **Sikorsky S-70i** *Black Hawk*, are multi-purpose, able to move troops and equipment, or scout land or sea for threats. Some, such as the **Bell AH-1 Cobra** and the **Kamov Ka-52** *Alligator*, are designed to attack mostly ground targets, using weapons such

BOEING CH-47D CHINOOK

Including rotors, aircraft is 30.2 m (99 ft) long

Westland Sea King HC4 UK 1979

Boeing CH-47D Chinook USA 1982

Wide rear cargo ramp *allows large items to be loaded*

Kamov Ka-52 *Alligator* Russia 1996

Bottom set of rotor blades *spins in the opposite direction to the top set*

Rotorless tail

Armoured body *can withstand hits from gunfire*

More than **2,100** versions of the *Black Hawk* have been built since its first production in 1976.

Eurocopter UH-72 Lakota France 2004

Set of three tailfins

Cabin *seats up to 18 passengers*

Landing skids

Four-bladed tail rotor *helps in flight stability*

Cockpit doors *can be ejected in an emergency*

Landing gear *absorbs shocks*

Sikorsky S-70i *Black Hawk* Poland 2011

as cannons, rockets, or small guided missiles. Larger choppers can deploy troops, supplies, or equipment, or evacuate the wounded or civilians out of a warzone. The **Westland Sea King HC4** can carry up to 28 commandos in its cabin, while the **Boeing CH-47D Chinook** can seat nearly 55 troops, or carry 12,000 kg (26,455.5 lb) of cargo. The **Kamov Ka-25PL**, with two sets of rotors, one above the other, is designed to hunt and attack enemy submarines. The same role is performed by the **Mil Mi-14 BT**, which can carry one torpedo or eight depth charges.

Spacecraft

Spacecraft are machines that are launched by rocket engines, out into space. Many of them are unmanned probes, sent out to explore parts of the Solar System. A small number have been manned, and have carried more than 500 people into space. In 1969, an American **Apollo 11 spacecraft** was launched by a Saturn V rocket and carried three astronauts into orbit around the Moon. Two of them descended in the Lunar Module onto the Moon's surface.

Apollo 11 spacecraft

Engine nozzle

Fuel tanks ❯ Tanks within the Service Module supplied fuel to the main engine.

Service Module ❯ This module provided life-support systems and power for the crew, and housed the spacecraft's main engine.

Thrusters ❯ Small thrusters made fine adjustments to the spacecraft's movements.

Command Module ❯ The 3.2-m- (10.5-ft-) tall Command Module was the only part of the Apollo spacecraft to return to Earth. It orbited the Moon, while the astronauts completed a return journey to its surface in the Lunar Module, then separated from the Service Module and travelled back to Earth.

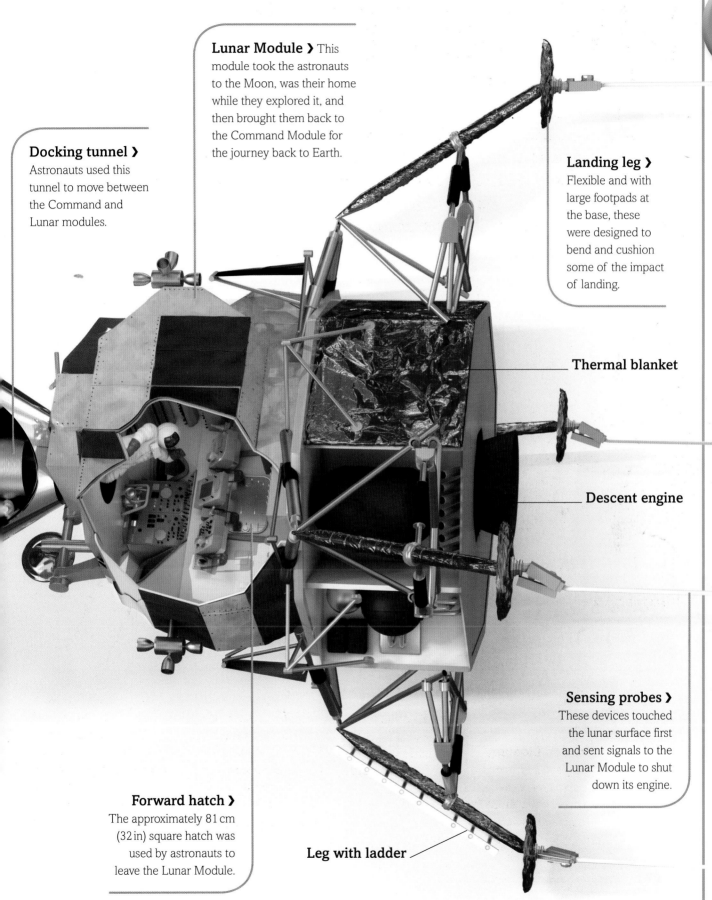

Lunar Module ❯ This module took the astronauts to the Moon, was their home while they explored it, and then brought them back to the Command Module for the journey back to Earth.

Docking tunnel ❯
Astronauts used this tunnel to move between the Command and Lunar modules.

Landing leg ❯
Flexible and with large footpads at the base, these were designed to bend and cushion some of the impact of landing.

Thermal blanket

Descent engine

Sensing probes ❯
These devices touched the lunar surface first and sent signals to the Lunar Module to shut down its engine.

Forward hatch ❯
The approximately 81 cm (32 in) square hatch was used by astronauts to leave the Lunar Module.

Leg with ladder

Launch vehicles

Nose cone

Second stage

Vostok-K Russia 1960

Single *rocket engine fires when second stage separates from first stage*

First stage

Saturn V USA 1966

Lunar module *of the Apollo spacecraft*

Third stage *separates from second, nine minutes after lift-off*

Launch vehicle *weighs 2.8 million kg (6.2 million lb)*

Space Shuttle Discovery USA 1990

Cabin *holds five to seven astronauts*

Payloads *can weigh up to 8.5 tonnes (9.4 US tons)*

Long March 2F China 1999

Saturn V's five rocket engines burned **12,710 litres** (3,358 gal) of fuel per second.

Shuttle's three rocket engines *propel it to speeds of more than 27,000 km/h (16,777 mph)*

Twin-bodied White Knight plane *carries SpaceShipTwo to launch altitude*

SpaceShipTwo *is released at 15,000 m (49,213 ft)*

LENGTH Short to long

Soyuz FG	49.5 m (162.4 ft)
Ariane 5	46–52 m (151–171 ft)
Saturn V	110.6 m (363 ft)

Enormous power is needed to overcome gravity and travel into space. So satellites and spacecraft are propelled by launch vehicles, with rocket engines and their own fuel supply. While rockets can only be used once, space shuttles are reusable.

To carry heavy cargos into space multi-stage launch vehicles are used, such as the two-stage **Long March 2F**, which carried the Shenzhou spacecraft in 2003, and the **Ariane 5s**, which have made more than 75 successful launches. Each stage of a launch vehicle has its own

Nose *holds Soyuz or Progress spacecraft*

Soyuz FG Russia 2001

Four booster rockets *19.6-m-(64.3-ft-) tall fire at launch*

Fairing *covers payload during launch, but opens to release craft or satellite once in orbit*

Atlas V USA 2002

Powerful boosters *fall away four minutes after launch*

Spacecraft's emergency crew escape system

A Delta IV Heavy weighs more than **200** female **elephants!**

Delta IV Heavy USA 2004

Each rocket booster *weighs 277 tonnes (305 US tons), when full of fuel*

Ariane 5 Multinational 2005

arianespace

esa   esa

cnes   cnes

Rocket boosters *fire for under 90 seconds at launch*

Virgin Galactic SpaceShipTwo USA 2010

Dream Chaser USA
under development

Upturned wing *for gliding back down to Earth*

rocket engines, and falls away after its fuel is exhausted, leaving the remaining smaller, lighter vehicle to continue. The biggest lifter among current launch vehicles is the **Delta IV Heavy**, which can carry 28-tonne (31-US-ton) loads into Earth orbit. This is just a quarter of the load carried by the three-stage **Saturn V**, used for the Apollo Moon landings. Spaceplanes, such as the **Space Shuttle** *Discovery* and the **SpaceShipTwo**, are powered by rocket engines, but use their wings to glide back to the Earth after their mission.

Space probes

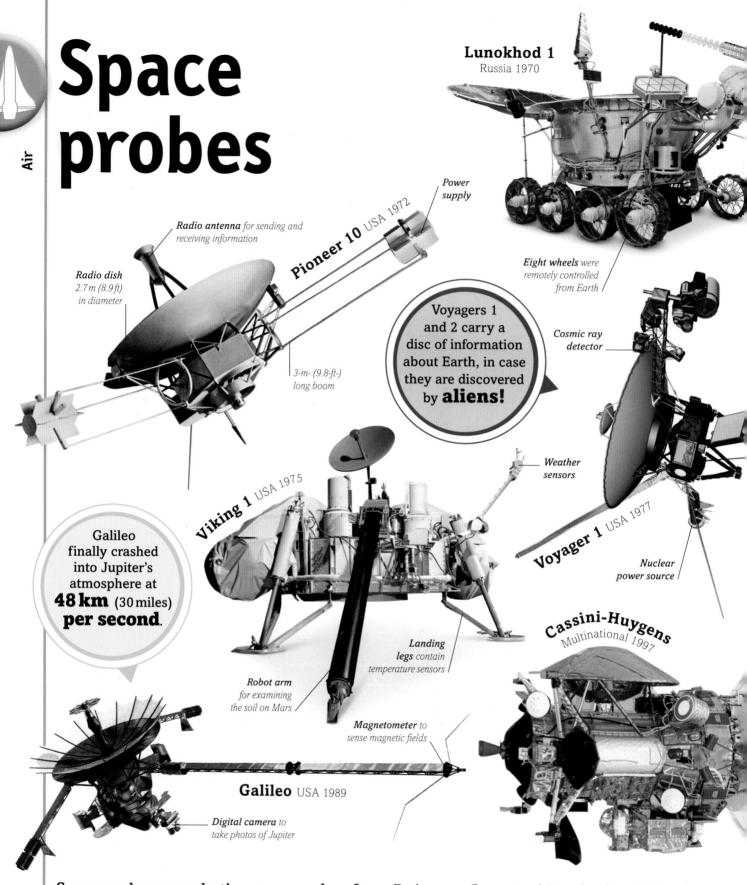

Lunokhod 1
Russia 1970

Radio antenna for sending and receiving information

Power supply

Pioneer 10 USA 1972

Radio dish
2.7 m (8.9 ft) in diameter

3-m- (9.8-ft-) long boom

Eight wheels were remotely controlled from Earth

Voyagers 1 and 2 carry a disc of information about Earth, in case they are discovered by **aliens!**

Cosmic ray detector

Galileo finally crashed into Jupiter's atmosphere at **48 km** (30 miles) **per second**.

Viking 1 USA 1975

Weather sensors

Voyager 1 USA 1977

Nuclear power source

Landing legs contain temperature sensors

Cassini-Huygens
Multinational 1997

Robot arm for examining the soil on Mars

Magnetometer to sense magnetic fields

Galileo USA 1989

Digital camera to take photos of Jupiter

Space probes are robotic, unmanned craft that explore planets, moons, asteroids, and comets, and send information and images back to Earth, using radio waves. The work of these probes has helped us to understand our Solar System.

Probes can fly past, orbit, or land on their target. **Viking 1** was the first long-term probe to land on Mars, sending back data until 1982. **Lunokhod 1** was the first successful rover, travelling 10.5 km (6.5 miles) around the Moon, while the **Curiosity Rover** continues to analyse

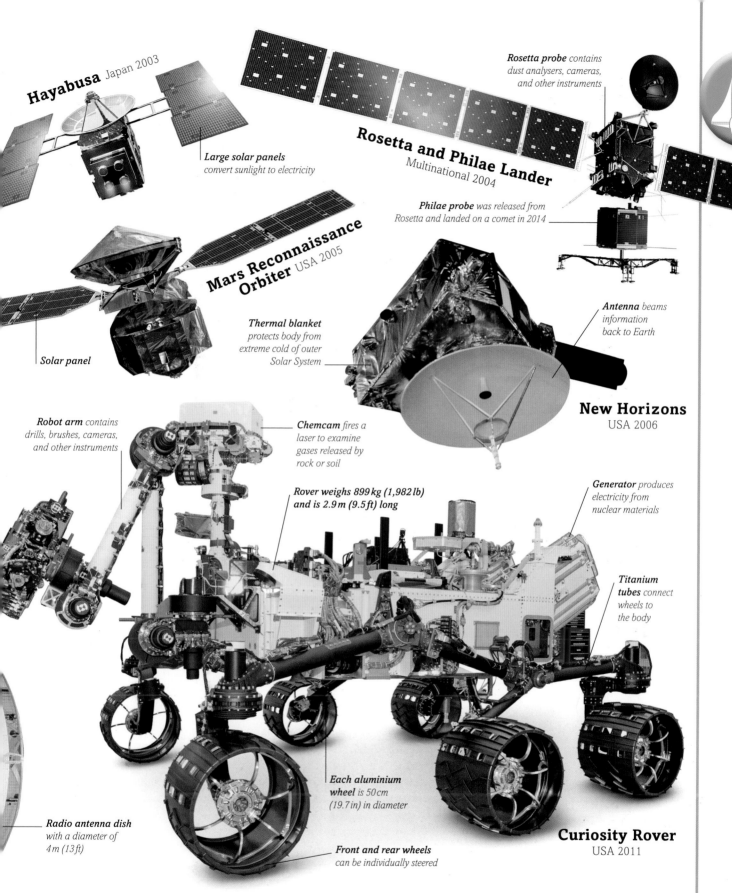

Hayabusa Japan 2003

Large solar panels convert sunlight to electricity

Rosetta and Philae Lander
Multinational 2004

Rosetta probe contains dust analysers, cameras, and other instruments

Philae probe was released from Rosetta and landed on a comet in 2014

Mars Reconnaissance Orbiter USA 2005

Solar panel

Thermal blanket protects body from extreme cold of outer Solar System

Antenna beams information back to Earth

New Horizons
USA 2006

Robot arm contains drills, brushes, cameras, and other instruments

Chemcam fires a laser to examine gases released by rock or soil

Rover weighs 899 kg (1,982 lb) and is 2.9 m (9.5 ft) long

Generator produces electricity from nuclear materials

Titanium tubes connect wheels to the body

Radio antenna dish with a diameter of 4 m (13 ft)

Each aluminium wheel is 50 cm (19.7 in) in diameter

Front and rear wheels can be individually steered

Curiosity Rover
USA 2011

Mars's rock and soil with its in-built laboratory. **Pioneer 10** became the first probe to travel beyond the asteroid belt, when it flew towards Jupiter. Later, however, **Galileo** orbited the planet 34 times sending back many photos and measurements during its 14-year mission. Some probes have travelled even further. **New Horizons** reached Pluto in 2015, after a 9.5 year journey, while **Voyager 1**, launched in 1977, is now more than 19 billion km (11.8 billion miles) away from the Earth, and with Voyager 2 and Pioneers 10 and 11, has left our Solar System.

Out of this world

Door *opens to release parachute during Earth re-entry*

Spacecraft *measures 3 m (9.8 ft) in diameter and holds two astronauts*

Gemini USA 1965

Radio antenna *sends signals back to Earth*

Mercury USA 1961

Vostok 1 Russia 1961

Spherical descent capsule *holds a single cosmonaut in an ejection seat*

Recovery compartment *releases main and reserve parachutes to bring capsule safely back to Earth*

ISS is 108.5 m (336 ft) wide

Main capsule *is 2 m (6.6 ft) wide and 3.5 m (11.5 ft) tall*

Solar panels *attached to solar observatory with cameras taking pictures of the Sun*

Orbital module, *where the cosmonauts live during the mission*

Skylab USA 1973

Soyuz Russia 1967

After losing one of its solar panels, astronauts erected a large **sunshade** to keep Skylab cool.

Descent module *carries cosmonauts back to Earth*

Orbital workshop *contains crew beds, a shower, and a toilet*

Fewer than 600 people have travelled into space. The first astronauts, known as cosmonauts in Russia, orbited Earth in tiny, one-person space capsules. Later astronauts travelled to the Moon, and to orbiting space stations, where they could live and work.

In 1961, Yuri Gagarin became the first spaceman, with a 108-minute flight in the cramped 2.3-m (7.5-ft) capsule of a **Vostok 1** spacecraft. A month later, the USA sent Alan Shepard into space on board **Mercury**. Until space stations were built, early manned missions were short.

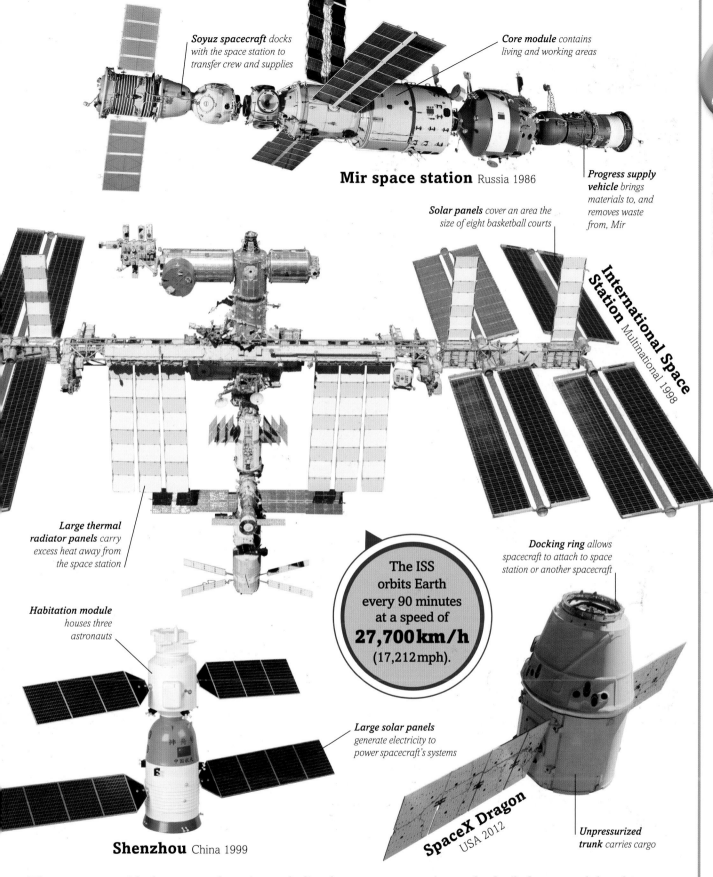

Soyuz spacecraft *docks with the space station to transfer crew and supplies*

Core module *contains living and working areas*

Mir space station Russia 1986

Progress supply vehicle *brings materials to, and removes waste from, Mir*

Solar panels *cover an area the size of eight basketball courts*

International Space Station Multinational 1998

Large thermal radiator panels *carry excess heat away from the space station*

Habitation module *houses three astronauts*

The ISS orbits Earth every 90 minutes at a speed of **27,700 km/h** (17,212 mph).

Docking ring *allows spacecraft to attach to space station or another spacecraft*

Large solar panels *generate electricity to power spacecraft's systems*

Shenzhou China 1999

SpaceX Dragon USA 2012

Unpressurized trunk *carries cargo*

Three crews, with three members in each, lived in the **Skylab** space station for a total of 171.5 days, performing 300 experiments. Cosmonauts inhabited the **Mir Space Station** for 12.5 years, with Valeri Polyakov spending a record-breaking 437 days, 18 hours in a row. Mir was the first space station to be built from modules that were put together in space. The biggest space station to date is the **International Space Station** (ISS), which needed more than 100 spaceflights, and 1,000 hours of spacewalks, to assemble. It has been manned since 2000.

LIFT-OFF!

Two thousand tonnes of spacecraft and fuel head into space, as space shuttle *Endeavour* thunders out of the launch pad at the Kennedy Space Center, in Florida, in 2009. From 1982 to 2011, shuttles made more than 130 successful spaceflights.

Each of a shuttle's two large, solid rocket boosters holds 450,000 kg (100,000 lb) of fuel, which is used up in the first two minutes. The shuttle's main engines continue burning, using all of the two million litres (530,000 gal) of fuel held in the 48-m- (157-ft-) long orange, external fuel tank by eight minutes after launch, when the shuttle is travelling more than 27,000 km/h (16,800 mph). This mission carried seven astronauts to the International Space Station, returning to Earth 17 days later.

GLOSSARY

Accelerate
To speed up and go faster.

Aerobatics
Acrobatics in the air, performed by aircraft for entertainment as well as in competitions.

Ailerons
Hinged surfaces, usually on an aircraft's wing, that can be raised or lowered to help an aircraft roll or turn.

Alloy
A mixture of two or more elements, at least one of which is a metal. Alloys often have useful properties, different to those of the elements from which they are made.

Amphibious
A vehicle that can travel both on land and in water.

Articulated train
A train with carriages linked together by a single, pivoting joint.

Autogyro
An aircraft with both a main rotor, for lift, and a propeller, to give forward thrust.

Battery
A store of chemicals in a case that, when connected to a circuit, supplies electricity.

Boiler
The part of a steam engine in which steam is produced.

Bonnet
A body panel, usually made of metal, which can open to reveal the vehicle's engine. Also known as a hood.

Boot
Also known as a trunk, a space for storage in a car.

Bow
The forward part of a vessel.

Bowsprit
A spar (pole) that extends forwards from a ship's bow.

Bridge
The part of a ship from where the captain controls the vessel.

Buffer
A shock-absorbing pad that cushions the impact of rail vehicles as they come together.

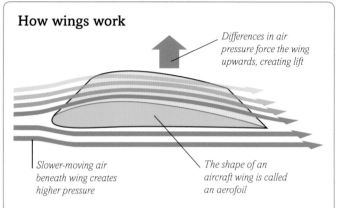

How wings work

Differences in air pressure force the wing upwards, creating lift

Slower-moving air beneath wing creates higher pressure

The shape of an aircraft wing is called an aerofoil

Lift
As the curved wing moves through the air, the air passing over the wing moves faster than the air passing beneath. Fast-moving air has a lower pressure. It is the slower, high pressure air beneath the wing that forces it upwards.

Bumper
A metal, rubber, or plastic bar fitted along the front and, sometimes, the back of a vehicle to limit damage if it bumps into something.

Cab
The part of a train or truck where the driver sits and controls the vehicle.

Class
A group of locomotives built to a common design.

Convoy
A group of ships or vehicles travelling together in formation.

Coupling
The parts, or mechanism, that allow railway locomotives to be joined together.

Derailleur
The part of a bike that moves the bicycle chain from one gear wheel to another when the rider changes gear.

Destroyer
A small, fast warship armed with guns, torpedoes, or guided missiles.

Diesel
A type of fuel made from oil used in many vehicle engines.

Disc brakes
A type of brake that uses pads to press against a turning disc, creating friction to slow the vehicle down.

Drag
A force of resistance on a vehicle as it moves through air or water, slowing it down.

Drone
Also known as an Unmanned Aerial Vehicle (UAV), a flying machine that either controls itself or is controlled remotely by a human operator.

Electromagnets
Magnets that are powered by electricity and can be switched on or off.

John Deere 6150 RH

How aircraft climb or dive

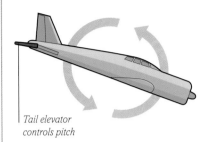

Tail elevator controls pitch

Wing ailerons control roll

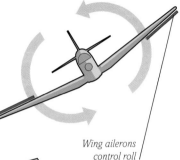

Tail rudder controls yaw

Pitch

To pitch (climb or dive), the pilot pushes or pulls the control column, raising or lowering the elevator flaps on the plane.

Roll

To roll, the pilot moves the control column to the left or right, which raises the ailerons on one wing and lowers them on the other.

Yaw

To yaw (turn) left or right, the pilot turns the upright rudder on the aeroplane's fin.

Elevator

A control surface on an aircraft that causes the plane to raise or lower its nose and climb or dive.

Excavator

A vehicle used at building sites to dig holes using a steel bucket attached to a long arm.

Exhaust

A tube that channels waste gases away from a vehicle's engine and out into the open air.

Firebox

The section at the rear of a steam locomotive boiler where the fuel is burned to heat the water in the boiler.

Flaps

Moveable parts of the rear edge of a wing that are used to increase lift at slower air speeds.

Fly-by-wire

An electronic flight control system used in aircraft instead of mechanical or machine-operated controls.

Foremast

The mast nearest the front of a ship.

Four-wheel drive (4WD)

Where power from the engine is used to turn both the front and back wheels of a vehicle.

Freight

Goods transported in bulk by truck, train, ship, or aircraft.

Friction

The force that slows movement between two objects that rub together. Brakes create lots of friction to slow down a vehicle.

Fuselage

The main body of an aircraft, to which the wings and tail are attached.

Galley (ship)

A fighting ship propelled by oars, and sometimes sails, used in the past in the Mediterranean Sea.

Gear

Toothed wheels that are used in trucks and cars to change the amount of speed or force used to turn wheels.

Generator

A machine that creates electricity.

GPS

Short for global positioning system, this refers to a navigation system that uses signals from a group of space satellites to work out a vehicle's position on Earth's surface.

Hatchback

A small car with a rear door and window covering the boot area.

Horsepower (hp)

A commonly used measure of the power of a vehicle's engine.

Hull

The main body of a boat or a ship.

Hybrid

A vehicle that has both a petrol engine and a second source of power, such as an electric motor.

Hydraulics

A system that uses liquid to transfer force from one place to another, to operate a vehicle's brakes, for example.

Internal combustion engine

A type of engine in which fuel and air are mixed and burned (combusted) inside cylinders to produce power.

Lift

The force created by air moving over a wing or rotor blade to keep an aircraft rising through the air.

Locomotive

A wheeled vehicle used for pulling trains. Electric locomotives rely on electricity provided by an external source, while steam and diesel locomotives generate their own power.

Maglev train

Short for magnetic levitation, a train that works by being raised above special tracks and moved forward by the power of electromagnets.

Ducati 916SPS

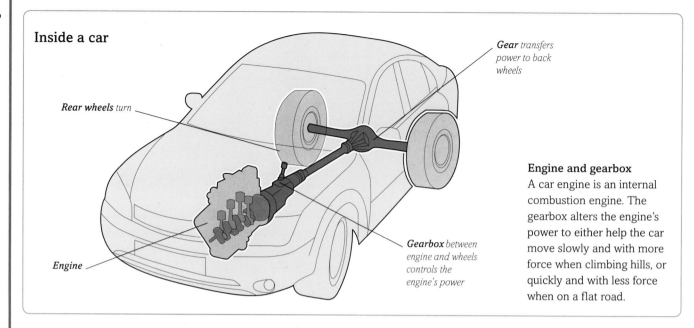

Inside a car

Gear transfers power to back wheels

Rear wheels turn

Engine

Gearbox between engine and wheels controls the engine's power

Engine and gearbox
A car engine is an internal combustion engine. The gearbox alters the engine's power to either help the car move slowly and with more force when climbing hills, or quickly and with less force when on a flat road.

Motocross
A type of motorcycle sport where riders race around laps of a cross-country course full of bumps and dips.

NASCAR
Short for National Association for Stock Car Auto Racing, a popular type of car- and truck-racing competition on tracks in North America.

Off-road
To travel in a vehicle away from roads and over tracks, trails, or open ground.

Orbit
The path of one object around a larger one under the influence of its gravity, such as that of a space probe around a planet.

Outboard motor
A detachable engine mounted on a boat's stern.

Outriggers
Bars that extend out from the side of vehicles, such as cranes or canoes, to provide support and help the vehicle balance.

Payload
The load carried by an aircraft or space launch vehicle, which include both passengers and cargo.

Pollution
Waste products that reach the air, water, or land and can do damage to the environment or the health of living things.

Probe
An unmanned vehicle travelling into space to a planet, moon, comet, or other body in order to collect information.

Propeller
A set of blades spun by an engine to power a vehicle.

Radar
The system of bouncing radio waves off objects to measure their distance, or reveal objects that cannot be seen.

Road-legal
A car, motorbike, or truck equipped with all the features required to make it suitable for use on public roads.

Roll bar
A strong frame or tube above the head of a driver or passenger that protects them should the vehicle roll over during an accident.

Roll cage
A strong frame inside a vehicle that protects people sitting inside.

Rocket engine
An engine that burns fuel along with oxygen or oxidiser (oxygen-producing chemicals) to produce a stream of gases. The rocket engine carries its own supply of oxygen or oxidiser.

Rotor blades
Long, thin aerofoils that are spun by a helicopter, or other rotorcraft, to produce lift.

Rudder
A vertical plate or board that can be moved to steer a vessel or help turn an aircraft.

Saddle
The seat on a bicycle or motorcycle, where the cyclist or rider sits.

DHR B Class No. 19

Japanese cargo vessel

Shunter
A small locomotive used for moving wagons or carriages around a railway yard. Also known as a switcher.

Solar panel
A device that converts energy from sunlight into electricity.

Sonar
A system for detecting and locating objects, particularly under water, using sound waves.

Spoiler
A device on a car or aircraft, often shaped like a wing, which alters the airflow around the vehicle to generate more drag or downforce. Often found on racing cars, to keep them gripping the ground.

Spokes
The rods or bars that connect the centre, or hub, of a wheel with its rim.

Stern
The rear part of a boat or a vessel.

Streamlined
A streamlined object has smooth curves so that air or water flows easily, increasing movement.

Suspension
A system of springs and shock absorbers on a vehicle to help give a smooth ride over bumps and dips.

Supersonic
To fly faster than the speed of sound. The speed of sound is about 1,236 km/h (768 mph) at sea level.

Thrust
The force that pushes a powered aircraft through the air, usually generated by an engine.

Tiller
A horizontal bar or handle attached to the rudder of a boat to allow a sailor to steer it.

Tonne
A unit of measurement equal to 1,000 kg (2,204.6 lb).

Torpedo
A self-propelled underwater weapon with an explosive warhead that is launched from a ship or submarine and travels towards a set target.

Turbocharger
A device that uses waste gases to boost an engine's power.

Waterline
The level normally reached by the water on the side of a ship.

Wheelhouse
The part of a ship or boat that holds the ship's wheel, which is used for steering the vessel. In larger ships, the wheelhouse is part of the structure known as the bridge.

VTOL aircraft
Short for vertical take-off and landing, VTOL refers to aircraft that can use their thrust to head straight up into the air like a helicopter, and so do not require a long runway.

Yard
A long pole, or spar, attached to a ship's mast to which the top of a square sail is fixed.

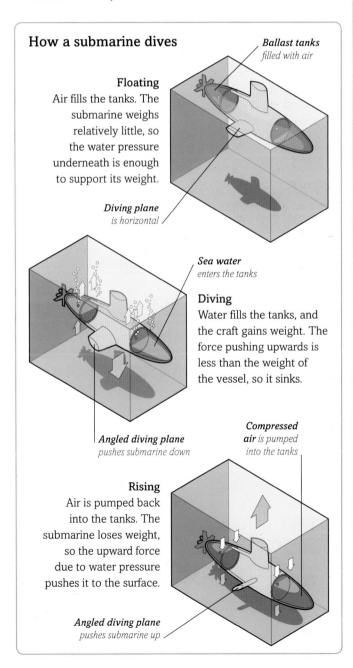

How a submarine dives

Ballast tanks
filled with air

Floating
Air fills the tanks. The submarine weighs relatively little, so the water pressure underneath is enough to support its weight.

Diving plane
is horizontal

Sea water
enters the tanks

Diving
Water fills the tanks, and the craft gains weight. The force pushing upwards is less than the weight of the vessel, so it sinks.

Angled diving plane
pushes submarine down

Compressed air is pumped into the tanks

Rising
Air is pumped back into the tanks. The submarine loses weight, so the upward force due to water pressure pushes it to the surface.

Angled diving plane
pushes submarine up

Index

A

Adler (train) 127

Agamemnon, SS 172–173

Agenoria (train) 126

ailerons 199

airbags 50, 61

airboats 193

Airbus 221, 222–223

aircraft 14–15, 198–235
  basic aeroplane design 198–199
  early 14, 200–205
  fighters and bombers 206–209, 212–215, 216–217, 227
  flying cars 80, 81
  helicopters 228–235
  jet 15, 212–215, 218, 221, 224–225
  light 218–219
  passenger 220–223
  racers and record-breakers 210–211
  reconnaissance 226–227
  seaplanes 216–217
  spaceplanes 238–239
  supersonic 15, 214–215, 224–225
  VTOL 15, 224, 225

aircraft carriers 182–183

airports 11, 106, 222–223
  Gatwick monorail 146, 147

airships 14, 201, 210

Akagi (ship) 182

Alfa Romeo cars 9, 67, 69

Allure of the Seas (ship) 13, 178–179

Alvin, DSV 189

ambulances 19, 107, 123, 233
  response bicycles 30–31

America (ship) 176–177

America's Cup 168–169

amphibious vehicles 82–83, 123, 217

Amundsen, Roald 165

animal power 18–21

Apollo 11 spacecraft 15, 236–237

Arcturus (ship) 176, 177

Argyllshire (ship) 172–173

Ariane 5 launcher 238, 239

Ark Royal, HMS 182, 183

Arleigh Burke, USS 184–185

Aston Martin cars 72, 74, 75, 80

Auburn Speedster 68

Audi Sport Quattro 86, 87

Austin Mini Seven 90, 91

autogyros 230, 232

auto polo 64–65

B

B-2 *Spirit* 208–209

B-52H Stratofortress 209

B&O Bo Switcher 140

Balloon trams 148

balloons, hot-air 14, 200–201

Batmobile 80–81

Beagle, HMS 164

Beagle Pup 218, 219

Bede BD-5J 218

Beechcroft A36 Bonanza 219

Bell aircraft 224–225

Bell helicopters 230–231, 233, 234

bendy buses 110–111

Benz Motorwagen 8, 62

Berlin U-Bahn 146–147

bicycles 22–37
  basic design 22–23
  early 24–25
  folding 30–31
  fun and speed 32–33
  mountain 9, 30, 34–37
  racing 22–23, 26–29
  recumbent 33
  safety 8, 25
  stunts and tricks 35, 36–37
  work 30–31

biplanes 198–199, 202, 204–205, 207

Bismarck, KM 180, 181

Blériot, Louis 203

Blitzen-Benz 98

Bloodhound SSC 99

Bluebird cars 8, 98–99

Bluebird K7 watercraft 191

BMW cars 68, 74, 90

BMX bikes 35

boats *see* ships and boats

Boeing 787-8 Dreamliner 221

Boeing B-17G Flying Fortress 208

Boeing E-3 Sentry 227

bombers 208–209, 216

Bond, James 80, 232

Bounty, HMS 164

bowsprit 161

Boyer, Lilian 204–205

BR Class 05 engine 132–133

brakes
  disc 60
  wheel 124

brig 167

Brough Superior SS100 56

Budd RDC railcar 136, 137

Bugatti cars 9, 66, 67, 68–69, 99

Bugatti railcar 134, 135

buggies 79

Buick cars 70–71, 96

bulldozers 121

buses 110–111
  horse-drawn 19
  trolleybuses 148–149
  water 176, 177

C

cabin cruisers 192, 193

Cadillac cars 70, 71, 97

CAF Urbos 3 tram 149

camels 20–21

camper van 84–85

Canadair CL-215 217

Cannondale racing bike 22–23

canoes 154–155, 157, 159, 192, 193

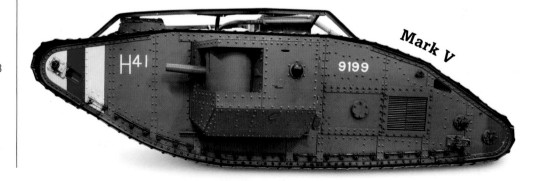

Mark V

RMS Titanic

caravans, desert 20–21

caravels 164–165

carriages, horse-drawn 18–19

cars 8–9, 60–101

amphibious 82–83

basic design 60–61

convertibles 88–89

crazy 80–81

dragsters 100–101

early 8, 62–67

family 60-61, 84–85

4x4s 86–87

fun 64–65, 78–79

luxury 96–97

1930s 68–69

1950s 70–73

racing 64–67, 72–77, 95

rally 74, 76–77, 78, 87

record-breaking speed 8, 9, 66, 75, 94, 98–101

small 90–93

sports 88–89

supercars 94–95

three-wheeled 90, 91, 92–93

Caudron G.3 226

Cessna aircraft 218, 219

chariots 18

Chevrolet cars 71, 73, 75, 88, 89

Chinook 235

Chrysler cars 70, 71, 96

clippers 165

coaches, horse-drawn 18–19

Columbus, Christopher 12, 164

compacters 121

concrete mixers 121

conning tower 187

construction sites 120–121

container ships 13, 174–175

Cook, Captain James 12, 160

cowcatcher 125

cranes 121

Crawler Transporters 108–109

CSCL Globe 13

Curiosity Rover 240–241

currachs 155

Curtiss JN-4 biplane 204–205

Curtiss-Robin J-1 210, 211

Cutty Sark (ship) 165

D

Daimler cars 62, 97

Dakar Rally 76–77

Darjeeling Mountain Railway 128

Dassault Mirage III 213

Datsun 260Z 89

Delta IV Heavy 239

Deperdussin Type A 203

diesel-electric engines 132, 135

diesel trains 9, 132–139, 150–151

diggers 120–121

dinghies, inflatable 192

dinghies, sailing 193

diving support vessel 175

DragonFly 333 helicopter 233

dragsters 100–101

Dreadnought, HMS 13, 180

dromon 163

drones 227

Duesenberg cars 63, 66, 67

E

Egypt, Ancient 155, 162

electric power 140–145, 148–149

Empire, PS 172, 173

Endeavour, HMS 160–161

engines

aircraft 199

diesel 9, 112, 132–139, 150–151

four-cylinder 41

internal combustion 8, 40, 60, 62, 110, 132

rear (in cars) 84

turbine 229

see also steam power

Eurofighter Typhoon FGR4 213

Ever Royal (ship) 174–175

excavators 120–121

exploration 12, 160–161, 164–165

F

F-14 Tomcat 214–215

F-22 Raptor 213

F-86A Sabres 212–213

Fairy Queen (train) 128

farm machinery 112–117

Ferrari cars 74–75, 88, 95, 99

ferries 176

Fiat Mephistopheles 98

firefighting vehicles 106

fishing boats 156–157, 174

Flatmobile 80–81

Flexity Swift trams 149

Flight Design CTSW 218–219

floatplanes 216

flying cars 80, 81

Flying Scotsman (ship) 130–131

Fluyt 165

Fokker aircraft 203, 206–207, 220

Ford

Cortina 84, 85

Escort RS1800 78

GT40 MKII 73

Model T 8, 63, 65

Mustang Fastback 88–89

forklifts 116, 117

Formula One (F1) 9, 72–73, 75

four-wheel drives (4x4s) 86–87

Fram (ship) 165

freight

ships 174–175

trains 138–139, 141

front-loaders 120–121

Fuji (ship) 173

Furious, HMS 182

fuselage 198

Kenworth C540

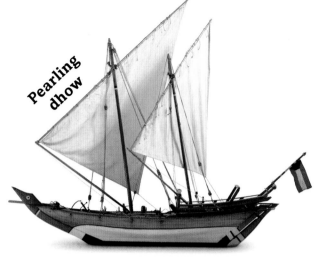

Pearling dhow

G

Gagarin, Yuri 15, 242
Galileo probe 240, 241
galleon 167
Gato, USS 188, 189
gears, bicycle 22, 34
George Washington, USS 183
Gipsy Moth biplane 198–199
gliders 14, 200–201
gondolas 157
Grand Princess (ship) 176, 177
Grand Prix Championships 67, 72, 75
Great Britain, SS 170–171
Gresley, Nigel 131
GWR streamlined railcar 134, 135

H

Hamilton, Lewis 75
Harley Davidson motorbikes 42–43, 46, 47, 48, 49, 54, 58, 59
Harrier ("Jump Jet") 15, 225
harvesters 116–117
hatchbacks 61, 84–85
Hawker Hurricane 207
helicopters 228–235
Hennessey Venom GT 95
Hillman Imp 84
Himiko (Water bus) 176, 177
Honda Super Cubs 44
Hong Kong Tramways 148–149
Hornet, USS 183

horse-drawn vehicles 18–19, 127
hovercraft 190–191
Hummer H3 87
huskies 18–19
hydrofoils 191

I-L

icebreakers 13, 175
ice-cream carts 31
Illustrious, HMS 182–183
Indian Railways 128–129, 141, 150–151
International Space Station 243
Inuit people 156, 157
Iwo Jima, USS 185
Jaguar cars 72, 73, 96, 97
Japanese trains 11, 142–143, 144–145
JCB Fastrac 115
Jeeps 9, 78, 79, 86
jet aircraft 15, 212–215, 218, 221, 224–225
Jet Skis 191

jetfoils 191
Junkers Ju87 *Stuka* 208
junks 163
Kamov helicopters 234, 235
Kawasaki Dragster 51
kayaks 156–157, 158–159, 192, 193
Kenworth C540 truck 102–103
Kirkliston, HMS 184, 185
La Reale (ship) 166, 167
Lamborghini cars 79, 94
Lancaster, Avro 208–209
Lancaster, HMS 184–185
Land Rovers 86, 87
Le Mans 24-Hour race 69, 73, 75
lifeboats 174, 175
Lil' Devil (truck) 118–119
Lilienthal, Otto 14, 201
Lincoln cars 68, 70–71, 96–97
Lindbergh, Charles 15, 210–211
liners, cruise 176–177, 180–181
Lockheed aircraft 206–207, 213, 224–225, 226, 227
locking, central 61
lunar module 236–237
Lunokhod 1 rover 240

M-O

Macchi Castoldi M.C.72 211
magnetic levitation (maglev) 11, 142, 143
Mallard (train) 11, 129
Mantis, BAE Systems 227

Mars probes 240–241
Mary Rose (ship) 12, 166–167
Maserati cars 67, 72
Massey Ferguson tractors 112–113, 115, 116–117
masts 160–161, 170–171
Mauretania, RMS 172–173
Mayflower (ship) 12, 164, 165
Mazda MX-5 89
MCC Smart Crossblade 79
McDonnell Douglas F-4 Phantom II 212–213
McLaren cars 74–75, 94, 95
MD900 Explorer 233
Mercedes-Benz
  cars 67, 68, 69, 70, 72, 85, 96–97, 98, 99
  trucks 104–105, 107, 121
Mercedes racing cars 74–75, 95
Messerschmitt
  aircraft 207, 211
  car 90
MG cars 68, 69, 88, 89
MiG aircraft 212, 213, 225
Mil helicopters 231, 232, 234, 235
Mini Moke 78, 79
mining 120–121, 126, 139
Mir Space Station 243
missiles 185, 187
Monge A601 184, 185
monoplanes 198, 203, 207
monorails 147
Monster Energy X-Raid Mini 76–77
monster trucks 118–119

JCB 3CX

Piper L-4h Grasshopper

mopeds 44–45

Mopetta Microcar 92–93

Morris Marina 84–85

Mosquito (de Havilland DH98) 208, 209

motorbikes 38–58

  basic design 38–39

  early 40–41

  fastest 56–57

  freestyle motocross 52–53

  long-distance beasts 58–59

  luxury features 59

  "naked" 38

  off-roaders 54–55

  racing 50–51

  road burners 48–49

  scooters 9, 44–45

  three-wheelers 46–47

  wartime 42–43

motorboats 192

motocross 52–53, 54–55

Motorrad 8, 40–41

narrowboats 192, 193

NASCAR races 73, 75

Nautile (submersible) 189

Nelson, Lord Horatio 167

New Horizons 241

Noble M600 95

Normandie (ship) 176, 177

North Carolina, USS 179

nuclear power 13, 186, 189

Oasis of the Seas, MS 177

Oldsmobile cars 62, 63, 84

Otso (ship) 175

OV-10 Bronco 226–227

P–R

P34 patrol boat 178–179

Pen-y-darren (train) 10, 126

Penny Farthings 8, 24–25

personal watercraft 191

Peterhansel, Stéphane 77

Peugeot cars 68, 69, 79, 84–85

Phoenicians 162, 163

Pioneer 10 probe 240, 241

Pitts Special S-2A 218–219

police transport 30, 233

  Harley Davidsons 46, 47, 48

Porsche cars 88, 95

powerboats 191, 194–195

propellers 170, 171, 191, 199

PRR Class GG1 train 140

Prussian Class P8 engines 129

Puffing Billy (train) 126

Queen Elizabeth II (ship) 176–177

Quimby, Harriet 202

racing

  aircraft 210–211

  bikes 22–23, 26–29

  cars 64–67, 72–77, 95

  motorbikes 50–51

  powerboats 194–195

  trimaran 168–169

rafts 156–157, 192

railcars 134–135, 136, 137, 141

rallies, car 74, 76–77, 78, 87

reconnaissance 226–227, 232

record breakers

  aircraft 210–211

  fast cars 8, 9, 66, 75, 94, 98–99

  flattest car 80–81

  motorbikes 56–57

  smallest car 90, 91

  tank 123

  trains 11, 130–131, 135, 136, 142–143

Red Bull Rampage 36–37

reed boats 154, 155

refuse trucks 106–107

Regensburg, SMS 178

Reliant Robin 91

Republic F-84C Thunderjet 212

Richthofen, Manfred von ("Red Baron") 206, 207

road-sweepers 107

Robinson helicopters 232, 233

Rocket (train) 10, 127

rockets 238–239

Rolls Royce cars 63, 96, 97

Romans 162, 163

Rough Diamond T 100–101

Routemaster, AEC 110, 111

rowing boats 155, 162–163, 192–193

RQ-4 Global Hawk 227

rudders 160, 198

S

Saab J35E Draken 212, 213

sailing ships 160–171, 174, 193

Saint Martin (island) 222–223

St Michael (ship) 166, 167

Salvonia (ship) 174, 175

sampan 156–157

Santa Maria (ship) 12, 164

Santissima Trinidad (ship) 167

Saratoga, USS 182

Saturn V 238, 239

Savannah, SS 13, 172

SBB Class Ce6/8 138–139

scooters, motor 9, 44–45

Sea King 228–229

seaplanes 216–217

Shepard, Alan 242

Shin Aitoku Maru (ship) 174, 175

Shinkansen "bullet trains" 11, 142–143, 144–145

ships and boats 12–13, 154–195

  aircraft carriers 182–183

  canoes and kayaks 154–155, 156–157, 158–159, 192, 193

  early 12, 154–155

  exploration 12, 160–161, 164–165

  fast 190–191, 193, 194–195

  flying boats 216–217

  international 156–157

  leisure 192–193

  passenger 176–177, 180–181

  racing trimaran 168–169

  rowing 155, 162–163, 192–193

  sailing 160–171, 174, 193

  steam 13, 170–173, 174

  steel 172–173

  trading 164–165

  warships 13, 162–163, 166–167, 173, 177, 178–179, 184–185

  working 174–175

shunters 136–137, 139

sidecars 42–43

Sikorsky helicopters 230, 231, 234, 235

Skylab 242, 243

skytrains 147

sleds 18

Sleeper Bus 111

SNCF TGV trains 142–143

snow ploughs 106, 107

solar power 13, 81

sonar 187

Sopwith Camel 206–207

space shuttles

Columbia 15

Discovery 108–109, 238, 239

Endeavour 244–245

space stations 242–243

spacecraft 15, 236–245

launch vehicles 238–239

manned 242–243

probes 15, 240–241

spaceplanes 238–239

SPAD SVII 206

speedway 55

Spirit of St Louis (aircraft) 15, 210–211

Spitfire, Supermarine 207

spy planes 227

SR71 Blackbird 225

Starling, HMS 181

stealth technology 209, 227

steam power

buses 110

cars 62–63

motorbikes 40

ships 13, 170–173, 174

tractors 114

trains 124–131, 139

trucks 104

steerage 170

Stephenson, Robert 10, 127

streetcars 140

Stumpjumper 9, 34, 35

Subaru cars 86–87, 90–91

submarines 13, 186–189

submersibles 188, 189

supercars 94–95

Supermarine Walrus 217

supersonic flight 15, 214–215, 224–225

SUVs (sports utility vehicles) 87

T

tandems 32–33

tankers 174, 175

tanks 122–123

landing craft 181

Thatcher Perkins (train) 124–125

Thrust SSC 9, 99

Titanic, RMS 13, 176, 177

Tom Thumb (train) 127

Top 1 Ack Attack 57

torpedoes 187

Tour de France 28–29

tow trucks 107

Toyota Yaris 60–61

tracks, caterpillar 115, 120, 122–123

tractors 112–117

trade 164–165

trains 10–11, 124–151

diesel 132–139, 150–151

double-decker 137, 143

driverless 147

electric 140–145

freight 138–139, 141

high-speed 11, 130–131, 142–145

steam 10, 124–131, 139

underground 10, 11, 129, 146–147

urban 146–147

trams 148–149

Trans-Europ Express 137

Trans-Siberian Railway 11

trawlers 174

tree fellers 107

Trevithick, Richard 10, 126

tricycles 25, 31, 33, 46–47

Trieste (submersible) 189

trimaran 168–169

triplane 203

trolleybuses 148–149

trucks 102–109

monster 9, 118–119

tugs 174, 175

Tupolev Tu-22M3 209

Turtle (submersible) 13, 188

turtle ship 166

tyres 22, 112, 114

U-V

U-boats 188–189

undercarriage 199

underground trains 10, 11, 129, 146–147

unicycles 32

unmanned aerial vehicles (UAVs) 227

Vancouver, HMCS 184, 185

Velocipedes 24-25, 40

Vespa scooters 9, 44–45

Vickers Vimy 210

Victory, HMS 167

Viking 1 probe 240

Viking longships 162–163

Vittorio Veneto (ship) 180–181

Volkswagen

cars 9, 74–75, 78, 85, 90

Kombi van 84–85

Voyager 1 probe 240, 241

W-Z

wagons 18–19

Wallis WA-116 232

Warrior, HMS 173

warfare

aircraft 206–209, 212–215, 216–217, 226–227

aircraft carriers 182–183

ambulance wagon 19

battle canoe 157

BSA Airborne bicycle 30, 31

cars 78–79

helicopters 234–235

motorbikes 42–43

ships 13, 162–163, 166–167, 173, 177, 180–181, 184–185

submarines 186–189

tanks 122–123

trucks 104

water taxis 157, 176

WaterCar Panther 82–83

Wendur (ship) 165

Westland helicopters 231, 235

whaling boats 156, 157

Williams-Renault FW18 73

windsurfing 193

wingwalking 204–205

Wright Brothers 14, 201, 202

Yakovlev Yak-38 225

Yamaha XJR 1300 38–39

Yamato (ship) 180–181

Zeppelins 14, 201

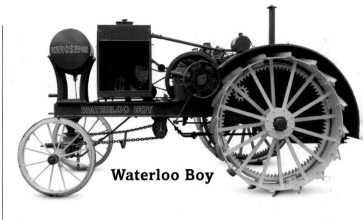

Waterloo Boy

LSER Class 395 *Javelin*

ACKNOWLEDGMENTS

Reviewer for the Smithsonian Institution:
Dr. F. Robert van der Linden, Curator of Air Transportation and Special Purpose Aircraft, National Air and Space Museum, Smithsonian

DK would like to thank:
Devika Awasthi, Siddhartha Barik, Sanjay Chauhan, Meenal Goel, Anjali Sachar, Mahua Sharma, Neha Sharma, Sukriti Sobti for design assistance; Kealy Gordon from the Smithsonian Institution; Carron Brown for proofreading; Jackie Brind for the index; Simon Mumford for photoshop work; Nic Dean for additional picture research; Charlie Galbraith for editorial assistance; Scotford Lawrence at the National Cycle Museum, Wales.

The publisher would like to thank the following for their kind permission to reproduce their photographs:

(Key: a-above; b-below/bottom; c-centre; f-far; l-left; r-right; t-top)

1 **Dreamstime.com:** Swisshippo. 4 **Dorling Kindersley:** James River Equipment (br). 5 **Dorling Kindersley:** IFREMER, Paris (cl); Ukraine State Aviation Museum (br). 6 **Dorling Kindersley:** National Motor Museum, Beaulieu (tc, br); Trevor Pope Motorcycles (tl); Adrian Shooter. **New Holland Agriculture:** (tr). 7 **Dorling Kindersley:** Musee Air & Space Paris, La Bourget (tr); Mr R A Fleming, The Real Aeroplane Company (tc); James River Equipment (br). **Photo used with permission of BRP:** (bc). 8 **Alamy Images:** Trinity Mirror / Mirrorpix (cr). **Dorling Kindersley:** R. Florio (br); The National Motor Museum, Beaulieu (ca). 9 **Alamy Images:** World History Archive (cra). 10 **Dorling Kindersley:** The National Railway Museum, York / Science Museum Group (c). **Science & Society Picture Library:** National Railway Museum (bl). 10-11 **Dorling Kindersley:** The National Railway Museum, York (bc). 11 **Alamy Images:** epa european pressphoto agency b.v (br); Geoff Marshall (tl); Colin Underhill (tr). 12 **Dorling Kindersley:** The Mary Rose Trust, Portsmouth (clb); The National Maritime Museum, London (c, bc). 13 **Dorling Kindersley:** The Royal Navy Submarine Museum, Gosport (bl); The Fleet Air Arm Museum (cla). **Getty Images:** Philippe Petit / Paris Match (tr). **Science Photo Library:** Mikkel Juul Jensen (br). 14 **Dorling Kindersley:** The Shuttleworth Collection, Bedfordshire (cra); The Shuttleworth Collection (br). 15 **Alamy Images:** B Christopher (bl). **Dorling Kindersley:** Brooklands Museum (cb); Yorkshire Air Museum (tl). **ESA:** ATG medialab (br). **Getty Images:** Education Images / UIG (tr). 16-17 **Alamy Images:** Sergii Kotko. 18 **Corbis:** John Harper (cb). **Dorling Kindersley:** B&O Railroad Museum (cl). 19 **Dorling Kindersley:** The National Railway Museum, York / Science Museum Group (cr). 20-21 **Corbis:** Christophe Boisvieux / Hemis. 24 **Corbis:** Hulton-Deutsch Collection (tr). **Dorling Kindersley:** The National Cycle Collection (cra, clb). 25 **Dorling Kindersley:** The National Cycle Collection (cra, c). **Getty Images:** Science & Society Picture Library (tl, tr, cr). **Science & Society Picture Library:** (cb). 26 **Dorling Kindersley:** The National Cycle Collection (tr). **MARIN BIKES:** (clb). 27 **Dorling Kindersley:** The National Cycle Collection (tr). 28-29 **Getty Images:** AFP / Pascal Pavani. 30 **Corbis:** Ashley Cooper (tr). **Dorling Kindersley:** The National Railway Museum, York (tl); The Combined Military Services Museum (CMSM) (cl). 31 **Dorling Kindersley:** The National Cycle Collection (tl). **Dreamstime.com:** Hupeng (crb). **Getty Images:** Peter Adams (cr). **iStockphoto.com:** DNHanlon (tr). 33 **Pashley Cycles:** (cr). 34 **Dorling Kindersley:** Trek UK Ltd (clb). **First Flight Bicycles:** (tr). 35 **Alamy Images:** pzechner (clb). **Gary Sansom, owner of bmxmuseum.com:** (crb). **MARIN BIKES:** (tr). 36-37 **Getty Images:** Tommaso Boddi. 38-39 **Dorling Kindersley:** David Farnley. 40 **Dorling Kindersley:** The Motorcycle Heritage Museum, Westerville, Ohio (c). **Getty Images:** Science & Society Picture Library (tr). 41 **Dorling Kindersley:** Phil Crosby and Peter Mather (cra); The Motorcycle Heritage Museum, Westerville, Ohio (clb). 42 **Dreamstime.com:** Photo1269 (tl). 42 **Don Morley:** (cl). 42-43 **Dorling Kindersley:** The National Motorcycle Museum (crb). 43 **Dorling Kindersley:** The National Motorcycle Museum (t, ca, cr, cb); The Motorcycle Heritage Museum, Westerville, Ohio (cl). 44-45 **Dorling Kindersley:** Micheal Penn (t); Scootopia (cb). 44 **Dorling Kindersley:** Stuart Lanning (c); The Motorcycle Heritage Museum, Westerville, Ohio (cla). 45 **Dorling Kindersley:** George and Steven Harmer (clb, cr); Neil Mort, Mott Motorcycles (cb, crb). **BMW Group:** (cra). **Honda (UK):** (tr). 46 **Dorling Kindersley:** (tr); National Motor Museum, Beaulieu (tl); Micheal Penn (crb); Tony Dowden (clb). 47 **Carver Technology BV:** (tr). **Corbis:** Transtock (cl). **Dorling Kindersley:** Alan Peters (tl). **Dreamstime.com:** Amnarj2006 (crb). 48 **Dorling Kindersley:** Carl M Booth (crb); The National Motorcycle Museum (tc); Charlie Owens (c); Charlie Garratt (cr, clb); Rick Sasnett (cl). 49 **Dorling Kindersley:** George Manning (cl, cr, crb); Harley-Davidson (tr); Ian Bull (clb). 50 **Roland Brown:** Riders for Health (clb). **Dorling Kindersley:** The Deutsches Zweiradmuseum und NSU-Museum, Neckarsulm, Germany (c). **Honda (UK):** (crb). 51 **Dorling Kindersley:** Adam Atherton (cl); The Deutsches Zweiradmuseum und NSU-Museum, Neckarsulm, Germany (t); Mark Hatfield (c); Palmers Motor Company (crb/Aprilia). **Honda (UK):** (crb). 52-53 **Corbis:** Erik Tham. 54 **Dorling Kindersley:** The Motorcycle Heritage Museum, Westerville, Ohio (tl); The National Motorcycle Museum (tr); Trevor Pope Motorcycles (crb). 55 **Dorling Kindersley:** National Motor Museum, Beaulieu (cl); The Motorcycle Heritage Museum, Westerville, Ohio (t); Neil Mort, Mott Motorcycles (cr); Trevor Pope Motorcycles (clb, crb). 56 **Dorling Kindersley:** Brian Chapman and Chris Illman (c); The Motorcycle Heritage Museum, Westerville, Ohio (tl); The National Motorcycle Museum (tr); National Motorcycle Museum, Birmingham (cra). 56-57 **American Motorcyclist Association:** (b). **www.ackattackracing.com:** (crb). 57 **Dorling Kindersley:** Beaulieu National Motor Museum (tr); Pegasus Motorcycles (crb). **Marine Turbine Technologies, LLC(www.marineturbine.com):** (cr). 58 **Dorling Kindersley:** The National Motorcycle Museum (tl); The Motorcycle Heritage Museum, Westerville, Ohio (tr); Tony Dowden (b). 59 **Dorling Kindersley:** Alan Purvis (cla); Michael Delaney (tl); Wayne MacGowan (tr); Phil Davies (clb). **ECOSSE Moto Works, Inc.:** (clb/Ecosse). **Honda (UK):** (crb). **MV Agusta Motor SpA:** (cr). 60-61 **Giles Chapman Library.** 62 **Alamy Images:** Werner Dieterich (cl). 63 **Dorling Kindersley:** Colin Laybourn / P&A Wood (tr); National Motor Museum, Beaulieu (tl); Haynes International Motor Museum (b). **Getty Images:** Print Collector (cl). 64-65 **Getty Images:** ullstein bild / Robert Sennecke. 66 **Alamy Images:** pbpgalleries (crb). **Art Tech Picture Agency:** (clb). **Corbis:** Car Culture (c). **Dorling Kindersley:** Ivan Dutton (br). 67 **Dorling Kindersley:** National Motor Museum, Beaulieu (tl). **Louwman Museum-The Hague:** (crb). 68 **Dorling Kindersley:** Colin Spong (clb); The Titus & Co. Museum for Vintage & Classic Cars (c). **Louwman Museum-The Hague:** (tr). 69 **Alamy Images:** Tom Wood (c). **Art Tech Picture Agency:** (b). **Dorling Kindersley:** National Motor Museum, Beaulieu (t). 70 **Alamy Images:** Esa Hiltula (cl). **Dorling Kindersley:** The Titus & Co. Museum for Vintage & Classic Cars (cla). 70-71 **Dorling Kindersley:** The Titus & Co. Museum for Vintage & Classic Cars (t). 71 **Corbis:** Car Culture (clb). 72 **Alamy Images:** Phil Talbot (cl). 73 **Dorling Kindersley:** National Motor Museum, Beaulieu (tr). **Getty Images:** Heritage Images (crb). 74-75 **Alamy Images:** ImageGB (t). **Courtesy Mercedes-Benz Cars, Daimler AG:** (b). 74 **Alamy Images:** pbpgalleries (clb). 75 **Alamy Images:** Tribune Content Agency LLC (c). **Dreamstime.com:** Warren Rosenberg (ca). **Courtesy of Volkswagen:** (cr). 76-77 **Corbis:** Transtock. 78-79 **Dreamstime.com:** Len Green (c). 78 **Alamy Images:** Mark Scheuern (clb). **Art Tech Picture Agency:** (ca). **Suzuki Motor Corporation:** (c). 79 **Art Tech Picture Agency:** (cra, tr). 80 **Alamy Images:** Buzz Pictures (clb); ZUMA Press, Inc (cla). **Dorling Kindersley:** Chris Williams (c). **Louwman Museum-The Hague:** (tr). 80-81 **Alamy Images:** Mark Scheuern (c). **Getty Images:** Jason Kempin (crb). 81 **Dreamstime.com:** Ermess (crb). **Getty Images:** UK Press / Justin Goff (tl). **Rex Features:** Andy Willsheer (ca). **Terrafugia/www.terrafugia.com:** (c). **Toyota (GB) PLC:** (crb/Toyota FV2). 82-83 **WATERCAR.** 84-85 **Art Tech Picture Agency:** (c). 85 **Alamy Images:** Motoring Picture Library (cr). 86-87 **Alamy Images:** Mark Scheuern (c). 86 **Art Tech Picture Agency:** (crb). **LAT Photographic:** (cl). **Giles Chapman Library:** (cla, cr). **Louwman Museum-The Hague:** (tr). 87 **Corbis:** Car Culture (ca). **Volvo Car Group:** (tr). 88 **Alamy Images:** Phil Talbot (b). 89 **Alamy Images:** Motoring Picture Library (ca). **Dorling Kindersley:** Brands Hatch Morgans (crb); Gilbert and Anna East (c). 90 **Alamy Images:** West Country Images (cla). **Dorling Kindersley:** National Motor Museum, Beaulieu (tr, crb). **Louwman Museum-The Hague:** (cb). 90-91 **Alamy Images:** Shaun Finch - Coyote-Photography.co.uk (b). 91 **Giles Chapman Library:** (tl). **Malcolm McKay:** (cra). **Renault:** (crb). **Tata Limited:** (cr). 92-93 **Alamy Images:** KS_Autosport. 94 **Dorling Kindersley:** Peter Harris (tr). **www.mclaren.com:** (c). 95 **© 2015 Hennessey Performance:** (crb). **Dreamstime.com:** Swisshippo (clb). 96 **Dorling Kindersley:** The Titus & Co. Museum for Vintage & Classic Cars (t). **Dreamstime.com:** Ddcoral (cla). 97 **Art Tech Picture Agency:** (cra). **Dreamstime.com:** Olga Besnard (cr). 98 **Giles Chapman Library:** (cr). **Courtesy Mercedes-Benz Cars, Daimler AG:** (cl). 98-99 **Flock London:** (cb). 99 **Corbis:** Bettmann (tr); Reuters / Kieran Doherty (c); Car Culture (clb). **Getty Images:** Science & Society Picture Library (tl). 100-101 **Corbis:** Leo Mason. 104 **Alamy Images:** Car Collection (clb). **Corbis:** Ecoscene / John Wilkinson (crb). **Dorling Kindersley:** Milestone Museum (tr, cla). 105 **Alamy Images:** Colin Underhill (t). **Dorling Kindersley:** DAF Trucks N.V. (c); DaimlerChrysler AG (clb). 106 **Dorling Kindersley:** Yorkshire Air Museum (cla); The Tank Museum (tr). 107 **Daimler AG:** (tr). **Dorling Kindersley:** James River Equipment (c). **Max-Holder:** (crb). 108-109 **Corbis:** Reuters / Rick Fowler. 110 **Corbis:** Demotix / pqneiman (tr). **Dorling Kindersley:** Newbury Bus Rally (cl, b). **Rex Features:** Roger Viollet (tl). 110-11 **Foremost, http://foremost.ca/:** (c). 111 **Alamy Images:** Oliver Dixon (cb). **Corbis:** Reuters / Brazil / Stringer (t). 112-113 **Dorling Kindersley:** Chandlers Ltd. 114 **Dorling Kindersley:** Paul Rackham (cl, clb); Roger and Fran Desborough (cla, cr). **David Peters:** (crb). 114-115 **Dorling Kindersley:** The Shuttleworth Collection (t). 115 **AGCO Ltd:** (cra). **Dorling Kindersley:** David Wakefield (t); Doubleday Holbeach Depot (cl); Lister Wilder (cr). **John Deere:** (clb). **New Holland Agriculture:** (crb). 116 **Dorling Kindersley:** David Bowman (t); Doubleday Swineshead Depot (cl). **John Deere:** (clb). 116-117 **Dorling Kindersley:** Doubleday Swineshead Depot (b). 117 **AGCO Ltd:** (tl). **Hagie Manufacturing Company:** (crb). **New Holland Agriculture:** (cla, tr, cr). 118-119 **Action Plus.** 120-121 **Getty Images:** AFP / Viktor Drachev (c). 121 **Dorling Kindersley:** DaimlerChrysler AG (tl); James River Equipment (crb). 122 **Dorling Kindersley:** Royal Armouries, Leeds (cra); The Second Guards Rifles Division (cr); The Tank Museum (cla, cl, tr). 122-123 **Dorling Kindersley:** The Tank Museum (b). 123 **Dorling Kindersley:** Royal Armouries, Leeds (cl, cra); The Tank Museum (tl, tr, crb, crb/Leopard C2). 124-125 **Dorling Kindersley:** B&O Railroad Museum. 126 **Dorling Kindersley:** Railroad Museum of Pennsylvania (c); The Science Museum, London (tr, clb); The National Railway Museum, York (cb). **Science & Society Picture Library:** National Railway Museum (cla). 126-127 **Dorling Kindersley:** The National Railway Museum, York / Science Museum Group (c). 127 **colour-rail.com:** (cra). **Dorling Kindersley:** B&O Railroad Museum (tl, tr, br); The National Railway Museum, York (cr). 128 **Dorling Kindersley:** B&O Railroad Museum (ca); The National Railway Museum, New Dehli (cb). 128-129 **Dorling Kindersley:** Adrian Shooter (cb); The National Railway Museum, York (ca, cb/Mallard). 129 **Dorling Kindersley:** Railroad Museum of Pennsylvania (br). 130-131 **Corbis:** Milepost 92 1 / 2 / W.A. Sharman. 132-133 **Dorling Kindersley:** Ribble Steam Railway / Science Museum Group. 134 **Dorling Kindersley:** The Musee de Chemin de Fer, Mulhouse (tl). **Steam Picture Library:** (bl). 134-135 **Dorling Kindersley:** B&O Railroad Museum (bc); Harzer Schmalspurbahnen (c, tc). 135 **Corbis:** Bettmann / Philip Gendreau (tr). **Dorling Kindersley:** Virginia Museum of Transportation (cr, crb). 136 **Dorling Kindersley:** B&O Railroad Museum (cl, cb); Virginia Museum of Transportation (cla). 136-137 **Dorling Kindersley:** Ribble Steam Railway / Science Museum Group (t); Virginia Museum of Transportation (ca). **Keith Fender:** (c). 137 **colour-rail.com:** (crb). **Dorling Kindersley:** The DB Museum, Nurnburg, Germany (tr). **Keith Fender:** (clb). 138 **Dorling Kindersley:** Didcot Railway Centre (tl); The National Railway Museum, York / Science Museum Group (cl); Railroad Museum of Pennsylvania (clb); The Verkehrshaus der Schweiz, Luzern, Switzerland (c). 138-139 **Dorling Kindersley:** Ffestiniog & Welsh Highland Railways (tr). 139 **Dorling Kindersley:** B&O Railroad Museum (c); Didcot Railway Centre (cr); Eisenbahnfreunde Traditionsbahnbetriebswerk Stassfurt (clb). **Keith Fender:** (crb). 140 **Dorling Kindersley:** B&O Railroad Museum (tl); Eisenbahnfreunde Traditionsbahnbetriebswerk Stassfurt (crb); Railroad

Acknowledgments

Museum of Pennsylvania (clb); The National Railway Museum, York (ca). 140-141 **Dorling Kindersley:** The National Railway Museum, India (t). 141 **Dorling Kindersley:** DB Schenker (b); The Musee de Chemin de Fer, Mulhouse (tr); Railroad Museum of Pennsylvania (cra); Eisenbahnfreunde Traditionsbahnbetriebswerk Stassfurt (cb). 142 **Alamy Images:** Kevin Foy (cr); Colin Underhill (tl). **colour-rail.com:** (cl). **Keith Fender:** (cra). **Brian Stephenson/RAS:** (b). 143 **Alamy Images:** epa european pressphoto agency b.v (crb); Iain Masterton (tr). **Dorling Kindersley:** Hitachi Rail Europe (cra). **Dreamstime.com:** Tan Kian Yong (cl). **Keith Fender:** (cr, clb). 144-145 **Alamy Images:** Sean Pavone. 146 **Alamy Images:** Danita Delimont (ca); Alan Moore (clb). **Brian Stephenson/RAS:** (clb/berlin u-bahn). 146-147 **Dreamstime.com:** Alarico (cb). **Siemens AG:** (t). 147 **Alamy Images:** dpict (cl); Iain Masterton (tr). **Bombardier Transportation, Bombardier Inc.:** (cr). **WSW mobil GmbH:** büro+staubach (crb). 148 **Alamy Images:** Jon Sparks (clb). **Dreamstime.com:** Yulia Belousova (crb). 149 **Alamy Images:** RIA Novosti (br). **CAF, CONSTRUCCIONES Y AUXILIAR DE FERROCARRILES, S.A.:** (cra). **Image supplied by Transport for Greater Manchester and taken by Lesley Chalmers.:** (tl). 150-151 **Corbis:** Stringer / India / Reuters. 152-153 **Alamy Images:** Tracey Whitefoot. 154 **Dorling Kindersley:** Exeter Maritime Museum, The National Maritime Museum, London (cl); National Maritime Museum, London (b). **National Maritime Museum, Greenwich, London:** (cra). 155 **Dorling Kindersley:** Exeter Maritime Museum, The National Maritime Museum, London (ca, clb); National Maritime Museum, London (t). **National Maritime Museum, Greenwich, London:** (c, b). 156 **Dorling Kindersley:** National Maritime Museum, London (cla, bl, cr, crb). 156-157 **Dorling Kindersley:** Exeter Maritime Museum, The National Maritime Museum, London (ca). 157 **Alamy Images:** Eye Ubiquitous (cr). **Dorling Kindersley:** Maidstone Museum and Bentliff Art Gallery (t); National Maritime Museum, London (crb). **National Maritime Museum, Greenwich, London:** (clb). 158-159 **Lane Jacobs**. 160-161 **Dorling Kindersley:** National Maritime Museum, London. 162 **Dorling Kindersley:** National Maritime Museum, London (clb); The Science Museum, London (cla). **Getty Images:** DEA / G. Nimatalah (crb). **Science & Society Picture Library:** (cr). 162-163 **Dorling Kindersley:** National Maritime Museum, London (t). 163 **Dorling Kindersley:** Pitt Rivers Museum, University of Oxford (cb). **National Maritime Museum, Greenwich, London:** (crb). 164 **Dorling Kindersley:** The National Maritime Museum, London (cla, c); Virginia Museum of Transportation (clb). **Rex Features:** Ilpo Musto (crb). 164-165 **Dorling Kindersley:** National Maritime Museum, London (c). 165 **Dorling Kindersley:** National Maritime Museum, London (cb); National Maritime Museum, London (cr). **The Fram Museum, http://www.frammuseum.no/:** (tr); **Michael Czytko, www.modelships.de:** (tl). 166-167 **Dorling Kindersley:** National Maritime Museum, London (ca). 166 **John Hamill:** (tl). **National Maritime Museum, Greenwich, London:** (bl). **www.modelshipmaster.com:** (crb). 167 **Dorling Kindersley:** Fleet Air Arm Museum (c). **National Maritime Museum, Greenwich, London:** (tl, br). **www.modelshipmaster.com:** (clb). 168-169 **Gilles Martin-Raget / www.martin-raget.com**. 170-171 **National Maritime Museum, Greenwich, London**. 172 **Dorling Kindersley:** National Maritime Museum, London (cla, cb). **Getty Images:** Science & Society Picture Library (t). 172-173 **Getty Images:** Science & Society Picture Library (c). **National Maritime Museum, Greenwich, London:** (cb). 173 **National Maritime Museum, Greenwich, London:** (t, cr, cb, crb). 174 **Dorling Kindersley:** National Maritime Museum, London (clb); RNLI - Royal National Lifeboat Institution (cr). **National Maritime Museum, Greenwich, London:** (cla, cl). 174-175 **National Maritime Museum, Greenwich, London:** (cb). 175 **Dorling Kindersley:** National Maritime Museum, London (c, cb). **National Maritime Museum, Greenwich, London:** (t). 176 **Dorling Kindersley:** National Maritime Museum, London (t). **National Maritime Museum, Greenwich, London:** (ca, clb). 176-177 **Dreamstime.com:** Jhamlin (crb). 177 **National Maritime Museum, Greenwich, London:** (t). **Used with permission of Royal Caribbean Cruises Ltd.:** (c). 178-179 **Corbis:** Joe Skipper / Reuters. 180 **Dorling Kindersley:** Fleet Air Arm Museum (cb); The Fleet Air Arm Museum (cla). **National Maritime Museum, Greenwich, London:** (cl). 180-181 **National Maritime Museum, Greenwich, London:** (c, cb). **SD Model Makers:** (t, ca). 181 **Dorling Kindersley:** Scale Model World (cb). **SD Model Makers:** (cr, tr). 182 **SD Model Makers:** (cla, ca, clb). 182-183 **Dorling Kindersley:** Model Exhibition, Telford (c, crb); Fleet Air Arm Museum (t); USS George Washington and the US Navy (ca). 183 **Alamy Images:** David Acsota Allely (cb). 184 **Alamy Images:** Joel Douillet (cr). **Dorling Kindersley:** Fleet Air Arm Museum (ca, cl). **SD Model Makers:** (cb). 184-185 **Dorling Kindersley:** Fleet Air Arm Museum (t). 185 **Alamy Images:** Jim Gibson (cr); Stocktrek Images, Inc. (cl). **Dorling Kindersley:** Scale Model World (cb). **Press Association Images:** (clb). **SD Model Makers:** (cla). 188 **Dorling Kindersley:** Fleet Air Arm Museum (cb); The Royal Navy Submarine Museum, Gosport (cla); Scale Model World (c). **National Maritime Museum, Greenwich, London:** (tr). **SD Model Makers:** (cra). 188-189 **Dorling Kindersley:** The Fleet Air Arm Museum (b). 189 **Dorling Kindersley:** IFREMER, Paris (cl); Scale Model World (t); The Science Museum, London (cla); Fleet Air Arm Museum (cb). **TurboSquid:** wdc600 (cr). 190-191 **Alamy Images:** Glyn Genin (t). 190 **British Hovercraft Company Ltd.:** (b). **Dorling Kindersley:** Search and Rescue Hovercraft, Richmond, British Columbia (ca). **LenaTourFlot LLC.:** (cl). 191 **123RF.com:** Suttipon Thanarakpong (crb). **Getty Images:** Science & Society Picture Library (cr). **Kawasaki Motors Europe N.V.:** (clb). **Photo used with permission of BRP:** (tr). 192 **123RF.com:** Richard Pross (cr). **Alpacka Raft LLC:** (tr). **Chris-Craft:** (tl). **Dreamstime.com:** Georgesixth (cb). 193 **Hamant Airboats, LLC:** (tl). **National Maritime Museum, Greenwich, London:** (tr, cl). 194-195 **Corbis:** Chen Shaojin / Xinhua Press. 196-197 **Dreamstime.com:** Bigknell. 198-199 **Dorling Kindersley:** Roy Palmer. 200 **Dorling Kindersley:** Musee Air & Space Paris, La Bourget (cl, c, cr); The Real Aeroplane Company (clb). 200-201 **Dorling Kindersley:** The Shuttleworth Collection (b). 201 **Dorling Kindersley:** Musee Air & Space Paris, La Bourget (cra, cl, c); The Planes of Fame Air Museum, Chino, California (t); Nationaal Luchtvaart Themapark Aviodome (cb). 202 **Dorling Kindersley:** Brooklands Museum (cla); The Shuttleworth Collection, Bedfordshire (t); Flugausstellung (cr); The Shuttleworth Collection (b). 203 **Dorling Kindersley:** Fleet Air Arm Museum (t); Nationaal Luchtvaart Themapark Aviodome (c); The Shuttleworth Collection (crb, crb/Avro Triplane). **U.S. Air Force:** (clb). 204-205 **Corbis:** Minnesota Historical Society. 206-207 **Dorling Kindersley:** Brooklands Museum (c); Planes of Fame Air Museum, Chino, California (cb). 206 **Dorling Kindersley:** Musee Air & Space Paris, La Bourget (cl); Flugausstellung (clb). **Richard Bungay(https://www.flickr.com/photos/98961263@N00/):** (tc). 207 **Dorling Kindersley:** Royal Airforce Museum, London (Hendon) (c); Yorkshire Air Museum (t); Planes of Fame Air Museum, Chino, California (crb); The Shuttleworth Collection (b). 208 **Dorling Kindersley:** Royal Airforce Museum, London (Hendon) (ca); The Real Aeroplane Company (tr); B17 Preservation (cl); RAF Museum, Cosford (clb). 208-209 **Alamy Images:** Anthony Kay / Flight (c). **Dorling Kindersley:** Gatwick Aviation Museum (cb). 209 **Dorling Kindersley:** Gatwick Aviation Museum (cra); Ukraine State Aviation Museum (cr, crb). **Getty Images:** Max Mumby / Indigo (t). 210-211 **Dorling Kindersley:** Royal Airforce Museum, London (Hendon) (c). 210 **©2015 National Air and Space Museum Archives, Smithsonian:** (crb). **Alamy Images:** B Christopher (clb). **Dorling Kindersley:** Musee Air & Space Paris, La Bourget (cla, cra, cl). 211 **Alamy Images:** Susan & Allan Parker (cr). **Dorling Kindersley:** Musee Air & Space Paris, La Bourget (tl, tr); Mr R A Fleming, The Real Aeroplane Company (clb); RAF Museum, Cosford (crb). 212 **Dorling Kindersley:** Royal Airforce Museum, London (Hendon) (t, ca); March Field Air Museum, California (cr); Flugausstellung (crb). **Dreamstime.com:** Gary Blakeley (clb). 212-213 **123RF.com. Dorling Kindersley:** Golden Apple Operations Ltd (cb). 213 **Dorling Kindersley:** RAF Coningsby (clb); Yorkshire Air Museum (t); City of Norwich Aviation Museum (cr); Flugausstellung (cl); Midlands Air Museum (ca). **Dreamstime.com:** Eugene Berman (crb). 214-215 **Alamy Images:** A. T. Willett. 216 **Dorling Kindersley:** Flugausstellung (cl); Fleet Air Arm Museum (cla); Brooklands Museum Trust Ltd, Weybridge, Surrey (tr); Gary Wenko (cr); Gatwick Aviation Museum (crb). **Dreamstime.com:** I4lcocl2 (clb). 217 **Alamy Images:** NielsVK (c). **Dorling Kindersley:** Musee Air & Space Paris, La Bourget (crb); Fleet Air Arm Museum (t); Ukraine State Aviation Museum (clb). 218 **Dorling Kindersley:** Planes of Fame Air Museum, Valle, Arizona (tl). 218-219 **Alamy Images:** Steven May (b). 219 **Alamy Images:** Susan & Allan Parker (br). **Dorling Kindersley:** Pima Air and Space Museum, Tuscon, Arizona (tl); The Real Aeroplane Company (tr). 220-221 **Dreamstime.com:** Songallery (cb). 220 **AirTeamImages.com:** (clb/Sud). **Dorling Kindersley:** Flugausstellung (b); Nationaal Luchtvaart Themapark Aviodome (cla, cra). 221 **Dorling Kindersley:** Ukraine State Aviation Museum (t). 222-223 **Alamy Images:** Jim Kidd. 224 **Dorling Kindersley:** Midlands Air Museum (clb, b); RAF Museum, Cosford (c). **Science Photo Library:** Detlev Van Ravenswaay (cla). 224-225 **NASA:** (b). 225 **Alamy Images:** NASA Archive (tr). **Dorling Kindersley:** Flugausstellung (tl); Ukraine State Aviation Museum (c); Yorkshire Air Museum (cb). 226 **Alamy Images:** Thierry GRUN - Aero (t). **Dorling Kindersley:** The Shuttleworth Collection, Bedfordshire (c); The Shuttleworth Collection (crb). **U.S. Air Force:** (clb, b). 226-227 **Alamy Images:** aviafoto (ca); Kevin Maskell (cr). 227 **NASA:** Tony Landis (tr). 228-229 **Dorling Kindersley:** RAF Boulmer, Northumberland. 230 **Dorling Kindersley:** De Havilland Aircraft Heritage Centre (tl); The Museum of Army Flying (crb). 230-231 **aviation-images.com:** (cra). 231 **aviation-images.com:** (cla). **Dorling Kindersley:** Musee Air & Space Paris, La Bourget (tr, crb); RAF Museum, Cosford (ca); Ukraine State Aviation Museum (cb, cr). 232 **Dorling Kindersley:** Norfolk and Suffolk Aviation Museum (tl). 233 **Dorling Kindersley:** Musee Air & Space Paris, La Bourget (cla). **Dreamstime.com:** Patrick Allen (cra). 234 **Dorling Kindersley:** Ukraine State Aviation Museum (cla, cb). 234-235 **Dorling Kindersley:** Ukraine State Aviation Museum. 238 **Corbis:** Imaginechina (r). **Dorling Kindersley:** Bob Gathany (l). **Getty Images:** Bloomberg / David Paul Morris (crb). **NASA:** (cl, c). 239 **Alamy Images:** Konstantin Shaklein (l). **NASA:** (cl, cb); Kim Shiflett (c). **Science Photo Library:** Detlev Van Ravenswaay (r). 240 **Corbis:** Model of the nuclear powered interplanetary probe sent to Jupiter (cla). **NASA:** JPL-Caltech / University of Arizona (c); JPL-Caltech (cr); KSC (crb). **Science Photo Library:** Ria Novosti (tr). 241 **Corbis:** JPL-Caltech (cb). **ESA:** ATG medialab (tr, cra). **Getty Images:** AFP / Akihiro Ikeshita (tl). **NASA:** JPL (cla); The Johns Hopkins University Applied Physics Laboratory LLC (c). 242 **Corbis:** Richard Cummins (c). **Dorling Kindersley:** Bob Gathany (cl). **NASA:** (crb, clb); (tr). 243 **Dorling Kindersley:** ESA (t). **NASA:** (c, crb). 244-245 **NASA:** Sandra Joseph, Kevin O'Connell. 246 **John Deere:** (bl). 247 **Dorling Kindersley:** Beaulieu National Motor Museum (br). 248-249 **Dorling Kindersley:** Adrian Shooter (b). 249 **Dorling Kindersley:** National Maritime Museum, London (tl). 250 **Dorling Kindersley:** The Tank Museum (br). 251 **Dorling Kindersley:** National Maritime Museum, London (tl). 252 **Dorling Kindersley:** National Maritime Museum, London (tl). 253 **Dorling Kindersley:** The Shuttleworth Collection (tl). 254 **Dorling Kindersley:** Hitachi Rail Europe (bl); Paul Rackham

All other images © Dorling Kindersley
For further information see: www.dkimages.com